Oxford

Cities of the Imagination

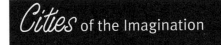

Cities of the Imagination

Oxford

A cultural and literary companion

David Horan

INTERLINK BOOKS
An imprint of Interlink Publishing Group, Inc.
New York • Northampton

First published 2000 by
INTERLINK BOOKS
An imprint of Interlink Publishing Group, Inc.
99 Seventh Avenue • Brooklyn, New York 11215 and
46 Crosby Street • Northampton, Massachusetts 01060

Library of Congress Cataloging-in-Publication Data

Horan, David.
    Oxford : a cultural and literary companion / David Horan.
      p. cm. — (Cities of the Imagination)
    Includes bibliographical references and index.
    ISBN 1-56656-348-8
    1. Oxford (England)—Description and travel. 2. Oxford (England)—
Social life and customs. 3. Literary landmarks—England—Oxford
4. Oxford (England)—In literature 5. Oxford (England,—History.
1. Title II. Series.
DA690.O98H57 1999
942.5'74—dc21   99-38631
                                              CIP

Design: Baseline Arts Ltd., Oxford
Cover images: Catriona Davidson; Chris Donaghue/The Oxford Photo Library; Gernshelm
Collection; Harry Ransom Humanities Research Center, The University of Texas at Austin;
British Motor Industry Heritage Trust.
Printed and bound in Canada
10 9 8 7 6 5 4 3 2 1

To request our complete catalog,
please call us at 1-800-238-LINK or write to:
Interlink Publishing
46 Crosby Street, Northampton, MA 01060
e-mail: interpg@aol.com • website: www.interlinkbooks.com

Contents

Foreword

*"Morse had never enrolled in the itchy-footed regiment of adventurous souls,
feeling little temptation to explore the remoter corners even of his native
land; and this principally because he could imagine few if any places closer
to his heart than Oxford – the city which, though not his natural mother,
had for so many years performed the duties of a loving foster-parent."*

—*The Remorseful Day*

For "Morse," read me.

It was in the early sixties when with a co-author I first visited
Oxford to meet the publisher of two sixth-form text-books we had
written. The publisher was Robert Maxwell. He was courteous and
charming to us. I called him "sir," I think. I will say no more.

On that first brief visit I saw little of Oxford and my impressions
were predictably neutral. But I do recall looking at the city from the
high ground of Headington Hill Hall and wondering what it was really
like down there – and quite certainly not concurring with Jane Austen's
crabby complaint: "I never was but once in Oxford in my life and I am
sure I never wish to go there again."

I did go again.

In fact, a few years later I found myself in Oxford permanently.
After thirteen years as a schoolmaster, I was gradually becoming too
deaf to cope with the demands of classroom teaching; and in 1966 I
was appointed to the Oxford Delegacy of Local Examinations (so very
sadly now defunct) to take responsibility for O-level and A-level
examinations in English, Greek, and Latin. I remained there for
twenty-two, mostly very happy years.

The first Morse novel was published in 1975, with the first TV
adaptation screened twelve years later. The gods smiled broadly on both
enterprises; and a few years after my retirement I could (I suppose) have
moved to almost any part of the world I wished: to Vienna, Venice,
Salzburg, the Italian Lakes…The reason for my staying put was – and

remains – a simple one: I just could not think of anywhere I would rather spend the rest of my life than Oxford.

One way or another I have received a good many awards and accolades, including a citation presented to me by the Lord Mayor and Oxford City Council who wished to place on record their appreciation of my work, and to express their gratitude that "in his novels Colin Dexter has shown our City as having a distinct and separate identity from its famous university."

Yes, of that I am proudest of all; and in turn I have felt it a privilege, like so many others, to be able to write about what for me has increasingly become "our City."

Many books have been written about Oxford. And justifiably so, since both Town and Gown provide an inexhaustible source of material. *Another* book, though, Mr Horan? No, not just "another" book, but one that brims with unusual and unexpected delights. Its chapters look at Oxford from twelve different angles, with attention focused, initially, on such individual luminaries as Cranmer, Johnson, C.S. Lewis, and the rest; and then broaden out to include fascinating information about so many aspects of the city. The result is that reading the book is rather like going into a supermarket with a short shopping-list, and then picking up a whole trolley-load of extra items along the aisles.

I find this book extremely readable and full of fresh insights. And with David Horan as her guide, Miss Austen might well have recanted on her rare lapse of good taste. As for Gerard Manley Hopkins, he found that his love for Oxford ever "grew more sweet-familiar."

For "Hopkins," read me.

Colin Dexter

Preface

Everyone who writes on Oxford seems to feel the need to apologize for adding another book to the already well-stocked shelves devoted to England's most exciting city. There are no apologies for this book, however. It isn't a history of Oxford and its university, for no-one would be so foolish to attempt that in so short a space; and I have left out much about college histories and architecture. What I have tried to do in this book is tell something of the story of Oxford through the lives and thoughts of those who have lived and worked here. Some, like Percy Shelley, were here only a matter of months; others like Lord Nuffield and J.R.R. Tolkien, spent almost their entire lives in the city.

This book can be used as a guidebook, for the landmarks identified and the lives featured are grouped geographically; the city and its suburbs are split into twelve sections, each centred on a location connected with one important figure in Oxford's history. Of the twelve, only the earliest, St Frideswide, was (presumably) born in Oxford, and only Frideswide, Cranmer and C.S. Lewis died here. All the others passed through and are therefore representative of the thousands of people who have spread Oxford's name around the world; for the city owes its fame, and the university its wealth, to its exports, those who spent three or four formative years at the university, went on to fame, power and influence and looked back with affection on their Alma Mater.

There is little original research in this book, for no city in the world has been so thoroughly chronicled and memorialized. I have instead worked my way through a vast library of specialist volumes, biographies and autobiographies and newspaper cuttings, often having to dig deep to sort out contradictory accounts of the same event. Some of the stories included here are so famous that they will be instantly recognized; rather more, I hope, will be less familiar, and a few, perhaps, even surprising.

Among all this reading, I found some authors I learned to trust and hereby acknowledge my debt to them and unhesitatingly recommend their books to anyone who wants to find out more about Oxford. They include: Jan Morris's *Oxford*; Miles Jebb's *The Colleges of Oxford*; Geoffrey Tyack's *Oxford: an Architectural Guide*; Derek Honey's *Oxford Pubs, Inns and Taverns*; John Blair's *Anglo-Saxon Oxford*; and Christopher and Edward Hibbert's monumental *Encyclopaedia of Oxford*.

Living in a city made famous by its dissemination of knowledge, the people of Oxford are invariably willing and eager to pass on information: much of what follows originated in conversations and meetings over the past sixteen years, where someone has said to me, "Did you know...." My thanks go to all of those people, many of whom I cannot even remember. My deepest debt, however, is to my wife, Nancy, who has shared all the burden of the writing of this book without any of its pleasure.

David Horan
Oxford, October 1999

Introduction

For more than a thousand years, Oxford has played a central role in English history. Before the first student took his first lesson at the university, saints walked here, kings were crowned here and parliaments debated here. Situated close to the heart of England and connected directly with London via that great natural route, the Thames (whatever your guidebooks say, nobody today calls it the Isis), Oxford has long been an alternative capital city – Charles I tried to rule from here during the Civil War, while Parliament held London – and no Nazi bombs fell on the university during the Second World War because, it is said, Hitler had decided to make Oxford the headquarters for his occupation of Britain.

Over the centuries, Oxford University has been home to many of Britain's greatest names in their formative years (there are two universities in the city now and Oxford Brookes already has a reputation among the newer universities to match that which its older neighbor has long held among the traditional establishments). Dozens of British Prime Ministers – including seven out of the last ten – were educated here and many students from abroad have benefited from the Oxford experience before going on to high office in their own countries. With the election of Bill Clinton, the university was at last able to boast of an old boy as President of the United States – although, of course, many Oxford men played a vital role in the establishment of the original American colonies.

In religion, as in politics, many of England's greatest thinkers either taught or were taught at Oxford and it is impossible to understand the development of the city and the university without appreciating the close ties with the Church over the centuries. The university grew up in St Mary's Church in the High Street and its first chancellor was Robert Grosseteste, Bishop of Lincoln. Many Archbishops of Canterbury learned their theology in the city's colleges: some, like Edmund Rich, were recognized as saints; others like Thomas Cranmer and William Laud, were executed as heretics or traitors. Great medieval theologians like John Duns Scotus and John Colet spread their ideas here, and rebels like John Wyclif and William Tyndale nursed their grievances.

Because Oxford produced so many church leaders, it tended to be conservative and even reactionary. Consequently, when Henry VIII – furious at the Pope's refusal to allow him to divorce his first wife, Catherine of Aragon – set up his own church and ordered his mercenaries to remove every last trace of Catholicism from the land, the destruction in Oxford was appalling. St Frideswide's Priory became part of the new King Henry VIII College; Oseney Abbey, Rewley Abbey, St Bernard's College, Gloucester College and Durham College were all destroyed; and the teaching brothers of the Augustinian, Dominican, Franciscan and Carmelite orders were run out of town.

But the Reformation was slow to win over the minds of Oxford, and when Henry's daughter, Mary Tudor, came to the throne in 1553, bringing the Roman Catholic faith back with her, it was in Oxford that she found the clerics to prove that the Protestant reformers Cranmer, Latimer and Ridley were heretics. In the seventeenth century, that great reforming chancellor, William, Archbishop Laud, was considered too Catholic by the Puritans who had taken over the government and his beheading was a significant step towards the Civil Wars of the 1640s. In the eighteenth century, John Wesley, a Fellow of Lincoln College, developed a new form of Anglicanism, which took religion to the industrial poor. After his death, it became the worldwide movement known as Methodism. For much of the nineteenth century, Oxford was aflame with religious debate and argument when Newman, Keble and Pusey, the founders of the Oxford Movement, made theology fashionable again and created a schism in the Church of England, between Anglo-Catholics and evangelicals, which exists to this day.

For more than 200 years, anyone who wanted to teach at Oxford as a Fellow of one of the colleges, had to be a Church of England clergyman. This inevitably led to a plethora of priests who were more committed to learning than to religion. Among these was that "slithy tove," Charles Dodgson (aka Lewis Carroll), who made a token gesture to the Church in order to keep his job for life at Christ Church, submitting willingly to ordination as a deacon, but refusing to be made up to full priest. In the wake of the Oxford Movement, and after a parliamentary commission, things changed rapidly and radically: Fellows no longer had to be Anglican priests; students no longer had to declare their belief in the

Thirty-Nine Articles of Faith of the Church of England; Non-Conformists and even Roman Catholics were allowed into the university.

Looking at the dust jackets of the books in any library or bookshop, it seems as though half of all authors have been through Oxford – or at least that half of all Oxford graduates have written a book – many of them set in Oxford. In 1989 Judy G. Batson identified 533 Oxford-based novels and the number has steadily risen since then. There have, though, been some seriously good writers here. William Shakespeare never attended the university, but he knew Oxford well, for he used to stop over with his friend John Davenant at the Crown Tavern in Cornmarket, as he passed back and forth between the theatres of London and his family in Stratford-upon-Avon. John Donne called Oxford home for a while, as did Dr Johnson and Percy Shelley, Gerard Manley Hopkins and Oscar Wilde, Swinburne, Arnold and Clough, Eliot, Yeats and Auden and those Oxford Inklings, C.S. Lewis and J.R.R. Tolkien.

Science too has been nurtured here: Robert Boyle worked out his laws of gas expansion; Robert Hooke identified the human cell; Edmund Halley predicted the return of his comet; Howard Florey developed penicillin, the world's most effective drug; and Stephen Hawking, probably the greatest scientific mind of our day, was born and educated in Oxford.

It is not all work, though; Oxford has a fine history of sporting achievements. The annual boat race against Cambridge is still a major national sporting occasion, although all those taking part are amateurs and unknown to the wider public. Oxford University footballers won the FA Cup in 1874 and were runners-up on three other occasions. It was here that the Hon. Marshall Brooks became the first man ever to jump a height of six feet, and in 1954, Roger Bannister, a graduate of Exeter College, became one of the all-time sporting greats when he ran the first sub-four-minute mile on the Iffley Road athletics track.

Oxford University has no campus...or rather, it has more than thirty of them, for all the constituent colleges grew up as independent units and each is a little world to itself. What the visitor sees from the street might be impressive – Oxford has always attracted the finest architects – but it gives little clue of what lies behind the facade. It is only in an aerial photograph of the city that one sees how open and green it is, for all the older colleges are built on the quadrangle principle, with buildings on each side of a courtyard, usually grassed over and reflecting the medieval cloisters where monks did their studying and writing.

Every visitor to Oxford should try to get behind the street walls of at least a couple of colleges although, with the exception of those that charge for the privilege, it is not always easy. College porters in their lodges jealously guard the entrances, and opening hours, if they exist at all, are usually restricted to a couple of hours in the afternoons. Even then, it is surprising how often the porters "forget" to remove the "The College is Closed to Visitors" sign. But never forget that these are not museums; even if the buildings have been standing for hundreds of years, each college is still the home and workplace of hundreds of people.

If you can summon up the courage and do not look too obviously like a tourist, it is quite possible to just march in boldly and get away with it. The secret, of course, is not to linger and look about you or – heaven forbid – take out a camera. Some lodge porters know everybody and will challenge you before you have gone more than a few yards; but if you disturb nobody and do not get in the way, where's the harm in trying?

If all this seems to concentrate too much on the university, one has only to realize that no-one travels far to admire Oxford's shops or its civic architecture. There is a bustling little city going about its business at the same time as the university goes about its: but, despite 700 years of Town-Gown jealousies, it is still the city that makes more allowances for the university than the other way round. There is no escaping the university in any aspect of Oxford life. It is the history and tradition of the colleges that brings visitors and their wealth to the city centre, and the students generate the area's night life and entertainment – from live-music pubs in Jericho to the Playhouse and Holywell Music Room. Besides, a good proportion of Town is made up of people with strong connections with Gown; almost all dons now live out of college and the university is still a major employer in the city. Even the traditionally hostile city council usually has one or two college tutors among its members.

Nevertheless, the council still refuses to cater for visitors, with a wholly inadequate bus station, outrageously high parking fees and a traffic-management system that is the stuff of nightmares. And the city centre is shamefully short of places where visitors can sit and rest their weary legs. Although the city streets are full of a bewildering array of food outlets, mostly take-away, there is nowhere to sit and eat it. What few benches there are, are invariably occupied by vagrant alcoholics.

Oxford can be bewildering, tiring and even disappointing for some visitors, but for anyone with the time and the imagination to walk around and look and think, it is still the most magical place in England. There is more history per square foot in Oxford than anywhere outside the centre of London, and the spirits of hundreds of famous men and women still haunt the passages and alleyways. The main streets are horribly busy, but it is so easy to wander off into side roads and passages where the centuries melt away and one still gets a sense of the Oxford of the past. There are always gateways to peep through, walls to look over and unexpected corners to find; and for anyone wanting charms on a larger scale there is always the medieval magic of cobbled Merton Street and the domestic perfection of seventeenth-century Holywell; try either of these streets early in the morning or at dusk and their power is doubled.

Oxford is a place where important things happen and have been happening for hundreds of years. There is always more to find out about its buildings and the men and women who have lived and worked among them. The following pages offer a selection of insights into the people and places that have made Oxford a city of the imagination.

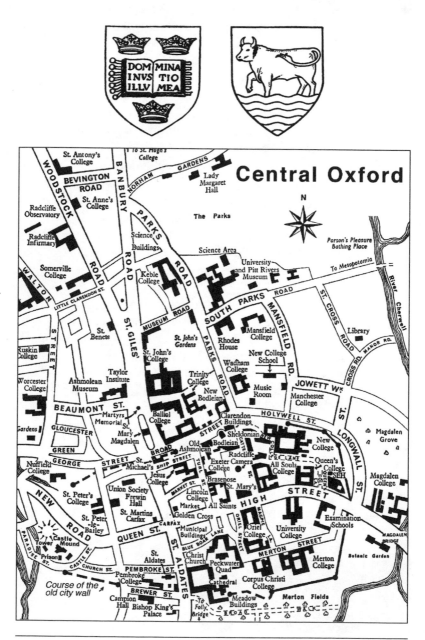

Central Oxford

CHAPTER ONE

St Frideswide's Oxford

"All the English people marvelled at such virtue in one so young"

"In old times, there was, in the city of Oxford a monastery of nuns where rests the most holy virgin Frideswide." So begins the earliest known version of the story of Oxford's own saint, written by the historian William of Malmesbury in 1125.

The old times of which he speaks go back to the eighth century, shortly after Christianity was brought to the Thames Valley and at a time when saints were thick on the ground. William of Malmesbury explains that Frideswide was a princess who spurned the advances of a royal suitor in order to devote her life to Christ. "But the king had set his heart on marrying the virgin and when prayers and flatteries had been spent in vain, he prepared to take her by force." Frideswide flees the city into a wood but is pursued and so she returns to Oxford "despairing of flight and too weary to go any further." She prays for protection and, as the young man passes through the town gates, he is struck blind. Realizing his fault, he begs her forgiveness and his sight is restored. He leaves Frideswide in peace and she lives out her days in a monastery in Oxford.

Two later versions of the story, again from the twelfth century, add details and local color. Frideswide is identified as the daughter of Didan, King of Oxford, who builds her a church, where she establishes a nunnery with twelve companions. Upon her father's death, the kingdom passes to Algar, King of Leicester, "a most villainous man and hateful to God," who demands Frideswide for this bride. The men he sends to seize her are struck blind but, even after Frideswide restores their sight, Algar is not impressed. Accompanied by two nuns, Frideswide is rowed up the River Thames to the town of Bampton, from where she goes into a wood called Binsey. By this time, Algar has reached Oxford and is struck blind at the city gates and remains blind for the rest of his life. In her hut at Binsey, Frideswide performs miracles of healing thanks to the miraculous powers of a holy well. Eventually she returns to Oxford, where she lives in sanctity, performing more miracles, until she dies on Sunday October 19 in the year 727.

The story of the pious virgin repelling a lustful suitor through God's intervention is a common one in the annals of the early saints, but most historians believe that at least some of Frideswide's story must be based on fact. Frideswide herself (unlikely as it seems, the name is pronounced Fried-swide, with the two syllables rhyming) is very much Oxford's own local saint and a church named after her existed on the site of the present cathedral from the eighth century. There was also a church and royal palace at Bampton in Saxon times and the hamlet of Binsey is today just outside the city boundaries. The churchyard there stands in a large oval enclosure which might have contained a daughter church to the priory. In the churchyard there is a holy well, which was for centuries a place of pilgrimage.

Frideswide's Oxford is the Oxford that can no longer be seen. The Victorian historian, J.R. Green, wrote that Oxford "had already seen five centuries of borough life before the first student appeared within its streets."

Ancient Oxford

The city is built on marshy ground where the rivers Thames and Cherwell meet and is divided by countless streams, runnels and backwaters. It is famous for its dampness, which gives rise to colds and chest infections. "Certainly Oxford is no good aire," said the seventeenth-century historian Anthony Wood. Around this uninviting spot, isolated prehistoric remains have been found; stone-age tools near Wolvercote, bronze-age bones under the University Parks and iron-age huts on Port Meadow. But there was no Roman Oxford; this city in which Latin was for centuries a passport to success was never home to those who wrote or spoke it naturally, though evidence of an important Roman pottery has been found in Headington.

Of course, the trouble with Oxford is that archaeologists rarely get the chance to dig there, for its most interesting sites lie impregnable beneath buildings that have stood for centuries and will presumably never willingly be knocked down. The historic heart of the city, however, is quite clearly built to a Saxon design, with four straight roads leading from the town gates to meet at the crossroads of Carfax.

Despite its damp and watery position, Oxford is at a site of strategic importance in southern England. It stands on that great artery, the Thames, halfway along a line between London and Bristol, and is the natural crossroads for a north-south route from Southampton on the south coast into the heart of England. In King Alfred's day, the Thames was the boundary between Wessex and Mercia, and Oxford was an important border settlement. As a trading post on the river and the site of a significant religious foundation, it grew in prosperity and, by the end of the tenth century, had a settlement of Danish immigrants who had come to England in the wake of the Viking raids. These were not invaders, but merchants and traders, giving a foretaste of the cosmopolitan flavor that Oxford would always have. In 1002, however, there occurred one of the most horrific events in Oxford's history.

The St Brice's Day Massacre took place on November 13, 1002, during the reign of King Aethelred the Unready, and was the result of mounting tension between the English and the Danish immigrants. Aethelred sent out a decree to the effect that all the Danes living in England "sprouting like cockle amongst the wheat" were "to be destroyed by a most just extermination." The Danes in Oxford were driven into, or took refuge in, St Frideswide's Church, whereupon the local populace set fire to it and destroyed it, murdering all the men, women and children inside. Perhaps because it happened a thousand years ago, perhaps because there are no contemporary accounts of it other than Aethelred's own, this monumental tragedy gets only a passing mention in most books on Oxford.

Among those murdered was Gunhild, the sister of Sweyn Forkbeard, King of Denmark, who responded by attacking England and gradually took over the whole country. The Danes, under Forkell the Tall, sailed up the Thames in 1009 and sacked Oxford where, in 1013, with Aethelred driven out of the country, Sweyn was declared King of England. Two years later, both rival kings were dead and an uneasy truce was agreed between Cnut, son of Sweyn, and Edmund Ironside, son of Aethelred, in which it was agreed Cnut would rule England north of the Thames and Edmund south of it. But Edmund was assassinated in Oxford in 1017 and Cnut became sole ruler.

Accounts of Edmund's death vary. According to one chronicler, he was killed by the mechanical figure of an archer which shot an arrow when touched; but the more commonly accepted story is that a disgruntled nobleman, Edric Streona, had his son hide in a cesspit in Oxford. When the King entered the privy, the youth stabbed him to death from below at his most unguarded moment. When Edric presented himself to Cnut to take credit for the deed, the Danish king promised to exalt him higher than any other English noble – he chopped off his head and displayed it on a pole from the highest battlement of his palace.

Frideswide's chroniclers said that, after King Algar's blinding at the city gates, Oxford was never a happy destination for any king. They must have had in mind Edmund Ironside's murder and perhaps the fact that Cnut's first son, King Harold Harefoot, crowned at Oxford in 1036, also died here four years later.

Oxford thrived and remained important, with a number of royal councils and parliaments held there and, by 1272, it ranked third in the country behind London and York in the amount of tax it had to pay. By that time, the royal palace of Beaumont was long-established outside the city wall. This had been built by Henry I, lived in by Henry II and was the birthplace of Richard I and King John.

Church and University

By now the university was also developing. Its beginnings undoubtedly lay in the religious houses that sprang up in the city for, in a largely illiterate land, the Church was the centre of knowledge and education, and almost all medieval scholars had a religious training. St Frideswide's Church was rebuilt after the massacre of the Danes and was replaced in 1122 by a priory which included a monastic school. Within a few years, Robert d'Oilly, son of the builder of Oxford Castle, established an Augustinian priory on land near the present railway station. This developed into Oseney Abbey in 1154 and was the third biggest church in England. In the early thirteenth century, St Francis of Assisi sent a group of friars to establish a centre in Oxford. Their message was so popular with local men that their numbers grew until they were able to build their own Greyfriars friary on land to the south of the castle, a site now covered by the Westgate shopping centre. The Cistercian monks established Rewley Abbey by the Thames to the west of what is now Worcester College; the Dominicans built an important teaching friary near Folly Bridge, and the Carmelites set up their training house in the grounds of the former Beaumont Palace.

Of all these important buildings, nothing remains except St Frideswide's which was incorporated into the cathedral. Everything else was destroyed in the reforming zeal that accompanied Henry VIII's Dissolution of the Monasteries in the 1530s, when he broke off the English church's connections with Rome. In their heyday, the religious foundations played host to many of the great theologians, philosophers and scientists of the time, including Robert Grosseteste (1175-1253), who was to become the first Chancellor of Oxford University, Roger Bacon (1214-92), so far ahead of his time that he was believed to be in league with the Devil, John Duns Scotus (c1264-1308), William of Ockham (1300-49), John Wyclif (1320-84), John Colet (1466-1519), and the Dutch humanist scholar Erasmus (1466-1536).

Not all the teaching took place within the abbeys and priories, however. Young men seeking an education came to Oxford where the masters from the religious houses would take them on as paying pupils. This gave rise to the academic halls which were the forerunners of the colleges. These halls were often simply town houses or were adapted from inns and would provide lodging and food as well as a room for lessons and lectures and housed between twelve and twenty students living and studying together. Originally a loose-knit collection of private enterprises, they gradually came under the control of the university. By the early fourteenth century, there were more than 120 academic halls within a couple of hundred yards of the University Church of St Mary the Virgin in the High Street.

Already the students formed a considerable proportion of Oxford's population, but this sort of education was still beyond the means of most people, so a number of wealthy donors set up funds to support poor scholars who wished to study at the university. This philanthropy was certainly behind John de Balliol's establishment of a hall for poor scholars in 1263, by which time William of Durham had already bequeathed 310 marks to the university to pay the rent for a dozen scholars at what was to become University College, and Walter de Merton, the Lord Chancellor of England had endowed a similar establishment, primarily for the sons of his seven sisters.

These new establishments, or colleges, included both masters and pupils and were backed by "endowments," the continuous financial support of rents in parishes that had been in the possession of the founder or his friends. This meant that the colleges became landowners – sometimes on a grand scale – and, even today, all over Britain people pay rent to Oxford colleges without really understanding why. The size and number of endowments varies from college to college so that some, like St John's and Christ Church, are fabulously wealthy, while others, like St Peter's and Keble, have almost no reserves to call upon. Today, of course, all are publicly funded through the university's huge government grant.

As the colleges came to the fore, the academic halls declined. Most colleges swallowed up a number of halls and by 1552 there were only eight left in the city. Today, only St Edmund Hall survives as an echo of the former situation, though it, too, is now a self-governing constituent college of the university.

These early days of Oxford are portrayed in Geoffrey Chaucer's *The Canterbury Tales* (1387-1400), in which England's first great poet contrasts student with scholar. Nicholas, star of *The Miller's Tale*, lodges

Warden, fellows and scholars of New College, c. 1463 (Bodleian Library)

with a carpenter in the city and seems to concentrate on music and wenching. On the other hand, the Clerk of Oxenford, one of Chaucer's pilgrims, is "hollow-cheeked and grave and serious," spends all his money on books and prays for the souls of those who have paid for him to attend the university, for "learning was all he cared for."

CHAPTER TWO

King Charles's Oxford

"The only city in England entirely at my devotion"

Charles I (1600-49) made Oxford the capital of England for three years
in the middle of the seventeenth century, while he was on the run from
Parliament in London. The university town became first a garrison
town, then a besieged town and finally, after Charles's defeat and
execution, it paid heavily for backing the losing side in the Civil War.

Charles Stuart was never supposed to become King of England. He
was born in Dunfermline, the younger son of the King of Scotland,
James VI and, even when his father was invited to unite Scotland and
England when the childless Elizabeth I died in 1601, the succession lay
through his older brother, Prince Henry. It was only when Henry died
in 1612 that the frail Charles – he had not been able to walk until he
was seven – prepared for power.

He was a cultured and accomplished young man but failed
completely to come to terms with the growing desire for more power to
be lodged in Parliament – as yet still far from a democratic institution.
That his belief in the "divine right" of kings to rule was sincerely held
there is no doubt, but it resulted in a stubbornness that offended and

often outraged his people. Charles's reign (1625-49) got off to a bad start, when he married a French Catholic princess, Henrietta Maria, at a time when the rising tide in the Church of England was distinctly Puritan. Under her influence he dissolved three parliaments in the first four years of his reign and then ruled without one for eleven years.

Problems grew and, in 1640, his troubles over taxes and the Scottish church, forced him to recall Parliament, which promptly got him to agree the Act of Attainment, stipulating that Parliament could not be dissolved against its own wishes. Everything Charles did antagonized Parliament, and Parliament's actions – including the execution of his advisor, the Earl of Strafford and the imprisonment of William Laud, Archbishop of Canterbury and reforming Chancellor of the University of Oxford – enraged him. Eventually, in late 1642, war was declared between the two sides. The first major battle took place at Edgehill, some thirty miles north of Oxford and resulted in a partial victory for Charles. Instead of rushing back to London to press home his unexpected advantage, the King stayed in Oxfordshire, capturing Banbury and Broughton castles and then stopping off at his palace at Woodstock before making a triumphal entry into Oxford, where he was regally received at Christ Church. After a few days he set off for London, only to find that the Parliamentarian troops had reached it first and secured it against him. So Charles returned to Oxford and set up his court there. It was an ideal choice for his capital, strategically placed near the centre of England, easily fortified, full of comfortable lodgings – once the students had been frightened out – and a source of wealth.

Charles set himself up in Christ Church and his queen moved into rooms at Merton; the Royal Mint was set up in New Inn Hall Street, and a gunpowder magazine in New College; the city's medieval walls were strengthened and new defences built; Port Meadow became a drilling ground for the soldiers and the colleges were ordered to hand over their gold and silver plate to be melted down and turned into coins to pay for the war.

Oxford, now barricaded and overcrowded, became an insanitary and dangerous place. Plague and typhus were constant companions and matters were worsened by a great fire which destroyed a quarter of the city in 1644.

The war itself did not go well for Charles and gradually his power base diminished. In 1645, Cromwell led his troops into Oxfordshire while Charles was in the north drumming up dwindling support. In his absence, Oxford was encircled by Parliamentarians who cut off all routes of supply to the city. The siege was lifted for a while and Charles returned for the winter, but in 1646, with things getting desperate, he disguised himself and fled in the dead of night. General Fairfax now demanded the surrender of Oxford, saying he "very much desired the preservation of that place (so famous for learning) from ruin, which inevitably is likely to fall upon it except you concur." On June 20, 1646, Fairfax entered the city and the surrender treaty was signed at Christ Church. The Royalist troops, over 3,000 of them, led by the dashing Prince Rupert, were given guarantees of safety to travel home or to the ports from where they could leave the country.

Charles was a beaten man, and was handed over by the Scots to the Parliamentarians who tried him as a tyrant, murderer and enemy of the nation. He was found guilty and, on a cold January afternoon in 1649, became the only British monarch to be put to death at the hands of the state.

Oxford now became a Parliamentarian stronghold, but there was new dissent in the ranks. A loose brotherhood of troops, known as Levellers, demanded that, with power having been taken from the king, it should pass further into the hands of the people, with votes for all "free" men, more frequent elections, religious tolerance and equality before the law. Cromwell, the great "libertarian," would not stand for this and the Levellers were sought out and purged. Two who led a revolt in Oxford, Private Biggs and Private Piggen, were executed by firing squad at Gloucester Green.

Christ Church

Visitors coming to Oxford without doing their homework have been known to stand at Carfax and ask "Where is the university?", unaware that it is all around them. Other visitors, however, have been known to come away from Oxford thinking they had visited the university, when in fact all they saw was Christ Church. And yet they would have been impressed. For Christ Church is the largest of all Oxford's colleges; it is colossally wealthy, it contains the university's largest quadrangle; its chapel serves as the cathedral for a diocese which covers three counties, and its list of alumni reads like a roll call of British history.

Christ Church, according to Oxford style, is never called Christ Church College and – although the largest city in South Island, New Zealand, was named Christchurch in 1850 by John Robert Godley after his former college – the name is always two separate words. Many people also know that Christ Church is known in Oxford as the House after its Latin name *Aedes Christi*, the House of Christ, but etiquette dictates that it is so called only by members of Christ Church. And to add further confusion to visitors, at Christ Church the Fellows are called Students and the students are best referred to as undergraduates.

Christ Church stands on the site of St Frideswide's eighth-century priory and owes its existence to Cardinal Thomas Wolsey (1475-1530). The son of an Ipswich butcher, Wolsey studied at Magdalen College, where he was ordained and from where he became chaplain to King Henry VII. Under the king's successor, Henry VIII, he gained tremendous power and wealth, revealing himself as a clever politician and careful diplomat. He was appointed Lord Chancellor of England in 1515, a post that gave him virtual control of Henry's domestic and foreign policies, and in the same year, already Archbishop of York, he was appointed Cardinal by Pope Leo X, giving him almost complete control over the Church in England as well. No commoner had held such power since the days of Thomas a Becket in the twelfth century.

And yet power brings enemies, and Wolsey was unpopular for his swingeing taxes to pay for the king's wars, while his ostentatious display of wealth brought resentment in the court. His downfall came when he was unable to supply Henry with the Pope's agreement to the king's divorce from Catherine of Aragon. He was stripped of his titles and charged with treason, but died as he journeyed from York to London to face trial and almost certain execution.

At the height of his power, Wolsey determined to build a college, Cardinal College, on a scale never imagined before in Oxford. He got the Pope to agree to the dissolution of St Frideswide's Priory in 1524 and started to build. Before his fall from power he had already erected the Great Hall, which was the largest and grandest in Oxford, and three-quarters of the enormous Tom Quad. The original plan for this quad had envisaged cloisters about it and a magnificent college chapel, although neither was ever built. When Wolsey's power and wealth were stripped from him, Henry VIII agreed to take on the project, which was to be known, inevitably, as King Henry VIII's College, but work continued slowly. It was not until 1546, when Henry moved the cathedral of his new Oxford diocese from Oseney Abbey to the former Priory Church, now to be known as Christ Church Cathedral, that Christ Church itself came into existence.

Wolsey's Great Hall with its magnificent hammerbeam roof, is used daily in termtime for meals for the undergraduates. It is open to visitors, and they marvel not only at the naturally-lit hall itself, but also at the array of portraits of Christ Church men around the walls. Above High Table are Wolsey himself, Henry VIII, both Queen Elizabeths and a number of recent Deans.

A late addition to Wolsey's Tom Quad is the magnificent tower, with its ogee-shaped dome, built above the gateway in 1681-2 by Sir Christopher Wren. Together with the Radcliffe Camera and Magdalen Tower, Wren's Tom Tower, as it is known, is one of the most recognizable of all Oxford landmarks. It contains the most famous and loudest of Oxford's many bells. Known as Great Tom, this bell, 85 inches wide and weighing seven and a half tons, was removed to Christ Church from Oseney Abbey. Anyone who spends an evening in Oxford will hear Great Tom, because it is rung 101 times at 9:05 every night. This is one of Oxford's eccentricities; the 101 derives from the original number of scholars at Christ Church and the time is 9pm Oxford time, for the city is one degree 15 minutes west of the Greenwich meridian and therefore five minutes behind Greenwich Mean Time. Tom's sonorous tolling can barely be heard these days above the sound of traffic in much of the city, but the story has it that the bell was muffled during the First World War for fear its sound would guide enemy zeppelins to Oxford.

From its very beginnings, Christ Church attracted distinguished men, including the soldier-poet Sir Philip Sidney (1554-86), Robert Burton (1582-1639), author of *The Anatomy of Melancholy* and Richard Hakluyt (1552-1616), the geographer whose first book, *Divers Voyages*

Touching the Discovery of America and the Islands Adjacent, describes English exploration in the New World.

During the seventeenth century, the college established itself as Oxford's premier seat of learning and wealthiest foundation. During the plague years of the 1620s the Court and Parliament were removed to Oxford with Christ Church as its headquarters and, of course, Charles I made the college his centre of operations during the Civil War.

Among the undergraduates in the second half of the century was William Penn (1644-1718), who went on to found the colony of Pennsylvania and its capital city of Philadelphia in the 1680s. Penn was converted to Quakerism while he was studying at Christ Church and was ordered to leave. He was in and out of jail for years because of his religious beliefs and his publications demanding greater tolerance for non-conformist religious groups, and he returned from North America in 1685 to aid persecuted Quakers in England. He was twice accused of treason but acquitted and returned to Pennsylvania in 1699 where, among other accomplishments, he issued the Charter of Privileges which guaranteed the religious freedom that he could not secure in England. He crossed the Atlantic once more, to spend his final years in England, where he died and is buried at Jordans in Buckinghamshire, only a short drive along the M40 from Oxford.

The philosopher John Locke (1632-1704), was a lecturer here from 1661-4 and a Student until the 1680s, when his friend Lord Shaftesbury fell from favor and went into exile. Locke, closely allied to Shaftesbury, was suspected of treasonable activity and put under close scrutiny at Christ Church. In the end, he too fled the country and in 1684 word came from Charles II that Locke should be expelled from the college. The Dean, John Fell, argued that there were no reasonable grounds for this: "He lives very quietly with us and not a word ever drops from his mouth that discovers any thing of his heart within. He seems to be a man of very good converse." Back came an official letter from the king demanding "that you forthwith remove him from his said student's place and deprive him of all the rights and advantages thereunto belonging." This time Christ Church gave in. After the Glorious Revolution of 1688, Locke returned to England to be feted but never came back to Oxford. In 1754 the college authorities tried to make some amends by commissioning a full-length statue of him for the library and acknowledging him as one of Christ Church's greatest sons.

Fourteen British Prime Ministers were educated at Christ Church, including Robert Peel (1788-1850) who was the first person ever to get a double First and, in 1828, William Ewart Gladstone (1809-98), who went on to become PM four times and one of the great reforming politicians of Victorian England. Until relatively recently, Oxford University sent its own Member of Parliament to Westminster; Peel served in this position as did Gladstone for a while. Gladstone was academically brilliant, also taking a double First in Classics and Mathematics and was considered the finest speaker the Oxford Union had ever seen. He was made an honorary Fellow of All Souls in 1858 and retained a lifelong love for Oxford. "To call a man an Oxford man," he said, "is to pay him the highest compliment that can be made to a human being."

A fellow undergraduate of Gladstone was Henry Liddell (1811-98), who stayed on to teach and became Dean of Christ Church in 1855. During his 36 years in the post, he totally reformed the college and became the pivotal social point for the entire university, receiving in the Deanery kings, princes and presidents from around the world. He was the father of Alice Liddell, the young friend of "Lewis Carroll," the maths don Charles Dodgson, with whom Liddell had a long and generally frosty relationship for more than forty years. They lived on opposite sides of Tom Quad, with Dodgson's last lodgings to the left of the gateway as you come in (he was allowed to build a photographic studio up against one of the chimney stacks on the roof) and the Deanery directly opposite, by the gateway to Peckwater Quad.

In one corner of Tom Quad were the rooms of the ultimate Oxford eccentric, William Buckland (1784-1856), professor of mineralogy and one of Britain's most important early geologists and fossil gatherers. His rooms were stuffed with his finds: rocks, bones and fossils, plus a veritable menagerie of creatures, both stuffed and live. He once alarmed a guest who inquired about the munching noise from beneath the sofa by telling him it was only the jackal eating some of the guinea-pigs.

Buckland, who went on to become Dean of Westminster Abbey, had a strongly developed sense of taste and claimed to have eaten his way through the entire animal kingdom – the nastiest thing he ever ate, he said, was mole and the next worst, a bluebottle. Dinner guests never knew what to expect (crocodile and battered mice both appeared on his menu) and he once told G.C. Bompas that he had had panther chops for dinner. The panther had been dead a while, he said: "But I got them to dig it up and send me some. It was not very good."

He claimed to be able to tell anything by its taste and horrified church authorities in Naples by licking blood stains said to have been left by a saint and declaring them to be bat's urine. But he really went too far in 1848 when dining with the Harcourts at Nuneham Manor. He was shown a shrivelled piece of flesh and asked to guess what it was, Buckland popped it into his mouth and "inadvertently" swallowed it, to the horror of his hosts who then revealed it was the heart of the Sun King Louis XIV, rescued for a family heirloom by an earlier Harcourt when revolutionaries raided the Val de Grâce royal church in Paris.

When the art critic John Ruskin (1819-1900) moved into Christ Church in 1837, his mother moved into lodgings at 90 High Street to keep him company and wrote daily to her husband of everything that went on: "I have nothing particularly to communicate but, judging by myself, I think you will feel easier when you know John is safe and well this morning." John visited her for tea and again after dinner most days. Having been educated at home, he was now mixing for the first time in his life with young men of his own age. He got on well with the titled set but also excelled at his studies, winning the university's famous Newdigate Prize for poetry in 1839. After graduating, his books, including *Modern Painters* and *The Stones of Venice*, established him as the most influential art critic of his day. His views were crucial to the design of the university's Natural History Museum (1855) and he was on hand to ensure that the workers were provided with books and started their day with prayers.

Ruskin felt that there was a special dignity in manual labor and started a road-building scheme in the village of Hinksey. This was not as silly a project as it has been made to sound, but was a practical plea for keeping the countryside beautiful. Ruskin noticed that carts cut across a pleasant green in front of some cottages simply because there was no proper track for them. So, with the landowner's permission, he proceeded to build one in the spring of 1874. Undergraduates, including Oscar Wilde and Arnold Toynbee, were invited to Corpus Christi College for diggers' breakfasts and then proceeded to work. He reminded them of "the pleasures of useful muscular work" as opposed to what he considered the wasted energies of the sports field. "Even digging rightly done is at least as much an art as the mere muscular act of rowing."

Ruskin had come back to Oxford in 1870 as the Slade Professor of Fine Art, when he was granted a set of rooms in Corpus. But, after the death of his child-sweetheart Rose La Touche in 1875, he struggled with depression and ill health. In 1878 he resigned the Slade professorship, immediately after the end of his celebrated court case with Whistler.

W.H. Auden (1907-73) was at Christ Church between 1925 and 1928. By the age of twenty he was already recognized as a poetic prodigy. Cecil Day Lewis, later to become Poet Laureate, was three years his senior yet "willingly became his disciple where poetry was concerned." Christ Church was too snooty to have a don to teach the new subject of English Literature, so Auden was sent to study with Neville Coghill at Exeter College. At their first interview, Coghill asked what Auden wanted to be in later life. "I'm going to be a poet," Auden answered. Coghill made some patronizing reply, only to be crushed by Auden "You don't understand at all. I mean to be a great poet." Yet Auden never applied himself to his studies and got only a third-class degree. According to the crime writer, J.I.M. Stewart, who sat opposite him during final examinations: "The tears were coursing down his pale and ample cheeks."

Most Oxford professors are appointed to their posts by their departments and hold the title for life. The great exception is the Professor of Poetry. This appointment lasts only five years and each holder is elected by Convocation – all Oxford MAs who care to turn out to vote. The post, although poorly paid, is usually seen as a great honor and there are usually a number of candidates, with the job often going to poets of international importance.

In 1956 Auden was elected to the post following Cecil Day Lewis. By this time, he was officially an American citizen, having emigrated at the start of the Second World War, and for this he faced considerable hostility in the Christ Church common room. During the election, Harold Nicolson, one of the other candidates, wrote to his wife Vita Sackville-West: "I do think it pretty cool for Auden to claim all the rewards and honours this country can give him while deserting her in the hour of danger."

During all his visits to the city while Professor of Poetry, Auden tried to make himself approachable to young poets. At 3pm every day he set off from his rooms for the nearby St Aldate's Coffee House where, he said, the only good coffee in Oxford was obtainable. He made it known he was available for conversation with undergraduates who wanted to show him their verses. Few dared approach him, but when in 1958 the young American beat poet Gregory Corso decided to speak to him, he distressed Auden by trying to kiss the hem of his trousers.

In 1969, Auden, now dividing his time between Austria and New York City, hinted that he would like to return to Christ Church. He observed:

> I'm getting rather old to live alone in winter and I would rather live in a community. Supposing I had a coronary, it might be weeks before I was found. In Oxford I should be missed if I failed to turn up for meals.

In January 1972, Christ Church offered him tenancy of a cottage in its grounds, known as the Brewhouse. When he arrived in Oxford from the U.S., the Brewhouse was not yet decorated for him, and he stayed at All Souls for a few weeks. He was happy to be back in Oxford, but saddened within two days when he was robbed in his rooms by a young man he had befriended. "I had to leave New York and come to Oxford to get robbed," he moaned, adding: "Compared with New York, Oxford is far more crowded and the traffic far noisier."

Auden gave a poetry reading in the hall of Balliol College which, to the organizers' surprise, was absolutely packed, with about 400 people attending and a further 200 being turned away. He charged no fee for this. However, he had few friends in the Christ Church common room and would stay there after meals drinking too much port or brandy. "Look here, if Auden wants to drink himself to death, please could you ask him to do so in the Brewhouse and not in the common room," one senior colleague implored. He became thoroughly disagreeable and consequently thoroughly depressed, and only stayed in Oxford for the

Tom Tower and the Tourist Trail (Oxford Times)

autumn and spring terms, going back to Austria for the summer. He died in Vienna the following September, just hours before he was due to return to Oxford.

The Cathedral

Christ Church today is the most visited of all the Oxford colleges, despite the steep admission fee (it is, of course, a fabulously wealthy institution). Enter via the gate in the middle of the Victorian gothic Meadow Buildings and note that anyone living in the Oxford diocese – that is anywhere within Oxfordshire, Buckinghamshire or Berkshire – is, quite rightly, entitled to claim free access to their cathedral. Once in here, the rest of the visitable parts of the college become immediately available.

Christ Church's chapel is England's smallest cathedral and, consequently, has a great feeling of being overcrowded – not just with visitors and monuments, for the architecture too seems to crowd in upon itself. There is probably less to interest the casual wanderer here than in any other English cathedral. Once the centrepiece, the shrine of St Frideswide has been put back together near the altar in the Lady Chapel. The thirteenth-century shrine was destroyed during the Reformation and St Frideswide's remains removed. Catherine Martyr, the wife of the Regius Professor of Divinity, was buried in her place, but when the Catholic Mary I succeeded in 1553, she had Catherine ejected and Frideswide put back. In Elizabeth I's reign, guilt was felt at the treatment of Catherine Martyr, and it was decided to please everyone by mixing the remains of Catholic Frideswide and Protestant Catherine and reburying them in the same grave. Today, no-one knows exactly where this grave is; the polished slate slab with Frideswide's name on it is more a symbol for devotion than an accurate marker.

Apart from three fourteenth-century tombs in rather poor condition, the most interesting feature of the cathedral is its stained glass, including the brilliant Becket window of 1320 in St Lucy's Chapel, and five windows by Edward Burne-Jones and William Morris, the Pre-Raphaelite artists who had been undergraduates together at Exeter College. Perhaps the most popular of these is the St Catherine window to the right of the High Altar, which is a memorial to Edith

Liddell, Alice's older sister, who died in 1876 only days after announcing her wedding. The face of the central figure, St Catherine, is Edith's.

Like all cathedrals, Christ Church is packed with memorials, but unless you are a Latin scholar, you will learn nothing from them, for there is barely a line of English recording the college's great men. Just inside the west doors, however, two large slabs have been set in the floor, commemorating John Ruskin, who is buried at Coniston, Cumbria, and John Locke, who lies in the churchyard at High Laver, Essex. Among those actually buried here are Edward Pusey (1800-82), one of the founders of the Oxford Movement, and the Irish philosopher George Berkeley (1685-1753). Berkeley lived in Holywell Street and died while his wife was reading to him from the Bible. Worried about being buried alive, he had left instructions that he was not to be interred until his body showed definite signs of decomposition.

Those who do understand Latin might still be perplexed by the memorial to possibly the cathedral's most interesting permanent resident. On one of the piers in the eastern side of the north transept stands a painted bust of a Jacobean divine and a scrolled inscription beneath which names him only as 'Democritus Junior'. This is Robert Burton (1577-1639), who was librarian at Christ Church and vicar of the nearby parish of St Thomas. He is best remembered as the author of *The Anatomy of Melancholy* (1621), one of the great English prose works of the seventeenth century. Burton himself was no stranger to melancholy (depression) and was known for his mood swings and sometimes as "a very merry person." His book, presented as a medical treatise, is actually an affectionate satire on the failings of learning and human endeavor. Burton found melancholy to be universally present, "an inbred malady in every one of us." Dr Johnson described it as the only book that could get him out of bed two hours earlier than usual. Every page was full of quotations from authors of all kinds: religious, the classics, historians, poets and travellers. "Democritus Junior" was the pseudonym under which the Anatomy was published; Democritus being the fifth-century BC Greek thinker known as the "laughing philosopher," amused by the follies of men. At a time when astrology was considered a perfectly acceptable form of study, Burton showed his ability in a most alarming way, dying on the very day he had predicted for himself.

Pass through Peckwater Quad to Canterbury Quad or slip in through the Canterbury Gate in Oriel Square and a signpost will direct you through a door in a suitably sober eighteenth-century building containing the library. Here one suddenly enters another world, stepping out of Georgian elegance into 1960s brutalism to the domain of the Christ Church Picture Gallery.

The collection, based on a magnificent gift of paintings and drawings in 1764 from an old member, General John Guise, is housed in a concrete bunker. Being underground may do wonders for keeping down the temperature and keeping the sunlight off the paintings, but there is something bizarre in the juxtaposition of these florid, mostly Italian, works in their ornate frames and the cold gray walls and concrete pillars of the 1964 gallery. The paintings, like so many in Oxford, are a largely second-division lot, but the collection of Old Master drawings is internationally famous and so wide-ranging that just a little can be shown at any one time.

Christ Church Meadows

Christ Church still has one last surprise and one last delight. Christ Church Meadow offers the sight of a herd of cows grazing on undeveloped grassland within 200 yards of the bustle, noise and activity of Carfax and the High Street. This land between the college and the River Thames has been jealously guarded by Christ Church against all plans for its development. It used to belong to St Frideswide's Priory and, whether lush in summer or flooded in winter, always offers a quick and easy escape from the trials of Oxford life. It is entered from St Aldate's through the War Memorial Gardens and then a perimeter walk breaks off to the right down to the Thames and up to its junction with the Cherwell. The main path passes in front of the Meadow Buildings and across to the Cherwell along Broad Walk. Until twenty years ago, when the trees were ravaged by Dutch elm disease, this double row of mature English elms was one of the great sights of Oxford. Today the visitor can only imagine the glory of the scene.

In the 1960s, it looked as though the tranquillity of the Meadows would be lost forever when the city council wanted to push a major road along the line of Broad Walk to relieve traffic congestion in the High.

The government backed the plan and it took two years and a huge outcry from university members past and present to get the idea scrapped. Speaking against it, Sir Colin Buchanan said:

> *I doubt whether there is another city in the world, still less a city which is a great seat of learning, which provides almost in its centre a comparable scene of pastoral remoteness and simplicity, isolated from motor traffic...it is not the matter of a minor open space, but of a splendid open area with long vistas and wide skies.*

His was a description which applies even today.

Almost a part of the meadows is Merton Fields, bounded by Broad Walk on one side and the open lane, Deadman's Walk, on the other. This was the route of medieval Jewish funeral processions, coming from the synagogue which stood near the site of Tom Tower, and going out beyond the city wall, skirting Merton College and up to the Jewish burial ground where the Botanic Garden is today.

Near the eastern end of Deadman's Walk, a metal plaque has been set into the wall, marking the site of the first ever man-made flight in Britain, a balloon ascent by James Sadler (1753-1828), a pastry cook turned laboratory technician who, less than a year after the Montgolfier brothers' first manned flight in France, took off from here on October 4, 1784 and landed some miles to the north-east of the city at Woodeaton.

Be careful though, before entering Christ Church Meadows, for a sign near the entrance warns:

> *Meadow Keepers and Constables are instructed to prevent the entrance into the Meadow of all beggars, persons in ragged or very dirty clothes, persons of improper character or who are not decent in appearance and behaviour and to prevent indecent, rude or disorderly conduct of every description.*

You are also not allowed in if you are carrying packages or bundles so as to obstruct the walks, flying kites, throwing balls, firing guns, fishing, catching birds or cycling.

The Meadows are a popular place to stroll for students wanting to gather their thoughts and for anyone wanting to clear their head. Marshal Gebhard von Blucher (1742-1819), who fought with Wellington at Waterloo and, it is said, saved the day when all was lost, was staying at Christ Church in 1814, where it is said he drank a full bottle of brandy before breakfast. He then walked off its effects with a stroll around the meadows, appearing a few hours later and showing no sign of having taken a drink.

St Aldate's and Folly Bridge

Beyond the entrance to Christ Church Meadows stands the St Aldate's police station, not the headquarters of Inspector Morse, but a building which has been filmed a number of times for scenes in the television series. Close up against it is the university Music Faculty and the Bate Collection of Musical Instruments. This cramped and badly displayed collection is almost certainly Oxford's smallest museum, but the importance of its content is way out of proportion to its size. The most comprehensive collection of Western musical instruments in England outside London, it is a living, working museum; the majority of instruments can be played – and are at regular intervals. Some pre-knowledge is assumed of visitors, but there is a great deal to catch the attention of the casual browser. Look out for Handel's own harpsichord, the small soprano trombone, and the original seventeenth-century recorder on which all school recorders have been based since. There are all manner of crumhorns, sackbuts, shawms and a veritable nest of serpents. Here too is the oldest Javanese gamelan orchestra in Britain, which is regularly played by an enthusiastic team of experts and beginners from the university and city.

South of here runs the Thames, crossed by Folly Bridge, the southern entrance to the medieval city and most probably the site of the original ox-ford. It takes its name not from the outlandish, castellated building known as Caudwell's Castle, built in Venetian palazzo style in 1849 by Joshua Caudwell, a wealthy eccentric who surrounded his home with cannons and classical statues. The original folly rather dates back to the thirteenth century when the bridge was known as Grand Pont – still the name attached to the roads on either side of the Abingdon Road to the south. This medieval folly was the original gateway with a tower built on the top by Roger Bacon, the Doctor Mirabilis, one of the earliest of Oxford's great scientists. It was known for centuries as Friar Bacon's Study and was pulled down in 1779 during a road-widening scheme.

Nearby stands the Head of the River Inn, the largest pub in Oxford and a former wharf house belonging to the boat builders Salter Bros. It takes it name from its position near the finishing post for the University rowing races, the winning boat of which is known as the Head of the River.

Back at the top of St Aldate's stands the pseudo-Jacobean style Town Hall which is the latest of several town halls and guildhalls to have stood on this site close by Carfax. It was outside here that the young Tony Blair got a taste of police strong-arm tactics when he took part in a demonstration against the National Front as an undergraduate. Just around the corner in Blue Boar Street and part of the Town Hall complex, is the council's Museum of Oxford in rooms that were previously the Oxford Public Library and on the site of the original Blue Boar Inn that gave the road its name. Among the exhibits here are some telling reconstructions of Oxford student rooms and domestic interiors, contrasting the wealth of North Oxford with the poverty of Jericho. Probably the most popular exhibit though, particularly with children, who are fascinated and horrified in equal proportion, is the skeleton of Giles Covington, a 22-year-old man hanged for the murder of a pedlar in Nuneham Woods in 1789. After his public execution at Oxford Prison, his body was cut down from the gallows, dissected at Christ

Folly Bridge and Bacon's Study (private collection)

Church anatomy school and his skeleton used thereafter as a teaching aid. Because Covington was convicted on the evidence of another suspect, there have been calls in recent years both for the case against him to be re-heard and for his remains to be given a proper burial. Given that so much of the history of Oxford is still standing, still occupied and still being used, it is hardly surprising that this cramped collection should be eternally overshadowed by the living museum outside its doors.

The Bear on the corner of Blue Boar Street and Alfred Street, claims to be the oldest pub in Oxford. Yet it is in fact not the original inn, but an ostler's house which was attached to it in 1606. It became an inn, known as the Jolly Trooper in 1774 and took over the name of the Bear Inn, which used virtually to fill Alfred Street when it closed in 1801. The staff have long kept up a tradition of cutting the end off customers' ties which are not represented in their collection of over 4,500. There is a free pint of beer as consolation for any tie destroyed.

Corpus Christi

The Oxford explorer hurrying between the glories of Christ Church and Merton easily overlooks little Corpus Christi College, tucked into the corner of Oriel Square between the two larger colleges. In the Civil War, it was simply a corridor between the two for Charles I in Christ Church and his queen, Henrietta Maria, in Merton. But it would be a shame to overlook completely one of Oxford's most attractive and delightful colleges. Its extremely compact ground plan belies the fact that no fewer than five academic halls had to be demolished to make room for it.

Corpus's Front Quad is certainly one of the most attractive in the university and Fellows Quad is the smallest. The most famous detail of the college is the sundial in the middle of Front Quad, which can be peeped at from the lodge gate, even when the college is closed to visitors. It was erected in 1581 and stands 26ft high in order to clear the shadows of the surrounding buildings. Unfortunately, its height makes its main dial very difficult to read from ground level. Even so, there are 26 other dials of various purposes dotted around the monument, which has been much damaged over the years by the antics of boisterous and drunken students and visitors who are irresistibly drawn to try to scale it and place various receptacles on its summit.

Corpus marks the transition from medieval into modern times at Oxford. It was founded in 1512 by Richard Foxe, Lord Privy Seal under Henry VII and Bishop of Winchester. Foxe originally intended a monastic college for Winchester monks, but his colleague Hugh Oldham, Bishop of Exeter, who foresaw the changes that would overcome the Church in the sixteenth century, persuaded Foxe to make his college a secular establishment. Foxe and Oldham together put up the money for the college.

From its earliest time, Corpus Christi had a modernist and liberal attitude. Foxe was a friend of the humanist scholar Erasmus and, under his influence, made Corpus the first Renaissance foundation in Oxford, giving great emphasis to the teaching of Latin and Greek. Erasmus himself proclaimed: "My mind foretells that in the future this college, like some holy temple dedicated to good learning, will be accounted among the chief glories of Britain in all countries of the world." Foxe himself went blind before the college was finished and the story is told that the first Fellows led the old man twice around Front Quad to make him think it much larger than it actually was.

Corpus is much associated with animals, thanks originally to its early benefactors. For decades a fox was kept chained in an outer courtyard to remind everyone of the founder, and three owls were maintained as a reminder of Bishop Oldham (the pun was on the pronunciation Owl-dham). In his own writings about the college, Foxe made heavy comparison to bees busy in their hive producing rich honey, and indeed bees were kept at Corpus for more than a century, their disappearance just before the establishment of Cromwell's Commonwealth being interpreted with hindsight as an omen. Add to these the pelican symbol of the college atop the sundial, and the tradition of Oxford's gentlest sporting competition, the annual tortoise race between the pets of Corpus Christi, Brasenose and Balliol, and the wildlife link is well established.

Corpus's most prominent literary association is through the relatively unknown Puritan President of the college, John Rainolds (1549-1607), who was one of the most important members of the committee of academics which translated and produced the King James Authorised Version of the Bible. There used to be regular meetings at Corpus to control the content of what was to be possibly the most influential book ever written in English.

A less welcome member of the college later in the seventeenth century was James, Duke of Monmouth (1649-85), the illegitimate son of Charles II. When the great plague struck London in 1665, Charles brought his court to Oxford and Monmouth lodged at Corpus, where his name was added to the list of members. However, twenty years later, after his failed attempt to claim the crown after his father's death, and his execution for treason, Monmouth's name was erased from all college records.

Other former undergraduates of note at Corpus include James Ogilthorpe, the founder of the state of Georgia, Matthew Arnold, poet, critic and Professor of Poetry at Oxford, and Robert Bridges, Poet Laureate.

Corpus is still one of Oxford's smallest and friendliest colleges, never shouting about its achievements, although academically its results have always been very good. Its liberalism lived on in the twentieth century: in the 1960s, before any of the men's colleges admitted women as members, Corpus allowed women as guests to meals in hall twice a term; undergraduates at the college led a campaign against the university buying shares in companies associated with apartheid South Africa and the college chapel was the first to allow denominations other than Anglicans to hold services in its chapel.

CHAPTER THREE

Cardinal Newman's Oxford

"Who could resist the charm of that spiritual apparition gliding in the dim afternoon light through the aisles of St Mary's?"

John Henry Newman (1801-90) was the most charismatic British churchman of the nineteenth century and the leader of the Oxford Movement which caused a revolution in the Church of England. He was born on February 21, 1801 and was accepted into Trinity College at the age of fifteen. After failing to get a first class degree, he took holy orders and was for a time curate at St Clement's, before, in 1826, being awarded a Fellowship at Oriel College, at that time the highest academic achievement possible in Oxford. In the senior common room at Oriel he came into contact with some of the best minds of the day, including the young Professor of Hebrew, Edward Pusey and John Keble (1792-1866), author of the enormously popular collection of verse, *The Christian Year*, which ran to over 95 editions in his lifetime. Keble was at the time considered "the first man in Oxford."

Newman was desperately shy but an enthusiastic churchman, contemptuous of Roman Catholicism. The Oriel group found they had much in common, especially their shared belief that the Church of

England had lost its way in leading the nation and was in danger of being sidelined by the secular authorities. This came to a head in 1833 when the government passed a statute abolishing ten Irish bishoprics. Keble, who by this time was Professor of Poetry, shook the university and the nation with a sermon "On National Apostasy" delivered in the university church of St Mary the Virgin in July 1833, in which he warned that Britain was moving away from God and called for a response from concerned Christians.

This was the first strike from the Oxford Movement, a collection of individuals who gathered behind Keble to fight for the future of their church. Their chief weapon was a series of pamphlets entitled *Tracts for the Times* (giving the movement its alternative name of Tractarianism) in which they elaborated their religious views. The Tracts were backed up by the weekly sermons at St Mary's, of which Newman had been vicar since 1828.

Newman served two congregations at St Mary's; the vice-chancellor and leading university figures attended in state in the morning and then at 4pm another service was held, attended largely by college servants and their families. It was at this afternoon service that Newman created his reputation as the greatest preacher of his age. He was no great orator, but the message of his sermons and the way he delivered them beguiled and bewitched his congregation. Gradually his Sunday afternoon sermons became the highlight of the university week, with undergraduates and the younger dons transferring from the morning service to pack the church to overflowing to hear him speak. The excitement was electric; some colleges even changed the times of chapel and meals in order to keep their students away from Tractarian meetings.

At the centre of the controversy was the pale, thin, ascetic figure of the vicar himself. Matthew Arnold wrote:

Who could resist the charm of that spiritual apparition, gliding in the dim afternoon light through the aisles of St Mary's, rising into the pulpit and then, in the most entrancing of voices, breaking the silence with words and thoughts which were a religious music – subtle, sweet, mournful?

Professor J.A. Froude of Brasenose claimed that Newman was a genius, "perhaps one of three or four at present alive in this planet." Even frosty Mark Pattison, Rector of Lincoln College, was caught up: "The force of his dialectic and the beauty of his rhetorical exposition were such that one's eye and ear were charmed."

The excitement and awe he provoked are unimaginable now. Young men in the university, known as Newmaniacs, took to copying his dress and his speech. J.C. Shairp remembered:

In Oriel Lane, light-hearted undergraduates would drop their voices and whisper "There's Newman!" when, head thrust forward, and gaze fixed as though on some vision seen only by himself, with swift, noiseless step he glided by. Awe fell on them for a moment, almost as if it had been some apparition that had passed.

And his message was increasingly that the Church of England, as part of the Catholic church created by divine authority, was more than just a human institution. He claimed that Anglican bishops were the true successors of the Apostles themselves, and that the Church of England needed to look back to its Catholic roots.

While Newman and his followers were creating their stir, not only in Oxford but in vicarages throughout the land, there was much opposition to what were seen as papist leanings. Newman brought it all to a head in 1841 when, in Tract 90, he suggested that the Thirty-Nine Articles of the Church of England, the creed to which any student had to agree before being accepted as a member of the university, fitted in with the beliefs of Roman Catholicism. This was too much for the bishops, the professors and the heads of the colleges. All further tracts were forbidden by the university and, for a while at least, the Tractarians were put to flight. As a result, several hundred clergymen left the Church of England and became members of the Roman Catholic church.

Newman's enthusiasm for the romanizing of the English church was a cover for the fact that he himself was drifting towards Roman Catholicism, and in 1842, with a small group of followers, he moved from St Mary's to its small sister church at Littlemore to the south of Oxford where he converted some abandoned stables into a "college" where he and his friends could live an austere semi-monastic life. In October 1845 he made the decision to become a Roman Catholic. Four of his companions at Littlemore had already made the break and, on October 9, Newman and two others were received into the Catholic church by Father Dominic Barberi.

It was a shattering blow that reverberated across England. John Keble said the spring had gone out of his year and Gladstone described it as an event of "calamitous importance." Within a year, Newman was accepted as a Catholic priest in Birmingham where he set up an oratory and thereafter became the guiding spirit in the rehabilitation of Catholics in English life. He did not return to Oxford until 1877, when he became the first honorary Fellow of Trinity College. Two years later he was made a cardinal. He died in 1890 and in Rome today the long slow process to have him declared a saint continues.

In Oxford, the Tractarians, now led by Pusey, suffered serious decline as a wave of liberalism swept through the Church of England and reforms did away with all religious tests including the need to swear allegiance to the Thirty-Nine Articles. Soon dons no longer needed to be Anglican clergymen or celibate, and the church's grip on Oxford was broken for the first time in 600 years. Newman's college buildings at Littlemore have been restored as a permanent memorial to him and serve today as a place of pilgrimage for both Roman and Anglo-Catholics.

The University Church of St Mary

The University Church of St Mary the Virgin in the High, is visited by more people every year than any other parish church in Britain. The present building dates largely from the fifteenth and sixteenth centuries, but there has been a church on this site since Saxon times. It was around St Mary's that the infant university grew up. In the early days before it built its own specialized meeting places, St Mary's was the centre of university life. Congregation House on the north-east side of the tower was built in 1320 specifically for meetings of Congregation, the University "parliament" and for storing the university archives. Examinations, which in the early days were largely oral, were carried out within the church; students had to dispute and debate in the porch and those seeking a divinity degree had to preach a Latin sermon.

It is difficult for the visitor used to the Gothic glories of parish churches in towns and villages across the country to appreciate the importance of this rather dull, surprisingly small interior, or to comprehend how much history has taken place here. It was in this broad nave that Archbishop Cranmer was brought for his final humiliation before being led to execution at the stake in what is now Broad Street. He was displayed to the assembled clerics and academics on a specially constructed platform against the pillar immediately opposite the pulpit. Even today, one can see where the stonework was chipped away to accommodate this cruel stage. It was here, a few years later, that Amy Robsart, the tragic wife of Queen Elizabeth's favorite, Lord Robert Dudley, was swiftly laid to rest. In the seventeenth century William Laud, Archbishop of Canterbury and Chancellor of the university was accused of preaching popery here. In the following century John Radcliffe, the university's greatest benefactor, was buried here and John Wesley, the founder of Methodism, preached as a Church of England minister from the pulpit and upset the university authorities with his ideas. And here, of course, in the nineteenth century, Newman stirred the young men of the university with his Sunday afternoon sermons.

There are two great architectural features of St Mary's; the first the astonishing baroque south porch leading on to the High, built in Archbishop Laud's time, with its candy-twist columns based on those of Bernini's great baldecchino in St Peter's in Rome. Above the entrance, stands a statue of the Virgin and child, a controversial "papist" icon, whose heads were shattered by a Parliamentary soldier before King Charles I's occupation of Oxford in 1642 – they were restored after the Monarchy itself was restored in 1660. The other feature is the great tower and its spire, completed in the early fourteenth century. There are four great aerial views of Oxford: from the Sheldonian Theatre, the towers of St Michael at the North Gate, St Martin's at Carfax, and St Mary's. This last undoubtedly has the finest views from the parapet where tower becomes steeple, looking across the heart of the university, down into All Souls and out across Christ Church meadows. Unfortunately, this is the most difficult climb of the four; more than half the ascent of 127 steps is up a narrow stone spiral staircase and the viewing gallery, also narrow, does not go right around the tower – when you have got to the end you have to turn around and squeeze past anyone who followed you up.

Despite the importance of St Mary's to the university, there is only one medieval tomb on display, that traditionally believed to be of Adam de Brome, the founder of Oriel College, which has always appointed the vicar of St Mary's. Unfortunately, this tomb is a reconstruction and only the lid dates from de Brome's time.

A marble slab in the floor near the sanctuary steps tells us that "in a vault of brick at the upper end of the choir of this church, lie the remains of Amy Robsart." In 1560, Elizabeth I, the daughter of Henry VIII and Anne Boleyn, had been queen of England for only two years. She was unmarried and a great prize for any man who could win her hand. The young queen's favorite was Lord Robert Dudley and he was ambitious. However, he was also married – to Amy Robsart. During 1560, foreign ambassadors at Elizabeth's court wrote home saying they had heard rumors that some evil would be done to Lady Dudley. She was staying at Cumnor Place just to the west of Oxford in the late summer when, one day, she sent all her staff (some say two ladies stayed with her) to a fair at Abingdon, while she remained in the manor house. When the servants returned, they found Amy dead at the foot of a staircase with her neck broken.

Accounts naturally differ, but there were enough who disliked

Cumnor Place (private collection)

Dudley to point the finger at him as a murderer freeing himself to marry the queen. Yet there were also suggestions that it was an accident or that it could have been suicide. Certainly, modern medical opinion has it that descriptions of Amy were those of a woman severely afflicted with cancer. But, of course, we want to think the worst because it makes for the best story. So Amy was buried hurriedly, without an inquest. Within a few years, Dudley was Earl of Leicester, but the queen, no doubt aware of the rumors, was certainly not going to marry him; she even suggested him as a husband for her doomed cousin Mary, Queen of Scots. In the event, Dudley went on to marry two other women – bigamously – and was for more than twenty years Chancellor of Oxford University. In 1588, he was appointed to lead the English forces against the Spanish Armada but died suddenly at Cornbury in north-west Oxfordshire.

The Radcliffe Camera
Behind St Mary's lies Radcliffe Square, the traffic-free area around James Gibbs's masterpiece, the Radcliffe Camera, the first round library in the world. It has been called the true heart of the university, but in reality nothing actually happens here and it is more a place that one passes through. True, the Camera itself, completed in 1748 (camera simply means chamber) is one of the two or three great buildings of Oxford, but it is not an area in which one feels one wants to linger for too long. The Radcliffe Camera is now an extension of the Bodleian Library – indeed the whole of the surface of Radcliffe Square between the two buildings lies only a few inches above the roof of the underground storage space in which some of the Bodleian's millions of volumes are stored. It is difficult to get inside the Camera, but if you can, you will recognize it as probably the biggest waste of space in Oxford; I mean internally, of course, where the wonderful domed area contains nothing but air, and the library shelves and working space take up a surprisingly small area.

Dr John Radcliffe (1650-1714), whose name crops up in Oxford more often than even Lord Nuffield, (Radcliffe Camera, Radcliffe Square, Radcliffe Observatory, Radcliffe Infirmary, John Radcliffe Hospital, Radcliffe Quadrangle, Radcliffe Road, Radcliffe Science Library) was not a great academic, nor even a long-serving inhabitant of the university. He was, like so many benefactors before and since, simply someone who passed through Oxford and then remembered it in his will. Radcliffe was a Yorkshire boy who came up to study at University College at thirteen, got an undistinguished arts degree and became a Fellow of Lincoln College at eighteen. He went on to study medicine and set himself up in practice in Oxford, where he achieved a surprising success with smallpox, the great scourge of the times. Radcliffe had little faith in fashionable blood-letting and instead insisted that fresh air should ventilate the sickroom.

By 1684 he had left Oxford and moved into practice in London where, despite the rudeness with which he treated his many patients, he collected a reputation and following and started amassing his huge fortune. He won the attention of the Court and saved the life of William III. Yet on being summoned to Queen Mary II, who was suffering from smallpox, he read the list of treatments she had already been given by other doctors and declared that she was as good as dead. He was right. When he died, he left his great fortune to the university, enough to build a new quad at his old college, £40,000 for the Radcliffe Library (Camera) and the rest to trustees who continued to spend it wisely, securing his name in Oxford's history. When one academic heard that Radcliffe had left money for a library, he described it as "like a eunuch founding a seraglio."

Brasenose College

Brasenose College (BNC in Oxford-speak) has one of the most enviable positions of all the colleges, with a frontage on the High Street (mock-medieval of c1900) and its main entrance on to Radcliffe Square. Its quads offer views of the spire of the University Church and the dome of the Radcliffe Camera, All Souls is only a stone's throw away, and it is the shortest of walks to the Bodleian Library and Sheldonian Theatre.

But for all that, Brasenose has rarely commanded a position among Oxford's most celebrated colleges; even today it is trying to shake off a nineteenth-century reputation for sporting excellence at the expense of academic standards.

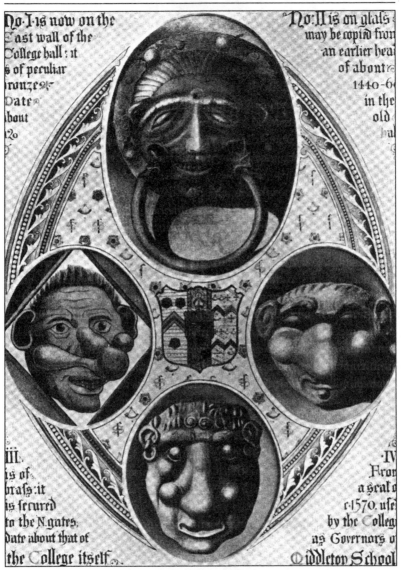

No·I·is now on the
East wall of the
College hall: it
is of peculiar
bronze:
Date
about
[2o]

No·II is on glass
may be copied from
an earlier head
of about
1440-6
in the
old
hall

III.
is of
brass: it
is secured
to the N.gates;
Date about that of
the College itself.

·IV
From
a seal of
c.1570. used
by the College
as Governors of
Middleton School

Brasenose door knockers (National Buildings Record)

The unusual name is inherited directly from Brasenose Hall, one of several academic halls on the site of the present college. The hall itself took its name from the great brass knocker in the shape of an animal's snout, which was attached to its main gate and first recorded in a document of 1279. In those days, academic halls shared special privileges with churches, and fugitives from the law could claim sanctuary within. One had only to clutch the ring through the brazen nose to be immune from prosecution.

However, in the 1330s, a time of considerable civil unrest in Oxford, a group of students and teachers sensibly migrated to the more peaceful surroundings of Stamford in Lincolnshire to set up an alternative university, taking with them the brazen nose. The king, Edward II, suppressed this rival establishment and the rebels were all sent back. But they left behind the knocker, now attached to Brasenose House, and there it stayed until 1890 when the building came up for sale. The College bought the whole property for the sake of the door knocker, which they duly brought home to Oxford. It now hangs above High Table in the hall. In the intervening centuries, Brasenose had had a near-replica made, probably to mark its foundation as a college, and that is what you can see today above the main gate in Radcliffe Square.

Brasenose was founded in 1509, the first Oxford college of the Tudor era. It was two Lancashire men who turned Brasenose from hall to college, William Smyth, bishop of Lincoln and Richard Sutton, a lawyer. Their northern beginnings led inevitably to a leaning towards undergraduates from Lancashire, Cheshire and Yorkshire, and it was to visit his fellow north countrymen that John Middleton (1578-1623), the 9ft 3ins wrestler known as the Childe of Hale, paid a visit. Middleton was inevitably a man of great renown and in 1617 he was called to the court of James I, where he wrestled with and beat the King's Wrestler. On his way back to Hale, Cheshire, he stopped over at Brasenose, where he left an imprint of his hand seventeen inches long according to one description – Samuel Pepys paid two shillings to see it in 1668. The college owns a lifesize portrait of the Childe of Hale and copies of the handprint.

Early students at the college included John Foxe (1516-87) whose *Book of Martyrs* played a vital supporting role in the English Reformation, the great dramatist John Marston (1576-1634), a contemporary of Shakespeare, and Robert Burton, author of *The Anatomy of Melancholy*. There were also several undergraduates who went on to play an important role in American history, including

Lawrence Washington, the great-grandfather of the first American President. He left behind him in 1619 a debt of 17s 6d (88p or less than a dollar and a half) in the college buttery, which was finally paid in 1924 by some visiting American lawyers. The Rev Thomas Adams, grandfather of Washington's successor, John Adams, was a Fellow of Brasenose but was deprived of his Fellowship during the Commonwealth for being a Quaker. Richard Bellingham, Governor of Massachusetts in 1641, was also a student here, as was James Noyse, whose second child, also James, was one of the founders of Yale University. Making a mark on the other side of the world was George Ferguson Bowen, the first Governor of Queensland, Australia.

Towards the end of the eighteenth century, the college gained for a while a reputation for academic quality. After the university subscribed to public examinations in 1800, Brasenose offered prizes to students gaining firsts or seconds and this both encouraged and attracted the finer minds of the time. It was in later Victorian times that Brasenose acquired its reputation as a sporting college, largely because the landed gentry associated at that time with the college were much given to sporting pursuits. Alumni of this time included William Webb Ellis (1805-72), who some years earlier at his public school, Rugby, had picked up the football during a match and run with it, thus, allegedly, giving birth to the game of rugby football. The college has produced two Prime Ministers: Henry Addington (1757-1844) was British premier between 1801 and1804 and, much more recently, John Gorton (b.1911) studied here before going on to become Prime Minister of Australia.

The biggest name associated with Brasenose in the nineteenth century was Walter Pater (1839-94), who is remembered by the college with a memorial plaque which has him surrounded by portraits of his peers – Leonardo da Vinci, Michelangelo, Dante and Plato – highly regarded indeed! Pater was the unlikeliest of heroes, yet this dapper, balding, repressed homosexual had a profound effect on generations of young Oxford men including Gerard Manley Hopkins and Oscar Wilde. Edmund Gosse said that "he was the most studied of English prose writers of his time." Pater, who studied at Queen's and became one of the first non-clerical Fellows of Brasenose, was the founder and genius behind the aesthetic movement of young men for whom art was life and life art, and whose desire for beauty led to affected speech and manners and flamboyant dress. They were ridiculed regularly by *Punch* magazine and in Gilbert and Sullivan's opera *Patience*, but in Oxford the effete style survived through the Brideshead generation of the 1920s until the Second World War. Oscar Wilde declared: "There is no Pater but Pater and I am his prophet," but Max Beerbohm found his lectures inaudible: "They were a form of self-communion; he whispered them."

Among writers associated with the college are the mystic poet Thomas Traherne (1636-74), the thriller writer John Buchan (1875-1940), who lived and is buried at Elsfield just outside the city and who died in Canada while serving as Governor General, and the Nobel Prize winner William Golding (1911-93). The two best-selling authors connected with the college, however, have more tenuous associations. In 1872 Thomas Humphry Ward, a Fellow of Brasenose married Mary Augusta Arnold, a twenty-year-old local woman. Neither is an instantly recognizable name, but Mary, as Mrs Humphry Ward (1851-1920) was the author in 1888 of a novel which took the English-speaking literary and intellectual world by storm. In its first year *Robert Elsmere* sold 40,000 copies in Britain and over 200,000 copies in America. In all, it passed a million copies in English and was translated into most foreign languages. The American writer Henry James said of it: "The book was not merely an extraordinarily successful novel; it was a momentous public event."

Mary Ward's three-volume novel about a young clergyman coming to terms with his loss of faith in the wake of the Oxford Movement led Tolstoy to describe her as the greatest English novelist of her time. The artist Sir Edward Burne-Jones enthused: "I never thought I should devour a book about parsons," and the most influential magazine of the time chose Prime Minister William Gladstone to review the novel.

Mind you, Mary did not exactly emerge from obscurity. As Mary Arnold, she was the granddaughter of Dr Arnold of Rugby, the most influential educationist of the century, and the niece of Matthew Arnold, poet, critic and Professor of Poetry at Oxford. Lewis Carroll wrote *Sylvie and Bruno* for Mary and her two sisters, one of whom married a Balliol man and made her the aunt of Julian and Aldous Huxley. After her marriage, she became secretary of the Oxford Association for the Education of Women, which led to the founding of Somerville College, but her feminism stopped short of giving women the vote, for she also founded the National Women's Anti-Suffrage League.

Jeffrey Archer (b.1940) is one of the more colorful characters associated with Brasenose in the post-war period. He was never a graduate, although he did not go out of his way to correct anyone who thought he was. In fact, he came to Oxford in 1963 as a PE master at a minor public school to study for a diploma in education and was attached to Brasenose. He excelled as an athlete and became president of the Oxford University Athletics Club as well as a ruthless publicist and fund-raiser. He threw his weight behind Oxfam's "Hungry Million" campaign and helped to raise a million pounds. His stunts in this good cause included bringing the Beatles to Oxford for the only time in their careers. But this was not for a concert, for they had donated something which Archer was able to auction to raise money and in return he secured them an invitation to dine at Brasenose with the Principal, Sir Noel Hall. The visit was an astonishingly well-kept secret at the height of Beatlemania, and John, Paul, George and Ringo had a quiet drink at Vincent's club in King Edward Street before going on to dinner at the college. After the meal, Sir Noel described the Beatles as "four exceptionally agreeable young men." Archer also staged a transatlantic dash to persuade President Lyndon B. Johnson to sign an album of Sir Winston Churchill's recorded speeches to be auctioned for Oxfam.

Archer went on to become a successful businessman and a Tory MP at 29. Five years later, however, he resigned from politics after losing his fortune in a dubious business venture. To make some money he sat down and wrote his first novel, *Not a Penny More Not a Penny Less*, in ten weeks. It sold a million copies in a year and Archer's new career was launched. He became an indefatigable supporter of the Conservatives outside Parliament and was appointed deputy chairman by Mrs Thatcher before being involved in an astonishing libel case which earned him £500,000, then the highest award in British history. Archer's new-found credibility brought him the chairmanship of the Conservative Party, a knighthood and then a peerage, before he set his sights on becoming the first elected Mayor of London.

Lincoln College

The delicious irony about Lincoln College is that it was set up by a man who persecuted the greatest free thinker of the English medieval church, John Wyclif – yet, 300 years later, the same college would produce the greatest free-thinking English churchman of modern times, John Wesley.

It was suggested that Richard Fleming had himself been attracted to Wyclif's teachings as a student, but by 1427 when, as Bishop of Lincoln, he obtained a charter from Henry VI to establish an Oxford college, he was notorious as the firmly orthodox churchman who had had Wyclif's body exhumed, burned and thrown into a nearby river. Fleming wanted to set up a little college to "train clergy in the true theology...to defend the mysteries of scripture against those ignorant laymen who profaned with swinish snouts its most holy pearls." His charter allowed him to take over three churches, All Saints in the High Street, St Michael at the North Gate and St Mildred's at the corner of Turl Street and Brasenose Lane. This last was immediately pulled down and the college erected on the site. Revenues from these three parishes served as Lincoln's small endowment and it was to remain one of the poorer colleges, and a theologically conservative one at that, throughout the Renaissance and the Reformation. Hugh Weston (Rector 1539-56) led the arguments against Cranmer, Latimer and Ridley in the University Church and was rewarded by Mary Tudor by being made Dean of Westminster. At least two members of the college were executed as traitors for holding Catholic allegiance during Elizabeth I's reign.

A late seventeenth-century Rector, Nathaniel Crewe (1633-1721) went on to be Bishop of Oxford, Bishop of Durham and eventually Baron Crewe. On his death, he left money to the university, £10 of which was to enable the Chancellor, plus heads of houses, doctors and professors to feast each year on champagne and strawberries before going on to the Encaenia degree ceremony at the Sheldonian Theatre. This bounty, known as the Creweian Benefaction, is used to this day. The university's greatest benefactor, Dr John Radcliffe, was a Fellow here from1670 to 1675, but on his death left his fortune to institutions other than Lincoln College, with which he had fallen out.

John Wesley (1703-1791) was born in Lincolnshire, one of nineteen children and came up to Christ Church in 1720. He was elected a Fellow of Lincoln College in 1726, and the rooms traditionally thought to have been occupied by him can be visited by arrangement with the bursar. Their restoration in 1928 was paid for by Methodists in the United States. Recent evidence has concluded, however, that these were not Wesley's rooms at all and that he lived in another part of the college altogether.

With his brother Charles Wesley (1707-88), the great hymn-writer, and a number of like-minded university men including George Whitefield (1714-70) of Pembroke, Wesley formed a religious group known as the Holy Club but perjoratively called the Methodists because they adhered strictly and methodically to religious ideas and practices. These included activities driven by social conscience, such as visiting prisoners at Oxford castle, reforming prostitutes and caring for the city's down-and-outs.

In the 1730s, the Wesleys and Whitefield travelled as missionaries to Georgia in the American colonies for three years with little success, although Whitefield later returned to acclaim. Back in England, John Wesley started his endless perambulation of the country, preaching outdoors to huge crowds, often of working-class people, and expounding his belief of personal salvation through faith. All his life, Wesley remained a minister of the Church of England and considered Methodism to be simply a movement within that church. He often returned to Oxford, where the Methodist ideals were maintained within a small group. He preached in many city churches, including the University Church. But after a sermon in 1744 which proved to be a stinging attack on idleness, gluttony, sensuality and general uselessness within the university, he found himself banned from that particular pulpit.

These were quiet times for Lincoln, even perhaps a decline, but academic fortunes and reputations improved under the liberal-minded Mark Pattison (1813-84), who brought a greater concern for scholarship and improved standards. Pattison was one of the strangest of the big names in Victorian Oxford. He came up to the top-dog college Oriel in 1832, but his second-class degree was not enough to earn him an Oriel Fellowship. Lincoln, meanwhile, offered him a post and he came into his own as an inspiring teacher and a conscientious tutor, although his colleagues thought him "unsociable, ungenial and morose."

Pattison certainly had his dark side as a tutor, as an eye-witness account of him in action suggests:

There was a timid knock on the door, and an undergraduate entered, with a sheet of paper in his hand, a theme or composition of some sort. Pattison beckoned the man to come forward, took the sheet and looked over it, puffing slowly at his cigar. Then he crumpled the page up in his hand, threw it in the man's face, and pointed to the door. The interview between pupil and tutor was over in a few minutes, without a word said on either side.

When he lost the election for Rector of Lincoln in 1851, Pattison was devastated: "I have nothing to which I look forward with any satisfaction; no prospects; my life seems to have come to an end, my strength gone, my energies paralysed and all my hopes dispersed."

In his memoirs, he makes a big fuss over losing this election but hardly gives a mention to the fact that he won the Rector's job ten years later and never even mentions that he was married the same year, at 48, to the 21-year-old Emilia Francis Strong. Whatever persuaded Emilia to marry the man remains a mystery; they lived apart for most of their marriage, although Mrs Pattison was a welcome relief at Lincoln Rectory for visitors who were having a difficult time with her husband. George Eliot was only one of many distinguished visitors who attended on the couple and it has long been thought likely that she based the desiccated marriage of Casaubon and Dorothea in *Middlemarch* on what she saw there. George Eliot's own record of her stay in Oxford focuses on some of her other meetings; with the daughters of Mrs Gaskell, the novelist; with Benjamin Jowett, about to be elected Master of Balliol; and with Walter Pater, whom she did not like at all. But she did enjoy a visit to the University Museum, where Professor Rolleston kindly dissected a brain for her.

Among distinguished Fellows in the twentieth century was the great medical researcher Howard Florey, while notable undergraduates included the poet Edward Thomas, the cartoonist Sir Osbert Lancaster, the thriller writer John Le Carre (David Cornwell) and Dr Seuss (T.S. Geisel) of *The Cat in the Hat* fame.

In 1970 Lincoln College shocked the townspeople of Oxford by claiming back one of the three churches originally adapted into Bishop Fleming's foundation, All Saints Church. The glorious white church with its "wedding cake" spire has been one of the great High Street landmarks since 1720, when it was built to replace the original Norman church that Fleming would have known. The spire of this church was declared unsafe in the 1660s and local inhabitants left their homes in fear. In 1700 it duly collapsed and destroyed much of the church. The new All Saints was claimed from Gown by Town in 1896, when the long-serving civic church of St Martin's at Carfax was demolished to widen the road. For seventy years, the University Church and the City Church were within a couple of hundred yards of each other on the High. By 1970 though, All Saints was in a state of disrepair. Lincoln College persuaded the Church Commissioners to declare it redundant and made plans to convert it into a library for the college. Despite the complaints of parishioners, the college opened its library in 1975 after huge renovations and refitting. The last remaining Lincoln church, St Michael at the North Gate, took over as the official city church.

The Mitre and the Chequers

Next to All Saints is the Mitre which, despite the claims of others, is the oldest surviving inn in Oxford. Several houses in the High and Turl Street were converted into the inn in 1310. Lincoln College became the owners in the fifteenth century and the present name derives from the headgear of the Bishop of Lincoln. During the seventeenth century, when being a Roman Catholic was a very dangerous occupation, Mass was often celebrated inside the Inn. In 1688 the landlord upset so many students with his Catholicism that a riot started here. All the windows were broken and the mob went on to raid every known Catholic house in the city. From 1671 until Victorian times, the Mitre was a major coaching inn on the run from London. It was here that the poet John Keats was dropped in 1817 when he came up to stay with a friend at Magdalen Hall. The original thirteenth-century vaulted cellar survives but most of the present building dates from 1630.

Closely related to the Mitre is the Chequers on the other side of the High. To reach it is to take a trip into the middle ages down one of the old medieval passages off the main road. The building here dates back to 1260 as a private house before it became the premises of a money lender, the sign of whose trade was a chequered board. It was rebuilt as a tavern in 1500 and much of that building remains today, known as the Chequers since 1605. In the eighteenth century curiosities and entertainments were put on at many Oxford inns. In 1757 a camel from Cairo was displayed at the Chequers, and in 1758 it shared the stage with the Siamese twins from Witney. By 1762 the inn had become almost a zoo, exhibiting fourteen large animals including a sealioness, a camel (clearly a popular beast), a racoon and "a very large fish," possibly a shark.

During the middle ages an underground passage led from this building under the High to the Mitre, and during the Dissolution of the Monasteries, soldiers acting for Henry VIII drove a group of monks into the tunnel and bricked it up at both ends. When the pub is very quiet, it is said, the screams of these dying monks can still be heard.

The High

Oxford High Street, known universally as the High, was described by Nikolaus Pevsner as "one of the world's great streets." It is wide and stretches in a great curve from Magdalen Bridge, past what used to be the city's East Gate, to Carfax. With a tower at each end, it is overlooked by six great colleges and two magnificent churches. It was never designed, but has evolved over a thousand years. There are shops old and new, grand and tacky, banks, pubs, hotels and, though not immediately obvious, a great deal of student accommodation. William Wordsworth (1770-1850) was a Cambridge man, but visited Oxford in May 1820 and wrote two sonnets on the city. He was greatly taken with High Street:

> I slight my own beloved Cam, to range
> Where silver Isis leads my stripling feet;
> Pace the long avenue or glide adown
> The stream-like windings of that glorious street.

It has been for the entire history of the university, the one great thoroughfare of the city. Now the Oxford Transport Strategy has removed the endless stream of motorized traffic, but merely created new problems for traders in the High.

The High, 1843 (Magna Gallery)

Oxford's Covered Market has a unique atmosphere, with its game-butchers and sausage specialist, its flower shops and book stalls, exotic fish and wonderful fruit and an ever-increasing number of eating places. Traditionalists are still drawn for good, simple fare to George's, the original market restaurant where one can still, on a weekday afternoon, see students sitting alone with an everlasting cup of coffee and reading their set texts on Jurisprudence or Anglo-Saxon. One of the joys of Oxford is that one need never be embarrassed to be found reading. Bill Bryson noticed this too: "I like to drink in the pubs, where you can sit with a book and not be looked on as a social miscreant."

The Covered Market owes its existence to the Oxford Mileways Act, passed in the 1760s with the intention of making the city's roads "more safe and commodious for traffic." One of the means of achieving this was to sweep the untidy and often unpleasant street markets out of St Aldate's (Fish Street) and Queen Street (Butcher Row). In 1774, John Gwynne's design for an off-street market between the High and Jesus College came into operation and gradually the number and diversity of stalls in the market increased. The whole thing was roofed over in late Victorian times.

The hall it created has wonderful acoustics and here, if you time it well, you can hear some of the best and most talented buskers in the whole of Europe but, thanks to pettyfogging regulations, only between 11am and 3pm, and even then "not Monday, Tuesday, Wednesday or Thursday."

All Souls

All Souls is something special; it is the neatest and most beautiful of the Oxford colleges, with those entrancing spires and pinnacles piercing the skyline. Its fifteenth-century frontage makes it the most genuinely medieval college building on the High and nowhere else do the "The College is Closed to Visitors" signs seem such permanent fixtures. In addition, it is the only one of Oxford's ancient colleges which takes no undergraduates – you have to prove yourself at one of the "lesser" establishments before you stand a chance of getting into All Souls – and academic brilliance is not the only requirement. Its Fellowships are the most coveted prizes in all the universities of the world: describe a man or woman as "a Fellow of All Souls, Oxford" and there is no need to ask anything more of their academic abilities. When T.E. Lawrence died – that is Lawrence of Arabia, the man who led the Arab revolt against Turkish rule during the First World War and who became an international hero and the subject of a multi-Oscar film – the only one of his achievements that his mother wanted emblazoned on the headstone of his grave in Dorset was "Fellow of All Souls College, Oxford."

The college name refers "the Souls of All Faithful People Deceased" and applies directly to the English dead of the Hundred Years War with France in the fourteenth and fifteenth centuries – it has been called "the noblest war memorial in England." It was founded in 1438 by Henry Chichele, Archbishop of Canterbury, at about the same time he founded St Bernard's College (later replaced by St John's). St Bernard's was to educate Cistercian monks, but All Souls would be a place of study for the non-monastic clergy. In a clever move, Chichele presented all the (hugely rich) land endowments he had gathered to the king, Henry VI, who in turn gave them to the college, thus becoming a co-founder. This suited both, as it cost Henry not a penny and also gave the college immediate top status. The land chosen was also a prime site, directly next door to St Mary's Church, still at that time the centre of university affairs.

An early Fellow was Thomas Linacre (c1460-1524), the scholar-physician who counted among his patients Erasmus, Sir Thomas More and Cardinal Wolsey and went on to found the Royal College of Physicians. Christopher Wren was a Fellow here from 1653 to 1661 under the Wardenship of Gilbert Sheldon (1598-1677), for whom he was later to build the "theatre" that carries his name. At All Souls, Wren was responsible for the huge – and, as one would expect, incredibly accurate – sundial, one of the most beautiful in the world, which can be glimpsed through the (always locked) gates in Radcliffe Square. The sundial stands on the wall of Hawksmoor's 200ft-long Codrington Library (Gothic outside, classical inside), which houses four portfolios of Wren's designs for St Paul's Cathedral and his plans for the rebuilding of London after the Great Fire of 1666.

It has been in the last 120 years that the quality of All Souls Fellowships has been established. After the 1914-18 war came a policy of inviting "distinguished senior students" to be associated with the college, and in 1964 a large-scale scheme was introduced to invite Visiting Fellows from the UK and abroad to spend up to twelve months there pursuing their research.

It is perhaps odd that such an august institution should also be the site of Oxford's strangest ritual, the Mallard Hunt. This only takes place once every hundred years, during the first year of a new century; though there is much doubt as to whether the Millennium hunt will take place. The ceremony is alleged to have evolved from the finding of a mallard duck in an ancient drain during the digging of the college's foundations in the fifteenth century – Archbishop Chichele, incidentally, had predicted such an event in a dream. The duck is celebrated in song every year at college feasts, but in the first year of the century, during their dinner, the Fellows pick up staves and torches and march off around the college buildings and grounds – on the roof as well – whooping and yelling for the bird. They are headed by a Lord Mallard who, at the end of their fun, produces a long stick with a dead duck spiked on the end of it and sings the Mallard Song so that it echoes across the Oxford night. Then the whole procession heads off for more drinks and conviviality indoors. Lord Mallard in 1900 was a young man called Cosmo Lang, who 36 years later as Archbishop of Canterbury persuaded Edward VIII that the country would not stand for him marrying an American divorcee and remaining King.

The Queen's College

Further down the High, one comes to The Queen's College and its imposing Palladian frontage. One of Oxford's little affectations, designed to sort out the readers from the gawpers, is that technically the college is not just Queen's but The Queen's (and don't confuse it with Cambridge's Queens' where the apostrophe is moved because it acknowledges two queens). The college gets its royal title because of some adroit sycophancy on the part of its founder, Robert Eglesfield, who in the mid-fourteenth century was chaplain to Queen Philippa of Hainault, consort to Edward III. She accepted, on behalf of all her successors as Queens Consort, that they should act as patroness to his new college, the sixth to be established in Oxford.

Certainly for the first 500 years of its existence, nobody ever referred to it as The Queen's College, but in the last years of the reign of Queen Victoria, the Provost, John Richard Magrath, officially added the definite article. In Oxford changes take a long while to become accepted and it is said that the university still refers to Queen's College in some of its official publications.

Queen's was never one of the richer colleges, and for a very long time it never rebuilt on the site that Eglesfield had bought, but simply adapted the old houses that already stood there. The great rebuilding came in the first half of the eighteenth century, when successive Provosts raised the money for a completely new look. Consequently, Queen's has more of a specific architectural identity than any of the other ancient colleges. It was long thought that the High Street facade and Front Quad behind it were the work of Nicholas Hawksmoor, successor to Christopher Wren and one of the finest of English architects. It now seems likely, however, that Hawksmoor's drawings were adapted by the Oxford master-mason William Townesend. He certainly was responsible for the cupola above the entrance to the college, keeping the rain off the statue of Queen Caroline of Ansbach, consort of George II, who put £2,000 of her own money towards the rebuilding. Caroline is perhaps rightly the most prominent queen in Oxford, for she was probably the most intelligent of the Queens Consort, constantly being reprimanded by her bluff German husband for spending too much time reading and behaving more like a schoolmistress than a queen.

The Queen's College, never a leader in academic or sporting leagues, nevertheless has a fame in the eating and drinking stakes, thus endearing it to successive generations of students. Queen's brewery was one of the most famous and the longest-lasting of all those attached to the colleges – they were necessary of course, in the early days when no-one dared to drink the water – and was still producing ale up to the outbreak of the Second World War. All special dinners at Queen's are announced by a trumpet fanfare and the college is host to two of the most famous of Oxford's celebrations. The first, at the start of the year is the Needle and Thread feast, named because each guest is presented with these articles, thanks to a dreadful pun on the French *aiguilles et fils*, which is supposed to sound like the name of the founder, Eglesfield...any excuse for a party has long been an Oxford tenet. The more famous junket comes at Christmas with the Boar's Head Feast. The tenuous derivation of this is supposedly a commemoration of the safe delivery of a Queen's student who, when attacked by a wild boar on Shotover Hill outside the city, thrust the copy of Aristotle he happened to be carrying into the beast's jaws and choked it.

King Henry V (1387-1422) was a scholar at Queen's in its early days and among the other great names associated with the college is that great reformer, John Wyclif, who was first Master of Balliol and later a teacher of philosophy at Queen's, where he worked on his own translation of the Bible into English. The college library holds the great actor David Garrick's own copy of Shakespeare's First Folio (there are more copies of this historic book in Oxford than anywhere else in the world), and other writers associated with the college include the dramatist William Wycherley (1641-1715), though he never took a degree. Jeremy Bentham (1748-1832), the philosopher and pioneer of Utilitarianism entered the college aged only twelve. The boy's rooms looked across to the churchyard of St Peter's in the East and he lived, he claimed, in continuous fear of ghosts. This was at a low point in the intellectual life of the college and indeed the whole university, and Bentham's severe judgment was: "Mendacity and insincerity – in these I found the sure, and only sure, effects of an English university education."

Howard Florey (1898-1968) became in 1962 the first working scientist to be appointed head of an Oxford college when he was made provost of Queen's. He is probably the university's greatest modern scientist, sharing the Nobel Prize for Medicine in 1945 for his work on penicillin. Florey was born in Australia and came to Oxford as a Rhodes Scholar when he was 24 to study medicine. He came back to the city in 1935 as professor of pathology and was quickly recognized as a brilliant researcher. Florey stayed quiet in the post-war years when Alexander Fleming was hailed as a hero for his discovery of the new wonder drug, penicillin. It was indeed Fleming, working at St Mary's Hospital in London, who noticed that spores of the mould killed a culture of virulent bacteria. Yet Fleming failed to realize penicillin's truly remarkable properties and it was Florey's team in Oxford which experimented with penicillin as a practical drug in the Radcliffe Infirmary. After tests on laboratory mice it was first used on an Oxford policeman who was dying from an infection caused when he scratched his face on a rose bush. He responded to the treatment, but supplies of the penicillin ran out and he died. But Florey had seen enough to know the drug's power and it went into manufacture, to be used to treat war wounds on the battlefields of North Africa in 1943. It was recently estimated that, so far, penicillin has saved thirty million lives.

One biographer put it: "Fleming was like a man who stumbles on a nugget of gold...and then goes off to look for something else. Florey was like a man who goes back to the same spot and creates a gold mine." Florey was knighted the year before receiving the Nobel Prize jointly with his Oxford partner Dr Ernest Chain and Fleming, and went on to become President of the Royal Society, Lord Florey, a member of the Order of Merit, and Provost of Queen's, in whose lodgings he died in 1969. Science and the state honored him, but ask the average person in the street about penicillin and it is still Fleming's name that most will give you.

CHAPTER FOUR

Shelley's Oxford

"They are very dull people here"

Percy Shelley (1792-1822) was the one who got away, the brilliant headstrong student who rebelled against Oxford University and against anything and everything the older generation stood for. He was the revolutionary who sought to shock, who got himself sent down from the university, who blazed a fiery trail as a poet and died a romantic poet's death, drowned in a storm off the coast of Italy.

Like so many student revolutionaries before and since, Percy Bysshe Shelley had his origins firmly in the privileged classes. He was born on August 4, 1792, near Horsham, Sussex, where his father, Timothy, was the Member of Parliament. From his schooldays onwards, young Percy stood aloof from and stood out from the crowd. At his prep school he drew attention to himself by his eccentric behaviour – like experimenting with gunpowder and blowing the lid off his desk during lessons. He went on to Eton, already England's most prestigious school, where he rebelled against the "fagging" system, which involved younger boys acting as servants for the older pupils, earned the nickname "Mad Shelley" and was mocked and bullied by his classmates. Although he was clearly a boy of tremendous intelligence and was fascinated particularly by scientific experiments, he was a strange individual who found it difficult to mix.

Consequently, when he came up to University College, Oxford in 1810, he was already firmly opposed to all forms of authority, he thought his father "the worst kind of tyrant" and felt abandoned by his mother. To reinforce his stand against the world, he was an anti-royalist, a vegetarian, opposed to marriage and, above all, an atheist.

It was unlikely, then, that his stay at Oxford would be a peaceful one. He arrived at this "stronghold of royalist tradition and prejudice," well versed in the radical English and French writers of the 1790s, addicted to German horror novels and surrounded by his chemical and electrical equipment. He appalled his scout (college servant) with the dreadful mess in which he left his rooms, and perplexed the tutor who told him he must read Aristotle, by asking: "But must I *care* about Aristotle?"

He was little affected by the life of the college, complaining "they are very dull people here." Academically things were not exactly strenuous. Officially, all he had to do was attend chapel every morning, translate into Latin once a week an article from the *Spectator* and visit his tutor once a term. So, instead he worked out his own timetable, whereby he would read for sixteen hours a day and, according to his friend, Thomas Hogg, sleep in the evening curled up like an animal in front of the fire before waking and working through the night on his scientific experiments. He grew his hair long when everyone else wore it cropped and he delighted in outlandish clothes.

It was his friendship with Hogg that sustained Shelley during his brief Oxford career, but it also brought about that career's premature end. Together they read beyond the texts set for them by the tutors, keeping up with the works of radical thinkers like David Hume, Voltaire, Tom Paine, Rousseau and William Godwin, Shelley's future father-in-law. They read and praised each other's poetry and developed their subversive atheism, the worst of all intellectual crimes in a university that valued religion so highly. Shelley's eccentricities continued and were sometimes too much even for Hogg to understand. On one celebrated occasion they were crossing Magdalen Bridge arguing over Plato's suggestion that the soul exists before birth, when Percy grabbed a baby from its mother's arms and started to question it about its memory of pre-existence.

By the start of their second term Shelley was writing what he described as "a systematic cudgel for Christianity," a 1,000-word essay which he had printed anonymously as the pamphlet *The Necessity of*

Atheism. He and Hogg persuaded the booksellers Slatter & Munday to display copies in the window of their shop just across the High from University College. Within twenty minutes, a Fellow of New College, the Rev Jocelyn Walker, had picked up and read the tract, was suitably enraged and ordered the cowed booksellers to burn all but one copy. That one copy was sent to the university authorities.

It did not take a lot of work to find out that Shelley was behind the pamphlet. He was called to a meeting of the Master and Fellows of University College, where he refused to answer questions about the authorship of the pamphlet on the grounds that it had been published anonymously. This gave the college the convenient excuse to expel him immediately for "contumacy in refusing to answer certain questions put to him." Hogg went to the Master to protest, but also refused to answer questions and was likewise expelled. A Fellow of the college, C.J. Ridley, later explained: "I believe no-one regretted their departure, for there were but few, if any, who were not afraid of Shelley's strange and fantastic pranks, and the still stranger opinions he was known to entertain."

Percy quarrelled with his father and eloped to Scotland to marry sixteen-year-old Harriet Westbrook. They had two children before the marriage collapsed and Harriet drowned herself in the Serpentine in London. He then married Mary, the daughter of William Godwin and the feminist author Mary Wollstonecraft, became a member of the notorious poet Byron's circle and fled to Italy leaving behind masses of unpaid bills. He revisited Oxford only once after his expulsion, and died eleven years later when his boat overturned during a sudden storm in Italy. He was cremated on the beach where he was washed up and his ashes were buried next to Keats in the Protestant Cemetery in Rome.

As Shelley's reputation as a poet grew during the nineteenth century, the college had to come to terms with the fact that one of its biggest troublemakers was also becoming one of its greatest attractions. He was finally acknowledged some seventy years after his death when University College was presented with the life-size marble sculpture that had been planned for his grave. The cemetery authorities declined to accept it, but the college was stuck with it. It is pure kitsch, a romanticized effigy of the naked poet as he was washed up on the shore, and the Fellows, aware that they could hardly put it in the chapel or in the middle of one of the quads, built a little shrine, tucked away down a dingy corridor, where it lies bathed in light from an overhead cupola. It has, of course, proved irresistible to over-excited undergraduates who have, from time to time, touched up parts of its anatomy with brightly colored paint.

University College

If any college was able to cope with a problem student like Shelley, it should have been University College, for it is generally agreed (outside the walls of Balliol and Merton, that is) to be Oxford's oldest surviving college. The claim is based on the will of William of Durham, who died in 1249, leaving 3,010 marks (about £200) to support a dozen scholars at Oxford University. The bequest was the first of its kind in England. Although the group was originally known simply as the Scholars of William of Durham, the name University College was soon applied, taken from University Hall, one of the buildings where the scholars lived.

Univ's claim does not – and has not for more than a century – have anything to do with King Alfred. Alfred, who was King of Wessex from 871 to 899 and was the first great hero of English history, was a learned king – it was even suggested that he could read and write, and so the idea of him founding a body of scholars is not ridiculous. But despite his local associations (he was born only fifteen miles away at Wantage and the Ashmolean Museum's greatest treasure is the Alfred Jewel), there was never any hint of a connection with either Univ or the university itself before 1381 when, during a costly dispute over property rights, certain Univ Fellows forged documents to suggest that King Alfred had founded the college and that the present king, Richard II, should therefore be its protector in this dispute. For some reason, the king went along with the college cause and the new "Aluredian" link served Univ well for centuries. During a dispute over appointing a new Master in 1727, Univ again appealed to the Crown, and the King Alfred fiction was established as a fact in law.

Some college authorities took this proof to heart, and in 1872 Univ celebrated its millennium with a huge banquet, at which their royal "patron" was toasted in elaborate style. Even then, however, not everyone could go through with the self-deception, and the historian E.A. Freeman excused himself from being present at the banquet, sending along in his place two old burnt cakes – a reference to the most famous folk story about King Alfred. The college celebrated its genuine 750th anniversary in 1999, hoping that anyone able to do simple arithmetic would overlook the embarrassing way it had got 250 years younger in the last 127 years

It is not Alfred's statue that graces the High Street frontage of University College, but those of the sister queens Mary II and Anne, among the least academically distinguished of British monarchs. Anne stands over the usual entrance to the college while her older sister guards the great double doors a little further down the High. Their father, the much-disliked James II, stands on the inner face of the gate tower, looking over Front Quad. This is one of only two surviving statues of Britain's last Roman Catholic monarch.

The Shelley Memorial lies behind a long featureless stretch of wall fronting the High, in the middle of which is a plaque to two great scientists: It reads:

In a house on this site between 1655 and 1668 lived Robert Boyle. Here he discovered Boyle's law and made experiments with an air pump designed by his assistant Robert Hooke, inventor, scientist and architect, who made a microscope and thereby first identified the living cell.

Boyle (1627-91), whose law about the inversely proportional relationship between the volume and pressure of a gas is familiar from school physics, was described by John Aubrey as "very tall...temperate, and virtuous, and frugal." Hooke (1635-1703), who invented many important scientific instruments, claimed that Isaac Newton's discoveries about gravity were based on ideas he had himself put forward years earlier and accused Newton of plagiarism, a complaint that history has failed to uphold.

John Radcliffe (1652-1714), the best-remembered of all Oxford's benefactors, was an undergraduate here and, although he went on to be a Fellow of Lincoln College, it was Univ he remembered in his will, leaving the money to pay for the building of a new second quadrangle. Among the distinguished clerics to study here, Archbishop George Abbot (1562-1633) and Professor C.H. Dodd (1884-1973) make a good pair. Abbott was part of the team behind the Authorized (King James) Version of the Bible and Dodd was the director of the translation of the New English Bible.

Two other themes in Univ's recent history are the links with the United States and with the British political Left. Dr Arthur Lehman Goodhart (1891-1978) of New York City was Master here between 1951 and 1963, the first American to be head of a college in either Oxford or Cambridge. Kingman Brewster (1919-88), of Long Meadow, Massachusetts, an ex-president of Yale, occupied the same post from 1986 to 1988. But the most famous American associated with Univ is the beleaguered President Bill Clinton (b.1946), who was attached to the college as a Rhodes Scholar in 1968-70. During his first year, he lived in a Georgian almshouse on Kybald Street at the back of the college. To see this, turn off High Street down what is now Magpie Lane but was, for some reason, referred to as Gropecunt Lane in the thirteenth century. Kybald Street, a cul-de-sac these last 500 years, runs off to the left. It is dominated by Parsons' Almshouse, bought by Helen and Frank Altschul of New York City and presented to Univ.

During the early part of the twentieth century, Univ gained a reputation as an aristocratic and gently socialist retreat. It has connections with two Labour Prime Ministers. Clement Attlee (1883-1967) came up in 1901 to read modern history. Most Oxford undergraduates who go on to make a name for themselves in politics head for the Oxford Union debating society, which they use as a showcase for their talents, but Attlee, later described sourly by Winston Churchill as "a modest little man with plenty to be modest about," was much too shy to ever speak at the Union. He was not at all political at this time and actually claimed that the well-to-do were "for the most part where they were because of their virtues." This, curiously, was the man who was to become the most radical Prime Minister in post-war Britain, whose government created the Welfare State and the once-glorious National Health Service, and which took into national ownership a fifth of the British economy, including the Bank of England and the railways.

Harold Wilson (1916-95), who was twice Prime Minister (1964-70 and 1974-6), was a Fellow here during the Second World War under William Beveridge (1879-1963) as Master. While he was at Univ, Beveridge worked on his radical plans to set up the Welfare State brought in by Attlee's government. To complete the circle, Arnold Goodman (1913-95), Wilson's legal adviser while he was Prime Minister, moved his ample proportions into the Master's lodgings from 1976 to 1986. One other left-wing politician to have studied at Univ was Bob Hawke (b.1929), the Australian Labour Prime Minister.

Like all Oxford colleges, Univ has its fair sprinkling of famous writers, including the poet Stephen Spender (1909-95) and the novelists V.S. Naipaul (b.1932) and Dornford Yates (1885-1960). Its most important scientist was Stephen Hawking (b.1942), the biographer of time itself. Hawking spent the first eight years of his life in Oxford, having been born in the city to which his parents had moved from blitzed north London during the Second World War. After schooling at St Albans, he returned to Oxford to read for a degree at Univ. His father wanted him to go into medicine but the young Hawking's interest lay in mathematics. This, however, was a subject not available at Univ, so he tried his hand at physics instead. The rest is history. After taking a First, he wanted to do research in cosmology, but was again thwarted because there was no-one in Oxford working in that area. So this time Oxford lost him to Cambridge where, since the 1960s, despite being confined to a wheelchair by motor neuron disease, he has established himself as one of the greatest physicists of all time.

Richard Ingrams (b.1937), founding editor of Britain's most influential satirical magazine *Private Eye*, came up to Univ after National Service in 1958 with illusions:

> One had the idea of Oxford being a very glamorous place. Full of eccentrics and aesthetes and witty people. But when I got there, there were just a lot of men in duffel coats wandering up and down the High Street.

With a hint of what was to come, Ingrams eschewed the established student journals *Isis* and *Cherwell* and took over a magazine called *Parson's Pleasure*. The very first issue produced a libel action, and eventually the magazine was banned by W.H. Smith – both events that Ingrams would grow used to in later years. During his time at Oxford, he met up with Paul Foot, John Wells and Auberon Waugh, all of whom were to become important elements in *Private Eye*.

Univ is one of the very few Oxford colleges to have a public thoroughfare running through it. Logic Lane was the subject of a heated argument between Town and Gown at the beginning of the twentieth century. At the High Street end, the college wanted to build a connecting bridge across the lane between two of its buildings. At first, local planning officials agreed to the request but, to safeguard their right to the ownership of Logic Lane, the council demanded £5 a year rent from the college. The college grandees refused this nominal payment, arguing that Logic Lane crossed their land and that they had maintained and repaired the lane since 1681, when the buildings on either side of it were built. The city councillors insisted that the ownership of all thoroughfares in Oxford had passed to the city under the terms of a charter issued in the reign of King John and, to spite the college, they removed the hinged post at the High Street end, which had prevented carts going up and down Logic Lane (and so disturbing the inhabitants). When finally the argument was heard in the High Court, the city was unable to prove that the lane was in existence at the time of King John and so the judge found in favor of the college and awarded costs against the city. By October 1905, the bridge was up. It cost University College £300 to build and cost the ratepayers of Oxford nine times as much to pay the legal bill.

In the days before the Randolph Hotel, Oxford's most important inn was the Angel, which stood on the corner of High Street and Coach and Horses Lane, as the east end of Merton Street was then known. It was a big place and did big business, with ten or more coaches leaving each morning after breakfast at its peak during the eighteenth century. Behind the inn were extensive stables, and horses were grazed overnight on the land beyond Magdalen deer park still known as Angel and Greyhound Meadow (the Greyhound stood across the High on the corner of Longwall). Many of the city's most important visitors stayed at the Angel, including King Christian VII of Denmark in 1768 and Queen Adelaide, consort of William IV, in 1835. The Angel was bought by the university in 1866 and demolished to build the new Examination Schools. A little of it remains, however. With a wonderful sense of continuity, the Oxford Bus Company uses part of what used to be the kitchens as a rest and refreshment room for its drivers.

The first coffee house in England was attached to the Angel Inn and opened by "Jacob the Jew" in 1650, and the luxuriously decorated Grand Café has a plaque commemorating it. In fact, the first recorded instance of anyone in England brewing coffee for their own use involved one Nathaniel Conopius at Balliol College, and coffee-drinking caught on in Oxford before London. The apothecary Arthur Tillyard sold the drink from his premises near All Souls in 1655 until after the Restoration, one of his best customers being Christopher Wren.

With the advent of transport from London to Oxford, newspapers from the capital were brought to the university city for the first time in any number and the coffee houses became the place to meet one's friends and catch up on the news. One commentator declared that a man might pick up more useful knowledge at Oxford's coffee houses than he could from his books in a whole month. In both Oxford and London, coffee houses became such lively places that Charles II in 1675 issued a Proclamation for the Suppression of Coffee Houses, but it was a decision which aroused so much immediate opposition that the proclamation was repealed eleven days later.

The Examination Schools

Because it is the university and not the individual colleges that gives degrees, it is the university that has to set the exams and find a place for students to be tested. In earlier times, this all took place in the Divinity School and off the neighboring Schools Quad but, by the middle of the nineteenth century, it was clear that new premises were needed and a competition for their design was won by T.G. Jackson, the most prolific of all Oxford architects. For the prestigious position on the site of the Angel Inn, he came up with a plan based on a Jacobean country house. The High Street frontage of the Examination Schools is magnificent, but it is only the entrance – all the business of exams takes place further back in the quieter environs of the beautiful open quad looking on to Merton Street. For much of the year, the visitor will see little activity around the Examination Schools, but be here in May and June when Finals exams are taking place and the bustle is tremendous. To take their exams, students must dress in "subfusc" – a formal outfit of black and white, with white bow ties for men and black stockings or tights for women and gowns for both. The air of formality, as undergraduates make their way to the Schools on exam days, gives a hint of the romance associated with Oxford, but the informality of the same area after the final finals offers a complete contrast. With the tension over at last, parties start in the street outside the Schools and city and university police have often had to step in to bring order to the High as champagne corks and party poppers fly.

Tucked into the corner of the Examination Schools is the Ruskin School of Drawing and Fine Art, founded by John Ruskin while he was Slade Professor of Fine Art in the 1870s. For 100 years it was tucked away in the Ashmolean Museum and, without Ruskin's leadership, declined to the point where it was considered little more than a finishing school for young ladies. There have been numerous attempts to kill it off – in 1959 there were letters to *The Times* from the likes of Jacob Epstein and Henry Moore in its support – but since 1978, when it moved to the present building (also by T.G. Jackson) with its wildlife frieze of intertwined vines populated by birds, squirrels and fruit, students have been accepted for a "serious" degree course in fine art.

The Botanic Garden

A visit to the Botanic Garden, tucked away below street level between the Cherwell and Rose Place, is often a disappointment to the day visitor to Oxford. Just getting in is daunting enough, with a long list of forbidden activities – no radios, no ball games, no dogs, no ice creams, no photography and no (greatest sin of all) tweaking off of cuttings and seedpods ("the police may be called"). And once inside, any visitor with summer thoughts of Britain in Bloom is likely to be underwhelmed by the displays, walking the paths between unkempt beds, often crowded with supremely unspectacular foliage.

What such visitors perhaps do not realize is that those elements which seem to detract from the garden are exactly the things which endear it to those who know it better. For this is most certainly not a public pleasure garden: it is the living storeroom and laboratory of a university department, it is there to provide specimens for biology and botany dons and students. It is also a sanctuary of calm for local people escaping the bustle of the High.

It was founded as the Oxford Physic Garden in 1621 and is the third-oldest in Europe. The original intention was to grow plants for their medicinal properties, but botany soon took over. The five-acre site, just outside the city walls, was previously the burial ground of Oxford's Jewish community, which had its centre near the site of the present Town Hall at the other end of High Street. After the expulsion of the Jews from England in 1290, the graveyard was taken over by the Hospital of St John the Baptist across the road where Magdalen College stands today. Magdalen leased the site to Henry Danvers, Earl of Danby, in 1621 and he appointed as the first Keeper John Tradescant, the seventeenth-century gardener whose collection of rarities formed the basis of the Ashmolean Museum.

The Botanic Garden (it was renamed in 1840) has long been Oxford University's main centre for the cultivation of plants brought from abroad as cuttings or seeds. Its most famous inhabitant was the first

Entrance to the Botanic Garden (Oxford Times)

Oxford Ragwort specimen (*Senecio squalidus*).The plant is not native to Britain, but was common on walls and roadsides in Oxford in the early nineteenth century, its very adaptable seeds having been blown from the Botanic Garden. From the 1840s it started to colonize the Thames corridor along the line of the Great Western Railway, with its seeds being carried in the trains' slipstream. From there it moved on to quickly establish itself in much of the country, always spreading first along railway lines. Although a weed, it has a delightful yellow flower and is not a killer of livestock like its poisonous cousin, Common Ragwort.

Except in high summer, entrance to the Botanic Garden is free and for anyone with time to spare or a particular interest, there is plenty to see. The glasshouses are usually the big attraction, offering the sight, rare in Britain, of sugar cane, rice, bananas and mangoes in various stages of maturity. Here, too, is that wonderfully ambiguous sign "Carnivorous Plants: Please Do Not Touch," leading one to wonder whether the restriction is to protect the plants or the visitors.

Merton Street

On the corner of Merton Street stands the Eastgate Hotel, the third in a series of inns built on the site of the drawbridged East Gate in the city's medieval fortifications. Further along, one comes to the stunning three-sided quadrangle of the Examination Schools and then the road turns at right-angles to open into one of Oxford's most perfect and evocative scenes. For most of its length between here and Oriel Square, Merton Street retains its pebble-pitched surface. There have been occasional plans to take up the cobbles or cover them with tarmac, but this would plainly be vandalism. Merton Street, according to Bill Bryson "an architectural treasure-house, one of the densest assemblies of historic buildings in the world," hangs on to its timeless atmosphere largely because it has very little motor traffic. This is partly because the road is a short-cut to nowhere and partly because it is really not a lot of fun driving over the cobbles.

The north side of the street contains a number of fascinating buildings including, at no.5, Postmasters' Hall, the birthplace and lifelong home of Oxford's most famous local historian, Anthony Wood (1632-95), who was educated at New College School and Merton

College. When he failed to win a Fellowship at his college, he devoted his life to antiquarian studies, spending most of his time shut away in Postmasters' Hall, in a closet-like room he constructed by the chimney in the garret. Here he produced a major work of Oxford history, the *Historia et Antiquitates Universitatis Oxoniensis* (1674) and *Athenae Oxonienses* (1691), a biographical encyclopaedia of writers and ecclesiastics – and also a wonderful source of lively and scandalous stories. Unfortunately, it was his undoing, for he suggested that the late Chancellor, the Earl of Clarendon, was in the habit of accepting bribes. The city was scandalized and Wood was brought before the university court in the Bodleian buildings, where he was expelled from the university and copies of the offending book were burned. A disagreeable fellow at the best of times, Wood now took fiercely against his surroundings, saying that Oxford "abounded with multitudes of ale houses...harlots, pimps and panders, bawds and buffoons, lechery and treachery, atheists and papists." He died not long afterwards and was allowed a last resting place across the road in the ante-chapel of his old college. Legend has it that he dug his grave himself, five years before his death.

Tucked in behind Postmasters' Hall stands one of the world's few remaining real tennis courts. For the visitor who has to be content throughout Oxford with tantalising glimpses through gates and archways into courtyards, gardens and quadrangles, there is nothing to be seen but the mysterious sign reading "OUTC the Real Tennis Court." Real or "royal" tennis was invented in medieval France and has been played in Oxford since the fifteenth century. Oxford has two surviving courts, though the one at Oriel, on which Charles I played during his time in Oxford, has not been used for tennis since the 1850s. The Merton Street court, however, still resounds to the play of a dedicated band of followers. It is the second-oldest surviving court in the country – the oldest being that of Henry VIII at Hampton Court.

Further along at no.4 and, unbelievably, sporting a tasteless, plastic numeral, stands Beam Hall, one of the few remaining buildings in the city to have served as a medieval academic hall. It is named after the thirteenth-century Chancellor of the university, Gilbert de Biham. After it ceased to be a home for undergraduates, it is reputed to have been the site of the first printing press set up in Oxford and thus the starting place for an industry which has given employment to Oxford men and women for 500 years. In the seventeenth century, Beam Hall was home to the physician Thomas Willis (1621-73), who was the first person to isolate diabetes and recognize asthma.

Merton College

The south side of the road is taken up by the multi-faceted facade of Merton College. Merton is solid, decent, conservative Oxford. It is not a noisy college like Christ Church or Balliol, not flashy like Magdalen or New College. Its greatest claim to fame is its antiquity. It might well be that Balliol and Univ can claim greater age by a few years, but there can be no doubt that Merton was the first real college as we know them in Oxford. It was the first self-governing community of scholars administering its own properties under its own statutes. Some years later, when the Bishop of Ely was founding the first Cambridge college, Peterhouse, he sent for Merton's statutes to use as a model.

William de Merton, the founder, was Chancellor of England under Henry III. He was a celibate priest himself, but had thirteen cousins and numerous nephews who all needed educating. But when it came to setting up an establishment for the de Merton boys, he was not sure whether to build it at Oxford or Cambridge, so he bought land in both places. Oxford came out on top in 1264, and to this day Merton College owns land at Grantchester, that most treasured corner of Cambridge.

In the early days, Merton became a nursery for bishops and during the fourteenth century produced four Archbishops of Canterbury. During the Reformation it remained largely loyal to Catholicism, although this was suppressed under Queen Elizabeth. But Catholic sympathies remained and, when Archbishop Parker imposed his own chaplain, John Mann, as Warden in 1562, the Fellows refused him entry at the gate. To this day, every new Warden of Merton has to hammer on the door of the college to be allowed in to take over.

Great names from the early days include Sir Thomas Bodley (1545-1613), who is buried in the college chapel and John Wyclif (c1320-84) who studied at Queen's and Merton, was briefly Master of Balliol and Warden of Canterbury Hall and was for a long time Professor of

Divinity and the most influential churchman in Oxford during the fourteenth century. Dubbed the "Morning Star of the Reformation," he was a forerunner of Martin Luther and spent much of his life in Oxford attacking the excesses of the Pope and his bishops, suggesting that they had too much power. Wyclif preached that a man's faith was between himself and God and needed neither the intervention of clergy nor the trappings of priestly power. He believed that one way of limiting that power was to have an English Bible, so that ordinary people could hear or read the scriptures for themselves and not need a priestly interpretation. Consequently, he supervised the first translation of the Bible into English and its distribution about the country by his followers, known as the Lollards. Although he was a thorn in the side of the Church hierarchy, Wyclif was tolerated until he attacked the doctrine of transubstantiation, the turning of communion bread into the very body of Christ. The Chancellor of the University forbade this argument in Oxford and when Wyclif disregarded him, the Archbishop of Canterbury called him to trial for heresy. But Wyclif died before this could be resolved. He was buried at Lutterworth in Leicestershire, a parish of which he held the living, but 41 years later his body was dug up, burned as a heretic and the ashes flung into the river.

During the Civil War, Merton was staunchly Royalist and provided lodgings for Charles I's queen, Henrietta Maria. Her rooms are still known as the Queen's Rooms. In that reign all was done with due decorum, although the same cannot be said of their son Charles II. When he moved the court to Oxford in 1665 to escape the plague in London, Charles's childless queen, Catherine of Braganza, took the Queen's Rooms, while his mistress Barbara Castlemaine, Duchess of Cleveland, had other rooms in the college and gave birth to one of Charles's illegitimate children while she was there.

Merton's Mob Quad is Oxford's oldest quadrangle and there are few places in the world better to get the feel of what life must have been like as a scholar in a medieval university. Here the student rooms crowd upon one another overlooking the quad, which is itself dominated from behind by the pinnacles of the chapel. What becomes clear is how the close, confined lives of the medieval students were dominated by the overwhelming influence of the church.

Recent times have thrown up many famous connections. Andrew Irvine (1902-24) might have been the first man to conquer Everest. He died on the mountain with his companion George Leigh Mallory, but nobody can tell for sure whether they died on their way up or coming down from the summit. Irvine was a Merton undergraduate at the time. Max Beerbohm (1872-1956), who wrote that immortal, if tedious, Oxford novel *Zuleika Dobson*, studied here and there is a room in the college dedicated to his memory. The American-born poet T.S. Eliot (1888-1965) was already a graduate of Harvard when he arrived at Merton in 1914 to write a thesis on the work of the philosopher F.H. Bradley, who was a Fellow at the college. Oxford was already emptying of undergraduates as the nation's young men were called up to fight in the trenches of France. Eliot's tutor, Harold Joachim, was a disciple of Bradley and in awe of the great man. Once, when an undergraduate was reading out an essay criticising aspects of Bradley's philosophy, Joachim stopped him and went and closed the window, in case the master should be passing and hear it. Eliot attended the meetings of an Oxford literary club known as the Coterie and it was here that he gave the first reading of his poem *The Love Song of J. Alfred Prufrock*. But he never really settled in Oxford, telling one friend that he relied on the company of women and in the university town there were none.

Other Merton poets included the Irishman Louis MacNeice (1907-63), who came up in 1926 during Oxford's period of "post-war deliberate decadence." "At the first party I went to," he wrote:

> there was no drink but champagne, a young man played by himself with a spotted stuffed dog on a string, and the air was full of the pansy phrase "my dear." I discovered that, in Oxford, homosexuality and "intelligence," heterosexuality and "brawn" were almost inexorably paired. This left me out in the cold and I took to drink!

The poet Edmund Blunden (1896-1974), was the ideal tutor for Keith Douglas (1920-44), the finest of the English Second World War poets. Douglas came up to Merton in 1938 from Christ's Hospital where he had been described as "the most brilliant and the most cantankerous of pupils." He went on to edit *Cherwell*, the undergraduate journal, but by the start of his second year Britain and Germany were at war and a friend recalls him announcing that he would "bloody well make my mark in this war, for I will not come back." He was killed in Normandy in 1944. J.R.R. Tolkien (1892-1973) was Merton Professor of English Language and Literature and lived in rooms at the college after the death of his wife, Edith, in 1971 until his own, two years later.

Merton Street opens out into Oriel Square, which should be another of the city's visual gems, surrounded as it is by the buildings of Christ Church, Corpus Christi and Oriel. Unfortunately, it has the air of a neglected backwater, little more than a jumbled car and bicycle park. Until the end of the Second World War, it was known as Canterbury Square, after the Canterbury Gate of Christ Church. The authorities at Oriel pleaded with the city council for the name to be changed, claiming that Oriel Square was the original name. Not to everyone's pleasure, the council agreed.

Oriel College

The names of the Oxford foundations are never simple and the full name of Oriel College is quite the most complicated, being "The Provost and Scholars of the House of the Blessed Mary the Virgin in Oxford, commonly called Oriel College, of the foundation of Edward the Second of famous memory, sometime King of England."

Oriel, then, is the first St Mary's College, the old St Mary's which forced William of Wykham to call *his* St Mary's "New College." It is the fifth oldest of the surviving Oxford colleges, being founded in 1326 by the Rector of St Mary's the University Church, Adam de Brome, a clerk to Edward II. That is where the St Mary link comes from. De Brome named the king as founder and the grateful monarch, soon to be brutally murdered in Berkeley Castle in Gloucestershire, made over a number of gifts to the new foundation, including the rectorship of the University Church. To this day, the Rector is appointed by Oriel and Adam de Brome's tomb stands in St Mary's.

The college takes its name from one of the early houses in which the Fellows were accommodated, called La Oriole, from its projecting upper window, the Latin name for which was "oratoriolum." Sir Walter Raleigh (1552-1618), that early explorer of North America, from where he brought tobacco and potatoes to Britain, was among the early students here.

Gilbert White (1720-93), the naturalist of Selbourne, was here in the dire days of the eighteenth century, but under the Provostship of John Eveleigh around the turn of the next century, Oriel sprang into prominence as the most respected and academically capable of all the Oxford colleges. Eveleigh developed the tutorial system through which dons maintain a close supervision of the undergraduates, the system upon which modern British university life has been based. He also made Oriel Fellowships the most sought-after mark of intellectual distinction within the university.

The earliest flowering of this intellectual elite was a group of Fellows known as the Noetics (from the Greek for intellectuals), which included Dr Thomas Arnold (1795-1842), later to be Britain's most famous and most influential public school headmaster at Rugby. But it was the generation after the Noetics that provided the finest manifestation of Oriel's academic talent, for it was in the senior common room here that the Oxford Movement had its genesis and powerhouse. Here, in the early nineteenth century, John Keble, John Henry Newman and Edward Pusey were all Fellows. Oriel also produced at around this time Oxford's most famous bishop "soapy" Samuel Wilberforce (1805-73).

The college went into decline after this, although tutors included the poets Arthur Hugh Clough (1819-61) and Matthew Arnold (1822-88), who was responsible for a number of images of Oxford which have been inextricably bound up with the city's attraction for visitors. He it was who called it "that sweet city with her dreaming spires" in his poem *Thyrsis*, and the "home of lost causes and forsaken beliefs" in his *Essays in Criticism*. In his poem *The Scholar Gypsy*, he re-invented a romantic Victorian drop-out from the seventeenth-century tale of an impecunious undergraduate who was forced to live a nomadic life, wandering the hills around Oxford and learning the mysteries of the gypsy life.

Matthew was the son of the Noetic, Thomas Arnold of Rugby, and studied at Balliol, where he won the Newdigate Prize for verse. He was elected to a Fellowship at Oriel, but his mother insisted he should take up a post in the Ministry of Education. There he was responsible for a vision that would lead to a school-for-all policy to rival the elitism of the public schools, but his first loves, poetry and Oxford, combined to attract him back as Professor of Poetry, a post he held for ten years, though it was so poorly paid that he was never able to move back to his beloved city.

In the twentieth century Oriel has been famous more for its sporting prowess – its boat club holds the record for the most consecutive wins in bumps races and this heartiness seems to have made up for the almost complete lack of intellectual distinction. The historian A.J.P. Taylor (1906-90) got a First at Oriel, but no thanks to his tutors. "I learned precisely nothing," he said. "I increased my knowledge of history, my understanding of it, not at all. I did not even learn how to write." The less enlightened also held out to make Oriel the last all-male college in Oxford, admitting women only in 1984. In this they were truly the sons of their nineteenth-century forebears, for it was Pusey who described the foundation of the first women's college as "one of the greatest misfortunes that has happened to us, even in our own time at Oxford."

It was, however, an Oriel student who made one of the most important changes to Oxford life, for Cecil Rhodes (1853-1902) was the man who opened up the university to the international world. Rhodes came to Oriel as a mature student (though only twenty) after he had been rejected by University College, and the Provost of Oriel admitted him with the grumble "all the colleges send me their failures." It took him eight years to earn his degree, largely because he was already bound up with financial deals in Africa and kept interrupting his studies to pop back to sort out problems there. Besides founding the Rhodes Scholarships for foreign students, the arch-imperialist who gave his name (for a while, at least) to a country, also left £100,000 to Oriel though, in doing so, he stipulated that a board of trustees must be consulted about the use of the money, "as the college authorities live secluded from the world and so are like children in commercial matters."

The trustees spent much of Rhodes' money on the Rhodes Building, built by Basil Champneys in 1910 as a foil to the Examination Schools at the other end of the High and to complete Oriel's newly acquired St Mary's quad. It replaced seven houses on High Street between Magpie Lane and Oriel Street and outraged a generation of Oxford citizens. The great colonialist himself stands on high, looking down past kings and bishops over to the entrance to the University Church. He appears again, bursting out of the side of a long, dull terrace in King Edward Street, where a plaque with a cameo bust reads: "In this house the Right Honourable Cecil John Rhodes kept academical residence in the year 1881."

In Oriel Street, opposite the side of the Rhodes Building, is Carter House, named in honor of the U.S. President Jimmy Carter. It was bought and restored in 1984, three years after Carter left office, through a gift from William Nelson Turpin of the President's home state, Georgia, who had been at Oriel in 1947. This forms part of Oriel's Island Site, a rabbit warren of student accommodation connected to the main college by a tunnel under the road. One of these buildings is the restored Tackley's Inn, where Adam de Brome housed his first scholars in 1326, and here too is the former real tennis court where Charles I exercised during the Siege of Oxford in the 1640s.

Drawing of Tom Tower, based on Wren's design (All Souls College)

CHAPTER FIVE

Sir Christopher Wren's Oxford

Si monumentum requiris circumspice

Christopher Wren (1632-1723) is the greatest of all British architects, revered as the man who designed and built St Paul's Cathedral, whose inspired dome dominated the London skyline for 250 years until the skyscrapers of our own time beat it for size, if not beauty.

As Surveyor-General to King Charles II, Wren was responsible for the rebuilding of London following the disastrous Great Fire of 1666, and the 51 churches he built in the capital between 1670 and 1685 constitute one of the most remarkable architectural achievements of all time. But, after London, Wren was most associated with Oxford. He was a student here and a professor, he carried out important scientific experiments here and married a local girl. Most importantly, he left the city with two of its most memorable buildings, the Sheldonian Theatre, described as "the most splendid room in Europe," and the eccentrically domed Tom Tower at the great entrance to Christ Church.

Christopher Wren was born on October 20, 1632 at East Knoyle in Wiltshire, the son of the rector, who was soon to take up the posts of Dean of Windsor and Registrar of the Order of the Garter. Christopher grew up at Windsor and mixed with the court of Charles I. His intellectual gifts were noticed as a child and he went up to Wadham College, Oxford in 1649, taking his first degree two years later and his Master's in 1653, after which he was made a Fellow of All Souls. There he stayed until 1661, despite being appointed Professor of Astronomy at Gresham College in London. His first contribution to the Oxford landscape was the huge and glorious sundial which he designed in 1659 for the wall of All Souls chapel.

Although this sundial is architectural in concept, it was really an extension of Wren's interest in constructing scientific instruments. Remember that by this time he had earned his place in Oxford as a mathematician, astronomer, mechanic and general all-around scientist. Since his student days, he had been one of a group of scientists who met regularly at Wadham to exchange ideas. They kept together when several members moved to London and were eventually to form the Royal Society, still the most distinguished scientific association in the world. Among Wren's projects were a weather clock, an "instrument to write double," new engines to raise water and new ways to print. He was the first to attach telescopic sights to astronomical instruments and developed measuring techniques which transformed the understanding of astronomy. And there was an improved microscope as well as all sorts of meteorological and surveying instruments. Interested in medicine, he did the drawings for an important book on anatomy and devised a method to transfuse blood from one animal to another.

The Sheldonian Theatre

It was not until the 1660s that he turned his hand to architecture when, now back in Oxford as the Savilian Professor of Astronomy, he was approached by Gilbert Sheldon, recently Warden of All Souls and about to become Archbishop of Canterbury and Chancellor of Oxford University. Sheldon wanted to give the university a building for official ceremonies such as conferring degrees. It is likely that Wren's interest in what was to become the Sheldonian Theatre was originally a mathematical and engineering problem, for his great achievement is in creating a vast floor space without the ceiling and roof having to be supported on obtrusive pillars. Architecturally, says Nikolaus Pevsner, it is "a young amateur's job, just a little confused."

Wren's U-shaped design was based on the antique Theatre of Marcellus in Rome, with a stage or platform at one end where the ceremonies could take place while the spectators were ranged in a tiered semicircle around the floor. The trouble was that Greek and Roman theatres were open to the elements, apart from a great tarpaulin which could be hauled across from side to side. Wren managed the same open arena but with a permanent roof. As the building was 70ft wide, the space could not be crossed by single wooden beams, so the young architect came up with a complicated series of trusses, taking the strain from the roof out into the supporting walls. This device is hidden from the spectators below by a ceiling painted with an allegorical scene of a great canvas being rolled back to show Truth triumphing over Envy, Hatred and Malice.

The Sheldonian Theatre can seat 2,000 people and does just that during the annual degree-giving ceremony and Encaenia, the high-point of the academic year, when honorary degrees are given to respected academics from other universities, celebrities in the arts and politics and, just occasionally, to businessmen who find the odd few million to benefit the university. Antonin Besse, who put up all the money for the creation of St Antony's and also helped out several less well-off colleges, was given such an honorary doctorate a few weeks before his death in 1951. Encaenia is held in June on the Wednesday of the ninth week of Trinity Term and is the best time to see Oxford University in all its pomp and ceremony, for all the bigwigs, from the Chancellor down, process in academic garb through the streets towards the Sheldonian.

Visitors to the Sheldonian are allowed to climb up into the roof space where Wren's wooden engineering can be admired. The floor here is so strong that the Oxford University Press was first housed here. Up from the roof area, one can climb to the cupola added in its present form in 1838. This is the most comfortable of the four great viewpoints over the city, if not the most dramatic.

Wren commissioned William Byrd, the Oxford stonemason, to carve fourteen great heads to stand in front of the Broad Street facade of the Sheldonian. No-one knows for sure what they are meant to represent, but they are universally known as the Emperors' Heads. One was removed to make way for Hawksmoor's Clarendon Building and the others have been replaced twice as the stone crumbled. In Max Beerbohm's satire *Zuleika Dobson*, they are referred to as the "Faceless Caesars." As Zuleika arrives in Oxford, her beauty is such that "as the landau rode by, sweat started from the brows of the Emperors."

During the 1660s and 1670s, Wren stayed in touch with Oxford even though he was now engaged in the rebuilding of London after the 1666 fire. He did work at All Souls, Trinity, St John's and Merton, but his second great contribution to the Oxford cityscape came in 1681 when he was invited by John Fell, the Dean of Christ Church, to complete the unfinished main entrance to the college in St Aldate's. He maintained the Gothic style of the lower part, but topped it with a tower with its now familiar but unique ogee-shaped cap. In later life, he came back to Oxford once more to make structural improvements to the Divinity School, which was beginning to suffer from the weight of Duke Humfrey's Library above it. While there, he replaced one of the windows in the centre of the north wall with a magnificent Gothic doorway which, when opened, led directly to the Sheldonian. Over the door are carved the letters CWA – Christopher Wren Architect.

Wren died at the great age of 91 in London in 1723 and was buried in the crypt of St Paul's Cathedral. On the wall above his grave a Latin inscription reads *Lector si monumentum requiris circumspice* – Reader, if you seek a monument, look around you. The same epitaph is as fitting in Oxford as it is in London.

All successful Oxford graduates can receive their degrees in the Sheldonian, but the writer Dorothy L. Sayers had to wait five years to get hers. It was not until October 14, 1920 that the first batch of women graduates were honored. With her on that day were Vera Brittain and Winifred Holtby.

Next to the Sheldonian stands the Clarendon Building designed by Wren's pupil, Nicholas Hawksmoor and built between1711 and 1713. It was paid for from the profits made by the Earl of Clarendon's book about the Civil War and was built as a printing works for the Oxford University Press. On top are seven lead figures of Muses made by Sir James Thornhill in 1717. Two, however, are fibreglass replicas given by Blackwell's bookshop (opposite in Broad Street) in 1974 to replace the originals which had fallen down. Unlike all the other university buildings in this area, visitors are not allowed inside.

The Bodleian Library

Standing between the Radcliffe Camera and the Sheldonian Theatre is the Bodleian Library complex, the precincts of which, with their heavy overlay of centuries of study and learning, make this the most awe-inspiring part of Oxford University. The Bodleian is one of the three English copyright libraries, which means it is entitled to a free copy of any book published in Britain. This has amounted over the centuries to an almighty collection of millions of volumes. Of course, they cannot all be stored in this old building. Most are, in fact, stacked in the New Bodleian on the other side of Broad Street, next to Blackwell's. Many more are tucked away on miles of shelving under Radcliffe Square and Broad Street. Other parts of the collection are housed in smaller libraries dotted throughout the city, and there is also a major store some miles to the south. Obviously this means that scholars in the Bodleian do not have instant access to all the books they need. But this does not put off the army of registered readers who take advantage of the resources of one of Oxford's greatest treasures. This is not, of course, a lending library; one has to read everything on the premises.

Apart from the quantity, the quality of the Bodleian collection is also stunning, ranging from the seventh-century manuscript of the *Acts of the Apostles* which was used by Bede, through the inevitable First Folio of Shakespeare, to the original manuscript of *The Wind in the Willows* bequeathed by Kenneth Grahame along with the copyright and the money brought in by it. Countless authors, churchmen and politicians have bequeathed their manuscripts and personal papers to the Bodleian for safe keeping.

The Bodleian buildings are ranged around the Schools Quadrangle, where even today one talks in whispers. Around its walls are the wide doors into the ancient schools, with their Latin names picked out in supremely elegant gold lettering on Oxford blue signs. Lectures and examinations were held here until the building of the Examination Schools in the High a century ago. Dominating the square is the Tower of the Five Orders, so called because each tier is fronted by columns designed in one of the five classical orders of architecture, starting with basic Tuscan at the bottom and becoming more elaborate as it rises through Doric, Ionic, Corinthian and Composite. The fourth tier has, instead of windows, a statue of King James I, the reigning monarch when the quad was built from 1613 to 1624. The King, who wrote treatises on smoking and demonology, is flattered as a major writer handing copies of his works to Fame and the University. It was James who said if he had not been a king, he would most have liked to be an Oxford man. At the west end of Schools Quad stands a bronze statue of William Herbert the 3rd Earl of Pembroke, University Chancellor 1617-30 and a patron of the arts – Shakespeare's First Folio was dedicated jointly to him and his brother, and Pembroke College is named after him. He stands guarding the entrance to the library itself.

One enters into the Proscholium, now occupied by the library's shop, and from here one can visit the Divinity School, one of the most beautiful and elaborate pieces of medieval architecture in Europe. This was the university's first purpose-built classroom, constructed between 1427 and 1488 for lectures and examinations which took place here with the candidates and examiners facing each other in the pulpits. The great glory of the Divinity School, obvious immediately as one enters, is the astonishing fan-vaulted ceiling of 1483, with its dramatic pendants and 455 carved bosses, some heraldic, some representational, all worth an inspection. The surprisingly low ceiling was installed to support Duke Humfrey's Library, built to house the great collection of manuscripts given to the university by Humfrey, Duke of Gloucester, the younger brother of King Henry V.

Through a door at the west end of Divinity School, one enters Convocation House, the panelled university parliament house, with its tiers of benches to hold the professors and dons, who met here below the Vice-Chancellor's throne to discuss university affairs. In the seventeenth century, this room also housed the national parliament on a number of occasions. When Charles I summoned them to Oxford in early 1644, the Commons met here and it was in this building that Charles II brought the MPs and Lords from plague-ravaged London in 1665 and again in 1685, when he dissolved parliament to prevent it from frustrating his plan to allow his Roman Catholic brother to succeed him as James II.

This room, unchanged in over 300 years, has often been used for filming costume dramas, including *The Madness of King George.*

Schools Quad (Oxford Times)

Off Convocation House stands the dark forbidding panelled chamber that is the Chancellor's Court. At its height, the university had almost complete legal power over its own members and would try and sentence them in this room. It was here that Anthony Wood was expelled from the university in 1691 for his defamation of the Earl of Clarendon in his *Athenae Oxonienses*.

Sir Thomas Bodley, the inspiration behind and financier of the schools and library building which surround Schools Quad to the east of the Divinity School, was a Fellow of Merton College. He was a scholar of Greek and Hebrew who received special permission to travel in Europe to learn other modern languages, and he bequeathed his own extensive library to the new university collection of books which were to be housed in the new buildings – which he never lived to see completed.

The final building in the area between Radcliffe Square and Broad Street is that housing the university's Museum of the History of Science, which was built about 1680 with the dual purpose of teaching science on the lower floors and containing Elias Ashmole's new museum above. The Ashmolean collection moved to its present home in Beaumont Street in 1845. Since 1924, the Old Ashmolean Building has housed the university's collection of historical scientific instruments. That original assortment has grown and now holds one of the world's most important collections of telescopes, microscopes, orreries, astrolabes, early medical instruments and the like. The whole thing has recently been restored and updated and will now perhaps cease to be one of Oxford's best-kept secrets. Among the exhibits can be found Lewis Carroll's photographic outfit and the astonishing lodestone known as the Countess of Westmorland's magnet. Dating from the 1750s it can raise 160lbs of metal. Possibly the best-known exhibit here is the blackboard used by Albert Einstein in a lecture at Rhodes House in 1931 to explain his Theory of Relativity. His chalked equations have been preserved intact. Among the medical exhibits are trepanning sets from the eighteenth century and an amputating kit of 1800. Here, too, is one of the original flasks of penicillin culture from Howard Florey's experiments.

The Oxford Story is the city's only real concession to commercial tourism and the people of Oxford tend to be quite snooty about it. However, for the first-time and short-stay visitor to the city, it continues to be an excellent, short introduction to the history of the university. Built here in Broad Street in 1987 with its back up against the city wall – an impressive part of which still exists here – The Oxford Story is a series of tableaux illustrating figures and events from various stages of the university's 750-year history. For about five pounds ($7.50), you can climb into one of the "time-cars," plug into the headset commentary and sit back for 25 minutes while being carried mechanically on a journey through time. The limitations of space mean that there are shortcomings in the extent of information about both the history of the place and the life of the university today, but this fun attraction is one of the very few in the city which will appeal to younger visitors. And, however restricted the amount of information imparted, it is almost certain to be more than the average visitor to Oxford used to take away.

As its name would suggest, the church of St Michael at the North Gate stands at the northern edge of Oxford's medieval city walls. Its tower, probably built just before the Norman Conquest, is the oldest structure standing intact in the city, although no trace remains of the Saxon church to which it was attached. From the thirteenth century, the tower was connected to the Bocardo Prison, above the North Gate. It was in a cell here that Archbishop Cranmer was held before being burned at the stake outside the city walls in 1556. It was probably from the tower itself that he was forced to watch the burning of Bishops Latimer and Ridley. The door of Cranmer's cell was preserved in St Mary Magdalen's, further up the road, but as this is now Oxford's most obviously Anglo-Catholic church, such a relic of Britain's most famous Protestant martyrs would fit uneasily there; so now it hangs in the tower of St Michael's.

It is possible to climb the tower for a view over the spires and pinnacles of the colleges to the east and the roofs of the business and retail sector of the city to the west. A new wide staircase has been installed which makes this the easiest climb of Oxford's four major viewpoints.

Jesus College

Of the three quiet colleges of Turl Street, Jesus College has been, outwardly at least, the quietest of all. This is largely because, for hundreds of years, it was a college almost exclusively peopled by undergraduates and Fellows from Wales, who created their own little enclave within the college and troubled the rest of the university little – except, that is, the men of Exeter College, across the road, upon whom they have carried out a long series of youthful pranks as part of an unneighborly rivalry (a rivalry that exploded into full-scale fighting in the "Turl Street Riots" of 1979). Oxford's Welsh college was also its first truly Protestant college, being founded in 1571, technically by Queen Elizabeth I but, in fact, by one Hugh Price, treasurer of St David's cathedral in Pembrokeshire. Price put up the money and did the work, but asked Gloriana to take the credit. He built his college on the site of the defunct White Hall, which had been one of the university's academic halls since the thirteenth century.

The college's alumni have created little excitement outside Wales, but within the principality have taken senior church and government posts. That great mystic poet, Henry Vaughan (1622-95), might have been attached to the college, though there is little proof. His twin brother, Thomas, however, was a Fellow in 1642. The only former students of international repute from Jesus, were Lawrence of Arabia and Britain's longest-serving Labour Prime Minister. Harold Wilson was an earnest young Yorkshireman when he came up to Jesus in 1934 and never had any time for the traditional student life. To be fair, he also had no money to pay for it. He lived an abstemious existence, managing to get his battels bill (college charges for food and drink) down to almost half the accepted level. The serious young Wilson felt smoking and drinking to be weaknesses to which he had no wish to succumb, an irony considering that his pipe became his trademark as Prime Minister.

When he first arrived at Oxford, Wilson was not committed to any political party. When he joined the Labour Club, he found the members were "very petty, squabbling about tiffs with other sections of the Labour Party instead of getting down to something concrete." But it was work that was most important to him and by 1937, when he got his First, he was accepted as one of the finest scholars of his generation. He failed twice however, to gain a Fellowship at All Souls and went instead to Univ, where Sir William Beveridge found him a junior research post. Wilson's son later became an Oxford don and in his retirement, the former Premier spent a good deal of time back in the city.

Thomas Edward Lawrence (1888-1935), who was hero-worshipped in the 1920s and 1930s as the Englishman who led the successful Arab revolt against the occupying Turks during the First World War, is one of Oxford's most famous sons. He was born in North Wales, the second of five illegitimate sons of Sir Thomas Chapman Bt, who took the name Lawrence when he fled to Oxford with his lover, the governess he had appointed to look after the four daughters from his marriage. T.E., or Ned as he was generally known, grew up at no. 2 Polstead Road, a semi-detached middle-class home just off Woodstock Road in North Oxford. He was educated at Oxford High School, in the the T.G. Jackson building on the corner of George Street and New Inn Hall Street, which is now the home of the university's Social Studies Faculty Centre. Here he failed the entrance examination to St John's College, but the accident of his birth in Wales made him eligible for a scholarship to Jesus, which he entered in 1907 to study history.

Apart from one term in college, he continued to live at home in Polstead Road, where a small, two-roomed building was built at the end of the long, narrow, rear garden so that he could do his university work. The little bungalow, now much enlarged, still survives and there is a plaque on the front wall of the house recording Lawrence's association.

His fellow undergraduates considered him rather strange and aloof – perhaps with good reason. One schoolfriend who went up to Jesus with him, E.F. Hall, recalled a visit from Lawrence, who walked in with a revolver in his hand and explained he had been trying to see how long he could go without food or sleep and had managed 45 hours. "I said, well let's get rid of this revolver, and he fired a shot down the Turl…I was quite frightened of him; that was the kind of thing that he did." Hall, who also remembered Lawrence sleeping in a coffin, joined him on his most famous Oxford escapade. Reading the works of the seventeenth-century Oxford historian Anthony Wood, Lawrence was intrigued by the story of a Saxon underground waterway flowing beneath the centre of the city – the Trill Mill Stream. Together, Lawrence and Hall found the entrance at Hythe Bridge, near Worcester College, and took a canoe along its full length by night, coming out in what is now the War Memorial Gardens at the edge of Christ Church Meadow. The journey took them twenty minutes.

In his last year at Jesus, Lawrence travelled to Syria for an archaeological dig, during which time he made observations of Turkish military movements for his tutor which were passed on to the Foreign Office. This spying experience earned him a place on another expedition to the area after he graduated, and this was the start of his escapades and adventures in the Desert War. His legendary exploits gave rise to an astonishing international adulation, and Lawrence, retiring and modest by nature, needed to get away from it. So a colleague with connections at All Souls managed to persuade the college to grant him a two-year Fellowship, where he could retire from the limelight and work on his account of the war, *The Seven Pillars of Wisdom*. He completed the first draft of the book in 1919, but the manuscript was lost (or, according to Lawrence, stolen) while he waited for a train at Reading station. In fact, Lawrence only stayed for one year at All Souls before being called back to the Middle East, but his great book was first printed in a private edition of just eight copies by *The Oxford Times*.

Exeter College

The first three Oxford colleges, Balliol, University and Merton, all still have a commanding presence in the city. The fourth oldest, Exeter College, is one of the less flamboyant and less exciting. The playwright Alan Bennett (b.1934) remembered: "My college, Exeter, was in 1954 a fairly modest – not to say undistinguished – establishment, which is precisely why I'd chosen it, as I would stand a better chance there, I reasoned, than at socially more exalted foundations such as Trinity." Bennett, who had rooms on the same staircase as the TV presenter Russell Harty (1934-88), became a junior don at Magdalen. Much of the time he was there he was playing in *Beyond the Fringe* in London and commuting to Oxford three days a week in order to teach. When, in 1962, the show went to Broadway, it put an end to his hopes of being a history don.

Exeter College was founded in 1314 by Walter de Stapeldon, Bishop of Exeter, who was later to become High Treasurer to the unpopular Edward II and was eventually murdered by the mob in London in 1326. For almost 100 years, it was known as Stapeldon Hall and, as its founder had left it few endowments, was one of the poorest institutions in the university. The original statutes for the college demanded that Fellows should only stay a maximum of thirteen years, before having to return to the Exeter diocese – Devon and Cornwall – to take up work in a parish. The effect of this ruling was that, with most scholars arriving at the college in their mid-teens, no-one aged much above thirty was ever attached to the hall and therefore the young, inexperienced crew was unable to make a mark in the wider university community. To escape being sent back to the West Country, the brightest among the Stapeldon Fellows simply transferred to one of the other colleges.

The name was changed to Exeter College in 1405, but fortunes did not improve until William Petre, an old boy of the college who made himself a great fortune as a deputy to Thomas Cromwell during the Dissolution of the Monasteries (he grabbed 36,000 acres for himself in Devon), decided in his retirement to rearrange and improve things at his old college. He changed the rules about Fellows' tenure of office, added a number of wealthy endowments, put new officers in post and donated his own library, which included the *Bohun Psalter*, a magnificent fourteenth-century illuminated book, owned in turn by Elizabeth of York, queen to Henry VII, and Catherine of Aragon, queen to Henry VIII and signed by them both. This great book served in a way as the royal "family Bible" and its Tudor inscriptions include the only reference in history to the birth date of Henry VII.

The college stayed devoted to the Catholic cause and this led to the martyrdom of two Fellows during Elizabeth I's reign, including the recently promoted St Ralph Sherwin, who was executed in 1581. Among other early alumni, Anthony Ashley Cooper (1621-83), the first Lord Shaftesbury and founder of the Whig Party stands out.

Exeter's cramped and restricted setting contains one remarkable jewel of architecture, the chapel built by Sir George Gilbert Scott in the 1850s, which he designed as a copy of Sainte Chapelle in Paris and whose scale dwarfs all else in the college's two main quads. The fleche, or thin turreted spire, of the chapel is a beautiful landmark on the central Oxford skyline. To erect his new chapel, Scott had to get rid of the rather fine seventeenth-century predecessor, which gave him so much trouble that he resorted to blowing it up with gunpowder.

Although academic prestige never really afflicted Exeter, it was a prominent sporting college in the nineteenth century, being among the first to promote rowing, opening only the third college cricket ground and masterminding the first athletics meeting in Oxford. Victorian dons of distinction included Francis Palgrave (1824-97), who compiled the *Golden Treasury of Lyrical Poetry*, the collection which for fifty years was the first-choice introduction to "great" English poetry in the nation's schools; and James Anthony Froude (1818-94) the younger brother of one of the founders of the Oxford Movement. He became a Fellow at Exeter in 1844, just before Newman converted to Roman Catholicism. Shortly after this event, Froude dramatically lost his faith, recording his agonies in two novels, both of which caused a scandal. *Shadow of the Clouds* (1847), featuring seduction, was considered so shameful by Froude's father, the Archdeacon of Totnes in Devon, that the old man went around the bookshops buying all the copies he could find and destroying them. *The Nemesis of Faith* (1849) was the story of a young Anglican priest who lost his faith and lusted after a married woman. This was a sensation and one of Froude's fellow dons at Exeter, the Rev William Sewell, publicly flung a copy of it into the fire. Froude was forced to resign his Fellowship and went to London to write for several magazines. By 1892, however, he had been forgiven and came back to Oxford as Professor of Modern History.

Among students here were R.D. Blackmore (1825-1900), author of the West Country novel *Lorna Doone*, the composer Hubert Parry (1848-1918) of *Jerusalem* fame and that pair of Pre-Raphaelite artists, William Morris (1834-96) and Edward Burne-Jones (1833-98), who were up as students together in the 1850s. Both remembered the city with affection – Burne-Jones wrote: "Oxford is a glorious place; godlike! at night I have walked around the colleges under the full moon, and thought it would be heaven to live and die here." Morris, bemoaning change, wrote:

> *Oxford in those days still kept a great deal of its earlier loveliness: and the memory of its grey streets as they were then has been an abiding influence and pleasure in my life...since then the guardians of this beauty and romance have ignored it utterly, have made its preservation give way to*

the pressure of commercial exigencies and are determined apparently to destroy it altogether.

Well-known twentieth-century figures who were undergraduates at Exeter included Zada Liaquat Ali Khan, the assassinated first Prime Minister of Pakistan; the actor Richard Burton (1925-84); Roger Bannister (b.1929), the first man to run a mile in under four minutes; and the author J.R.R. Tolkien (1892-1973).

The noble building on the corner of Broad Street and Holywell Street is the Indian Institute, and its facades are adorned by heads of tigers, elephants and Hindu deities. It was built in 1875 at the height of the British Raj's reign in India, with the aim of providing a meeting place at which one could learn about the sub-continent and Indians could learn about the mother country. Young men studying for the Indian Civil Service attended courses here. The Institute contained an Indian museum which swiftly overflowed with gifts sent by princelings from all over India. Most of this was transferred to the Ashmolean in 1968 when the university, sensing that India's importance to Britain and Oxford had diminished greatly, decided to take over the building for other uses. It now houses the history faculty library.

Hertford College

The novelist Evelyn Waugh (1903-66) was far from impressed with his time at Hertford College, describing its Catte Street frontage as looking like a large provincial bank; but then the university was not too impressed with Evelyn Waugh either; he only got a poor Third in history and spent much his time getting drunk and being silly with his titled companions. Their larks are sent up in the opening chapters of his first novel *Decline and Fall.* But Waugh also gave us *Brideshead Revisited,* the television dramatization of which brought visitors to Oxford in the 1980s looking for the Brideshead link, the way they came looking for Inspector Morse links in the 1990s.

Hertford is a young college with a long history. It began life as an academic hall, Hart Hall, which was taken over in 1283 by Elias de Hertford who passed it on to Walter de Stapeldon, the Bishop of Exeter. He lodged students here for a while during the building of his own Exeter College nearby. Thereafter, for much of its early history, it was a hall of residence for Exeter, prospering in the sixteenth century when its sympathies attracted boys from Roman Catholic backgrounds like the poet-priest John Donne (1572-1631), who matriculated here in 1584 at the early age of twelve.

In the eighteenth century, under the Principalship of Dr Richard Newton, Hart Hall was incorporated into the university as Hertford College, although it attracted very few endowments and lived perilously close to economic failure. Up in 1764 was Charles James Fox (1749-1806), who would go on to become one of the greatest of all British parliamentarians. Fox said of his time in Oxford: "To a man who reads a good deal there cannot be a more agreeable place." But he did not spend all his time reading and recalled an occasion when he leapt out of his study window to join fellow undergraduates in a pitched battle with local youths.

After Dr Newton's death, the young Hertford College went into terminal decline and, by 1805, with only two Fellows and no students, was closed down. At this time, Magdalen College was seeking to expand into the High Street site occupied by Magdalen Hall and bought the Hertford site with the intention of moving the academic hall there. A disastrous fire at the hall in 1820 speeded up the transfer. Magdalen Hall, rich with endowments, now sought to revive Hertford's college status and, with the money of Thomas Baring of the banking family, realized its wish as Hertford College rose again in 1874.

By now, all the medieval buildings of old Hart Hall were crumbling, and the new college turned to T.G. Jackson, who was establishing himself as Oxford's leading architect. He built most of the Catte Street facade we see today. It was Jackson, too, who solved the problem of occupying sites on either side of New College Lane (all the baths were on the north side and curfew was early). The structure he erected has become one of Oxford's most famous tourist landmarks. The Bridge of Sighs, named because of its similarity to the Ponte dei Sospiri in Venice, was objected to strongly by New College, which claimed it would ruin the view of the college from the Bodleian complex. They were right, of course, and it does; but it does so with a panache that has delighted visitors to the city for more than a century.

May Morning at the Bridge of Sighs (Oxford Times)

University dons are often portrayed as a stuffy lot, but sometimes they reveal surprising qualities. In 1968, the year of student unrest across Europe, the Hertford junior common room tried to bully the Fellows into allowing the undergraduates half the seats on the college's governing body. "In the unlikely event of this demand being refused," said the undergrads, "the JCR shall organize an incessant stream of violent demonstrations." The Fellows were not cowed by such post-adolescent threats and hit back with three points (and a splendid sense of the absurd):

1 The Governing Body refuses to enter into negotiations of any sort under duress or threat of violent action. 2 The Governing Body, in anticipation of such action, has made appropriate disposal of its exiguous funds and now has access to tear-gas bombs, truncheons, water cannon and other devices, the nature of which it is not expedient to disclose. 3 The Governing Body has among its members an expert on cholera and authority on sex hormones and one with a first-class certificate in automatic weapons. They have put their knowledge at the disposal of the Governing Body, which is prepared to exploit it ruthlessly in the suppression of overt violence.

Gavin Maxwell (1914-69), author of the nature classic *Ring of Bright Water*, came up to study estate management at Hertford in 1933. He was the grandson of the Duke of Northumberland and had been brought up in his isolated ancestral Scottish home, so Oxford hardly suited him at all. In his first year he associated with other Scottish noblemen, walking around town in tweeds and shooting shoes studded with nails, with spaniels and Labradors at their heels. He was really not interested in his chosen subject and failed his prelims at the end of his first year, having to resit them a year later.

But still he did not work, so he and his companions, faced with the disgrace of being sent down if they failed a second time, decided the only way they could pass would be if they were to steal a copy of the examination papers. As the lightest of the group, Maxwell was chosen to carry out the burglaries with the others acting as lookouts. So, less than a week before the exams, he found himself shinning up drainpipes into offices that were thought to be secure. Only one paper eluded their search, and so for that they covered their shirt cuffs with white paper on which they had written all the facts they required in tiny lettering, using yellow ink. "So we passed our preliminaries in this disgraceful manner," Maxwell recalled in middle age, "and we remained at Oxford for a further two years of idleness."

Just off New College Lane, beyond the Bridge of Sighs, lies possibly the best-known and most popular of all Oxford's pubs, the Turf Tavern. It has – possibly because of its situation in Bath Place, surrounded by small domestic buildings in the shadow of the high walls of New College – an air of great age, yet is really not that old. It was formerly a malthouse backing on to the city wall and became a cider house in about 1775, known at first as the Spotted Cow. It did not get its present name until 1845, when it was named after a nearby gambling hall where turf accountants (bookmakers) met. The pub itself is very small but, as most people seem to prefer to drink outside in the courtyard, this is hardly a problem. The passage leading beyond the Turf to Holywell Street is today called St Helen's Passage, though in former times it was known as Hell Passage, possibly a reference to the same gambling house or a descriptive name conjuring up the dark conditions under the city wall.

In Hell Passage in the 1850s – a wretched place then – lived a stable groom and his family. The groom was named Burden and his eldest daughter was to become one of the most famous muses in the history of British painting and to set the standard for what we still today think of as Pre-Raphaelite beauty. One evening, seventeen-year-old Jane Burden (1839-1914) and her younger sister Bessie were approached by two young men at a theatre in Oriel Street. The men were the artists Dante Gabriel Rossetti and Edward Burne-Jones and they were in Oxford to paint murals in the new Oxford Union building in St Michael's Street. Rossetti was struck by Jane's beauty and asked her to go around to his rooms in George Street the next day and model for him. Jane never turned up, because her parents objected, but Rossetti called at Hell Passage and persuaded the Burdens to let her come. Thus began a career for Jane, in which her abundant, flowing hair and large, dark eyes were to make her famous

Rossetti immediately drew her face for the giant figure of Guinevere in his mural at the Oxford Union. He set aside the sketches he had already made of Lizzie Siddal, his long-term favorite model and future wife. Jane was entranced by Rossetti, who took an intense interest in her own and her family's life. She was much in demand. William Morris, another of the Union painters, asked her to model for his picture of Iseult standing before a richly canopied bed grieving for the absent Tristram. Sitting for the shy Morris was much less fun than sitting for the exuberant Rossetti. However, Morris fell deeply in love and, when Rossetti had to leave Oxford to look after Lizzie Siddal who was ill in London, Morris took the opportunity of proposing to Jane. She accepted and, in April 1859, they were married at the church of St Michael at the North Gate. She was 19, he 25. From that day, Jane, who was to be loved all her days by both Morris and Rossetti, suppressed all references to her Oxford back-street origins, rarely coming back to the city, not even for her mother's funeral.

At no.7 New College Lane, stands the house of the astronomer Edmund Halley (1656-1742). Because he gave his name to the most famous of all comets, Halley is one of the best-known astronomers of all time. He worked out the predictions for the return of the comet that bears his name while he was Savilian Professor of Geometry at Oxford (1703-42). During that time, he lived in this house and built an observatory on the roof, which still survives. Halley was an all-round scientist of considerable note, although he left Queen's College without a degree at the age of twenty. He had by then already published a paper on planetary orbits and went on to make important discoveries about the earth's magnetic field, the optics of the rainbow and barometric pressure. But it was in the field of astronomy that he shone, being the first man to make a complete observation of the transit of Mercury and, in 1715, accurately predicting the path of the total solar eclipse. He was a friend of the older Isaac Newton and encouraged him to publish his revolutionary *Principia Mathematica* in 1687, paying for the printing himself. In 1720 he was appointed Astronomer Royal.

New College

New College Lane continues past the gate of New College and turns sharply right to become Queen's Lane. Together, they form a thoroughfare which, like Merton Street south of the High, gives the modern-day pedestrian a glimpse of what life in Oxford must have been like in earlier days. Though other colleges can happily be shortened to Merton, Balliol or Wadham, Oxford etiquette demands that you never speak just of New; the word college must always be tacked on – just the opposite, in fact, of Christ Church.

The first thing that becomes obvious to anyone who sees New College is that it is certainly not new. As a matter of fact, it is not called New College either. However, when its foundation stone was laid by William of Wykeham in 1380, it was the first new college in Oxford for nearly half a century and, although its official title was St Mary's College of Winchester in Oxford, there was already a St Mary's College (that now known as Oriel), so Wykeham's foundation was the "new" St Mary's.

It was also new in its approach and its concept. Its originality lay in the fact that it taught undergraduates and because it was designed as a quadrangle, with all the important elements of communal life – chapel, hall, library, chambers, bursary and Warden's lodgings, facing each other in an intergrated whole.

William of Wykeham (1324-1404) was Bishop of Winchester and a rich and powerful man. In fact, only a year after starting to buy land for the college, he was made Chancellor of England, the most powerful commoner in the land – although he soon fell out with Edward III, accused of embezzlement. His aim in building the college was to repopulate the clergy of England after the ravages of the Black Death. Wykeham had helped design Windsor Castle and also designed his college like a fortress. It is worth trying to get past the lodge porters, for New College offers a magnificent vision of what medieval Oxford life would have been like. Its grand, though severe, Great Quad is offset by the glories of the chapel and the delights of the gardens, famously incorporating a long stretch of the thirteenth-century city walls. The American writer Nathaniel Hawthorne (1804-64) was bowled over by them when he visited Oxford:

> *The gardens of New College are indescribably beautiful, – not beautiful in an American sense, but lawns of the richest green and softest velvet grass, shadowed over by ancient trees, that have lived a quiet life here for centuries. Such a sweet, quiet, sacred, stately seclusion...cannot exist anywhere else.*

New College Chapel which, despite the counter-claims of Christ Church, is the premier university setting to hear sacred music sung sublimely, has a couple of art treasures which were each in their day controversial. The great west window was designed by Sir Joshua Reynolds, first president of the Royal Academy, and painted by Thomas Jervais in the 1780s. Both artists appear as shepherds in the nativity scene in the upper half of the window. The Virgin Mary is a portrait of Eliza Sheridan, wife of the dramatist and, in her youth, the most famous singer in England. The seven Virtues portrayed in the lower half of the window were modelled from other society favorites of the day and look, according to Lord Torrington, like "half-dressed, languishing harlots."

Below the window stands the eight-foot statue of Lazarus carved by the anglicized American-born sculptor Jacob Epstein (1880-1959). It is a remarkably powerful portrayal of the biblical character, newly raised by Christ from the dead, still tightly wrapped in his burial bandages, but turning his head to gaze through the screen from the ante-chapel into the chapel itself. Its hulking presence can still come as a shock, even when one is familiar with it, and a good number of Fellows of the college have never come to terms with it. It was bought directly from the artist himself, by the Warden, Alic Smith, who spotted it in the artist's studio when sitting for a portrait bust. "You know," he told Epstein, "that would look very well in my college." New College only paid Epstein £700, which was a derisory sum in 1952. There was a hint of more to follow, but the artist never received another penny. The following year, however, he found his name added to those who were to be given honorary degrees by the university, and the sight of him in the Encaenia procession must have salved Smith's conscience somewhat.

That New College always did things on a grand scale is evidenced by the fact that the college cesspit (this was, of course, long before decent drainage) was the largest ever constructed in Oxford and did not need to be emptied during the first 300 years of the college's history. It was eventually "carefully excavated," filled in and chosen as the site for a student common-room.

So determined had William of Wykeham been that his new college should succeed that, once it was established, he built a feeder school for it, a grammar school in Winchester which went on to become one of the most influential private schools in the country. For centuries, New College operated a closed shop, taking all its Fellows and virtually all its undergraduates from Winchester. This insularity served the college well for centuries but was its undoing in the nineteenth century, when the spirit of "improvement" spread throughout the university in reaction to the demise of the previous century. New College remained aloof from these developments and insisted on retaining its right to set its own examinations for its own students. Consequently, as the standards and reputation of the university rose, New College sank back. After fights with the university and a parliamentary commission, change eventually arrived with Warden Sewell.

Sewell's successor as Warden in 1903 was the most famous name associated with the college and one of the few Oxford academics of the twentieth century to become a household name. Unfortunately, the Rev William Spooner (1844-1930) was celebrated neither for his research nor his administrative qualities. He achieved fame simply because he was the archetypal absent-minded Oxford don.

Spooner was the first non-Wykehamist (he never went to Winchester) to be admitted as a student to New College in the reforms of the 1860s and went on to become successively the first non-

Wykehamist Fellow, Dean and Warden. He steered the college through a time of difficult changes and turned down the chance to become Vice-Chancellor – top dog in the university. He was an unmistakable figure, an albino with an unusually large head and very short-sighted. He was a popular and gifted conversationalist, but had the unfortunate habit of transposing the initial letters or sounds of words, so that in chapel he famously announced the next hymn as "Kinquering Congs their Tikles Tate" or asked rhetorically: "Which of us has not felt in his heart a half-warmed fish?" These inadvertent malapropisms were seized upon and expanded upon by wits in London and the spoonerism was born. It has become an established comedy format and certainly many of the most outrageous spoonerisms – such as his red-faced error when a letter was never delivered and he meant to ask two servant girls "Which of you has missed the post?" – were never uttered by him.

Dr Robert Seton, a great friend of Spooner, revealed after the Warden's death in 1930 that he had admitted to him that he had sometimes made spoonerisms deliberately "to raise a laugh." He was, though, definitely absent-minded and much more likely to be true are the gaffes that included his questioning of a former student after the First World War: "Tell me, was it you or your brother that was killed in the war?" Professor Edward Morris Hugh-Jones, who also knew Spooner, agreed that most spoonerisms were apocryphal, but remembered the time when the Warden was invited to dinner in North Oxford. "During the evening," he said:

> it came on to rain quite heavily and his host and hostess pressed him to stay. It was far too cold and wet for Spooner to traipse all the way back to college, they said, and they would gladly make up a bed for him. They were as good as their word and briefly departed upstairs to see to the arrangements. When they came down again, their guest had disappeared. Suddenly there was a knock at the house door and there was Spooner, totally wet through, with a little bundle in his hands. 'My nightshirt,' he explained. 'I went back to college for it.'

Other famous names associated with New College include the *Forsyte Saga* novelist John Galsworthy (1867-1933), the diarist Parson James Woodforde (1740-1803), the playwright R.C. Sherriff (1896-1975), the anti-pornography campaigner Lord Longford (b.1905) and the Labour

Party politicians Hugh Gaitskell (1906-63), Richard Crossman (1967-74) and Tony Benn (b.1925).

Dennis Potter (1935-94) achieved fame as an undergraduate at New College in 1958, when he was filmed and interviewed for a BBC programme called *Does Class Matter?* Potter, who went on to become the finest playwright British television has produced, had crossed the traditional class divide when he came up to Oxford from working-class origins in the Forest of Dean. Always argumentative and with a lot to prove, he quickly made a name for himself, debating at the Oxford Union and in student journalism. In one article, he wrote disparagingly of:

> *the droves of bitterly disappointed Americans who descend on 'Axford, England' each summer. They are upset because the medievalism is not everywhere apparent except maybe in their hotel bedrooms, and are in danger of mistaking the city's glistening new Woolworth's for Balliol College.*

Looking back on his New College days in later life, he wrote: "There are those who hate Oxford because they never went there and those who loathe it because they did. I was decidedly in the latter category, but time has mellowed my feelings into something more ambivalent."

CHAPTER SIX

Oscar Wilde's Oxford

"Oxford is the capital of romance; in its own way as memorable as Athens, and to me it was more entrancing. In Oxford, as in Athens, the realities of sordid life were kept at a distance."

Oxford almost claimed Oscar Wilde for its own. He arrived in 1874, a brilliant scholar who had already taken a degree in Dublin, confident that he was intellectually superior to all those around him, and proceeded to whip through his studies and exams, taking a double First in Greats and winning the Newdigate Prize for poetry. He should have, and wanted to, stay on as a don, but the colleges would not have him. For Oscar, Oxford was heaven; a cloistered existence where he could always find someone to listen to his ideas on aestheticism and, above all, where there was a steady stream of beautiful, fresh-faced boys up from public school, who shared his joy in an all-male environment. In later life, he said he wanted to get to the point where he should be able to say "that the two great turning points in my life were when my father sent me to Oxford and when society sent me to prison."

Oscar Fingal O'Flaherty Wills Wilde (1855-1900) was born in Dublin on October 16, 1855, the son of an alarmingly short (Oscar was over six feet) doctor who was irresistible to women and consultant to royalty; he had treated Napoleon III and the Emperor Maximilian, and the boy was named Oscar after the King of Sweden, who had asked to be godfather to the son of the doctor who had cured him of cataracts. Oscar devoured books as a boy and he learned without difficulty, delighting particularly in Greek and Latin. At Trinity College, Dublin, he won many prizes for classics and his closest friend was John Mahaffy, Professor of Greek. Without effort, he won a scholarship to Magdalen College, Oxford.

In his early days in Oxford, the strongly built Wilde was almost a "hearty," enjoying, shooting, boxing and rowing, though he soon stopped this last: "I don't see the use of going down backwards to Iffley every evening." John Ruskin, the Slade Professor of Art, impressed him in his first year, and he became one of Ruskin's road-building party, enjoying hard labor in Hinksey village and insisting on being the one to push Ruskin's wheelbarrow for him. But at the end of the year, Ruskin went off to Venice and Wilde found himself falling under the influence instead of Walter Pater of Brasenose, who espoused the "art for art's sake" philosophy and was the inspiration of the aesthetic movement. Oscar embraced his ideas, turning to a more flamboyant way of dress, speech and mannerism, and held "beauty parties" in his rooms at which the conversation had to match the clothing and the decor, He decorated his rooms with objets d'art, including his collection of Pre-Raphaelite blue-and-white china, of which he made his celebrated remark "Oh, would that I could live up to my blue china!" Later he would boast that the Vicar of St Mary's opened a sermon with:

> When a young man says, not in polished banter but in solemn earnestness, that he finds it difficult to live up to the level of his blue china, there has crept into the cloistered shades a form of heathenism which it is our bounden duty to fight against and to crush out if possible.

Inspired by visions of handsome Greek youths, Oscar became more openly homosexual – although on one vacation back in Ireland he fell in love with a girl who went on to marry Bram Stoker, the author of *Dracula*. He affected a pose of indolence during the day, but worked furiously when no-one was watching and read of his First in mods in

The Times while breakfasting at the Mitre. In his finals, he ostentatiously asked for extra paper after the first hour of a three-hour exam and then walked out half an hour before the end – and still got the best First in his year. Although Oxford chose not to give him a Fellowship, he retained a love of it all his life; "I envy you going to Oxford," he wrote to a young friend. "It is the most flower-like time of one's life. One sees the shadow of things in silver mirrors."

After going down in 1878, he published poetry, then prose and, in the 1890s, built a reputation as the finest dramatist of his day. But his homosexuality was to be his downfall; he met Lord Alfred Douglas ("Bosie") when revisiting a friend at Oxford and outraged the boy's father, the Marquess of Queensberry with their relationship. Unwisely, he sued the Marquess for libel and lost, only to be tried himself for homosexuality. His conviction and imprisonment in Reading jail broke him spiritually and, of course, he was destroyed professionally. His last years were spent roaming Europe and he died in Paris, aged 45. His rooms overlooking the Cherwell at Magdalen have been turned into a bar and furniture store.

Magdalen College

Since its foundation in the fifteenth century, Magdalen College has been one of the biggest and most important colleges in Oxford. Its name offers more evidence for those who believe that pronunciation is Oxford's own snobbery and mispronunciation a clear way to identify an outsider. Forget all you know about Mary Magdalen, even though it is after this penitent that the college is named, Magdalen (like Magdalene College in Cambridge) retains the archaic pronunciation of Mawd-lin. To make matters worse, it lies on the banks of Oxford's "second" river, the Cherwell – that's Char-well, by the way, even though the people of middle and north Oxfordshire who live within its reaches pronounce it Chur-well.

If it had been up to its founder, Magdalen would not have stood on its riverside site at all. When William of Waynflete became Bishop of Winchester, he decided to endow a college in Oxford for the study of theology and philosophy and had his eye on the site across the road where the Examination Schools now stands. But events during the War of the Roses, set back his plans and he did not pursue the idea for another decade, during which time he had attained the position of Chancellor of England.

In this intervening ten years, Waynflete had managed to buy a bigger plot of land on the northern side of the High Street, but outside the city wall. It was the site of the Hospital of St John the Baptist, the traditional name for hostels for poor and needy travellers. The hospital had been founded by Henry III in the thirteenth century and was by now very run down. By fair means and foul, the college managed to attain property and land across the Midlands and the South of England, and the rents and tithes from its real estate made it, within 100 years, the wealthiest college in Oxford. During this time most of the buildings we see today were built, including Magdalen Tower, standing solidly and handsomely on the city side of Magdalen Bridge and still thought by many to be the most beautiful building in Oxford. Work started on building it in 1492, the year Columbus first reached the Americas.

Like so many other colleges, Magdalen's style swung back and forth during the Reformation, but during the Civil War a century later, it stood very firmly on the side of King Charles I against the Parliamentary forces. Its position across the bridge made it the first substantial building in the city on the London Road, and it became the headquarters of Charles's brilliant young general Prince Rupert (1619-82). But some still think of the college's greatest moment as the occasion when it stood up for its independence against a king. The king was the Roman Catholic James II who, on the death of the college President, Henry Clerke, in 1686, recommended as his successor one Anthony Farmer. Now Farmer was not a Fellow of the college and, to make matters worse, he was a Catholic and both these matters technically disqualified him from the job under the terms of the college statutes. So the Magdalen Fellows chose one of their own number, John Hough. James II was willing to back down over Farmer, but insisted that the Bishop of Oxford, Samuel Parker, should be a compromise candidate. The Fellows refused to accept him and a Royal Commission followed during which nearly all the top men at Magdalen came close to looking for new jobs. But James had trouble all over the country at this time and shortly after giving in and allowing Hough to take over at Magdalen, abdicated the throne in favor of his Protestant daughter Mary and her strange Dutch husband William of Orange. He then fled to Europe, never to return.

The greatest figure in the history of Magdalen was Martin Routh, who remained President until his death at 99. His 64 years in charge is far and away a record for any Oxford college, and the remarkable thing is that neither he nor Magdalen declined in reputation, even in his great old age. Routh spanned two eras in Oxford: the easy, complacent, lacklustre days of the eighteenth century, and the new, aggressively intellectual, Victorian era. A man who could both remember seeing Dr Johnson lost in thought in High Street and yet lived to fight the coming of the railways to Oxford, was clearly someone to take seriously. His attachment to the past went back even further, for he was proud to boast that he had an aunt who had known a woman who remembered seeing Charles I in Oxford. Routh was also reputed to have been the last man in England to wear a wig as part of his everyday dress – the wig itself is preserved in the college library. In later years he became a popular spectacle. On Sundays, people would gather at the gates of the college to see him make his way across the quad to chapel, a wizened little figure in full ceremonial dress. He was a scholar of real note and quite unflappable. When an anxious don told him that a Fellow of the college had committed suicide, Routh is reported to have replied: "Pray don't tell me who. Allow me to guess."

Perhaps because of its riverside setting, perhaps because of its spacious feel, Magdalen is still one of the most popular of Oxford's colleges, with students and visitors alike. Among the natural tourist attractions is the extraordinarily peaceful fifteenth-century Cloister Quad. Possibly nowhere in Oxford is quite so evocative of the romantic idea of busy clerics or committed scholars. A doorway from the cloisters leads out to an expanse of lawns before the New Building of 1733, and from there on to the Deer Park and Magdalen Grove, where the college has kept a herd of about forty fallow deer (one for each Fellow in Waynflete's original statutes) for 300 years.

The idea that John Betjeman (1906-84) would later be knighted and appointed Poet Laureate would have seemed laughable to his tutors at Magdalen in the late 1920s, as he was unable to take his studies seriously. This middle-class boy spent his time hob-nobbing with the more aristocratic undergraduates and developing his liking for the life of a *bon vivant*. Although he had been a pupil at Oxford's Dragon School and knew the city and its surrounding district so well, nothing suited him so much as life at Magdalen, where his college rooms on the second floor of New Buildings were "a kingdom of my own":

My wide-sashed windows looked across the grass
To Tower and hall and lines of pinnacles.
The wind among the elms, the echoing stairs,
The quarters, chimed across the quiet quad
From Magdalen tower and neighboring turret-clocks,
Gave 18th-century splendour to my state.

One of the young Betjeman's tutors was C.S.Lewis, and these two important figures of twentieth-century English literature did not get along at all well together. Lewis's bluff, beery style did not go down well with the aspiring aesthete, who delighted in striking poses as Oscar Wilde had done fifty years earlier. Under the statutes of the English faculty, he was entitled to take medieval Welsh as a special subject and, knowing there was no-one in Oxford fit to teach it, mischievously opted for it. This resulted in a tutor being brought from Aberystwyth once a week by train to teach him. It came to nothing of course, as all of Betjeman's formal studies came to nothing, when he failed his divinity exams and left the university without a degree.

Tucked within the present buildings of Magdalen College (behind the long wall in Longwall Street) is the site of Magdalen Hall, built in 1480 as the grammar school of the college. Although it later developed as one of the academic halls of Oxford, the grammar school itself survived and, to this day, is one of the prestigious private schools of the city, though now it is in Cowley Place on the other side of Magdalen Bridge.

During the twentieth century, the school produced a steady stream of middle-ranking academics and professional men, but in early times those associated with it had a bad habit of coming to a sticky end. At the end of the fifteenth century, Sir (St) Thomas More, Henry VIII's "man for all seasons," was supposed to have been a pupil here. Losing royal favor for refusing to accept Henry's authority over the Church in England or his divorce from Catherine of Aragon, he also lost his head, in 1535. He had clearly not learned the lesson of the school's former

Master, Thomas Wolsey (c1475-1530) who, only a few years earlier, had lost his position of power for similar reasons. Only a year after More's execution, another former member of the school, William Tyndale (c1494-1536) was burned at the stake for a number of heresies including having the temerity to translate the Bible into English.

During the seventeenth century, Magdalen Hall established a major reputation, with the philosopher Thomas Hobbes (1588-1679) and Edward Hyde, Earl of Clarendon (1588-1679) among its alumni. In 1817 the poet John Keats (1795-1821), who never attended any university, travelled up to Oxford with his friend, Benjamin Bailey, and stayed with him at Magdalen Hall, to get away from the pressures of London, where his first book of poetry had been poorly received. Keats arrived by coach at the Mitre and walked down High Street to Bailey's rooms at Magdalen Hall. He stayed five weeks and fell in love with the city. "This Oxford I have no doubt, is the finest city in the world," he wrote to his sister. "I am among colleges, halls, stalls, plenty of trees, thank God – plenty of water, thank heaven – plenty of books, thank the Muses." While in Oxford, he wrote the third book of his epic poem *Endymion*.

Magdalen College is the scene of one of the great events of the Oxford year, the May Morning celebrations. For hundreds of years, Magdalen's choristers have ascended the great tower at an unearthly hour on May 1, to sing an invocation to summer. Anthony Wood, writing in the seventeenth century, reported that the choristers "do, according to an ancient custom, salute Flora at four in the morning with vocal music of several parts." Undergraduates from other colleges and townspeople too, have always come to crowd Magdalen Bridge and High Street to hear the angelic voices from on high. What was just a local tradition gained national importance in Victorian times when the Pre-Raphaelite painter, William Holman Hunt, displayed his painting *May Morning on Magdalen Tower*, filled with portraits of the college's leading academics.

Nowadays, the early-risers do not have to rise so early, with the choristers starting their invocation at 6am. But many of the student listeners in the street below are not starting a fresh day so much as finishing a very tiring day. May Morning happily occurs at a time when college and university exams are coming to an end, when students are happy to shake off the yoke of learning for another year and when the pursuit of pleasure takes precedence over the pursuit of learning. The pubs open early on May 1 and alcohol-induced reverie plays a large part in the celebrations, including the formerly traditional foolhardy jumps from Magdalen Bridge into the chilly Cherwell below. The police have recently put a total ban on the Cherwell leap, thus ending a local tradition and removing the unedifying spectacle of the cream of Britain's intellectuals proving just how stupid they can be.

Magdalen Bridge itself, with its wide pavements, is the most noble entrance to the city centre. Oxford City Council has, for years, cherished a dream of keeping cars out of High Street and anyone who had to drive along it regularly knew what an obstacle course it could be. Yet Magdalen Bridge is a stretch of road one never associates with cars, although until 1999 the traffic was always heavy. It is a place for bicycles – which could appear four and five deep before and after the day's lectures – and an endless stream of pedestrians. It is not a bridge offering expansive vistas and the Cherwell is not the most exciting of rivers. To the north for most of the year there is no suggestion of the green walks that abound behind Magdalen's buildings, but only, on looking over the balustrade, a collection of punts, for this is the main tourist punting station, though the locals know to set off from the Cherwell Boathouse in North Oxford.

There has been a bridge across the Cherwell here since at least 1004 and there are those who insist – albeit unconvincingly – that this was the ox-ford that gave the city its name. The original was, of course, made of wood, but by the sixteenth century it had been replaced by one of stone, some 500ft long. It was from here that Queen Elizabeth I took her official leave of the city after her visit in 1566 and eighty years later Charles I left his besieged city for the last time, riding disguised over Magdalen Bridge to head for Scotland where he would surrender. The whole thing was rebuilt to its present style in the 1770s, at which time the roads out to Headington and Cowley were gated and a toll-house built to collect money to pay for the bridge's upkeep. In recent years it has undergone a thorough and expensive restoration, when feelings in the city ran high because not a penny for the work came from the coffers of the university.

The grounds of Magdalen College are almost unbearably beautiful, stretching along the Cherwell and managed for wildlife. Addison's Walk was named after the essayist Joseph Addison (1672-1719), whose rooms overlooked these meadows. He was a champion of natural landscape design, arguing that the works of nature are often superior to Man's creations. Addison was at the college between 1689 and 1711 and remembered these riverside groves in his essays for the *Spectator*, the

Magdalen College Tower on May Morning (Oxford Times)

work for which he is best remembered. The great meadow is a nature reserve where an Oxfordshire speciality, the beautiful snakeshead fritillaries, flower in great profusion in April and May. Because of their beauty they almost became extinct through overpicking in the nineteenth century and the plants at Magdalen have been protected since 1908.

The Cherwell and St Catherine's College

Addison's Walk runs northwards from the college buildings until it reaches Mesopotamia, a narrow strip of land lying between two branches of the River Cherwell and named, in a typical Oxford fashion, from the Greek meaning "between rivers" after the ancient land between the Tigris and the Euphrates in what is now Iraq. This stretch of the Cherwell is the most popular for students and visitors to try their hand at punting, in those strange, flat-bottomed boats, propelled by the use of a long pole pushing against the river bottom. What looks an easy occupation is, in fact, much more difficult and, for those who do not want to try themselves, there is usually a lot of fun to be gained from watching the antics of first-time punters trying to make progress up the river.

More experienced punters wanting to travel further upstream have to disembark beyond Mesopotamia at the weir where the river level changes abruptly and the punt has to be dragged or pushed up the Rollers, a series of metal tracks on the bank, before being put back on to the higher stretch of water. Close by the Rollers is Parson's Pleasure, the bathing place that has long been the subject of much mirth and much speculation. It has for centuries been used by male undergraduates and dons for swimming and, more recently, sunbathing, usually in the nude. C.S. Lewis loved the place. Parson's Pleasure, or Patten's Pleasure as it was first known, is screened on all sides except the river frontage. Ladies coming past in punts were either ordered to avert their eyes or else would get out of the boat and walk past the notorious spot. With the rise in public swimming pools – even in Oxford, where they are in perilously short supply – Parson's Pleasure lost much of its custom, if not interest. One former *habitué* told me: "By the end, the only men who went there were those who wanted to expose themselves to passing punts and those who delighted in the company of naked young men."

Not far away was Dames' Delight, a female and family equivalent of Parson's Pleasure, which was opened in 1934 and closed in 1970. Needless to say, the dames never followed the parsons' example by bathing in the nude.

The historian A.J.P. Taylor (1906-90) and his wife Margaret lived at Holywell Ford on the banks of the Cherwell. One night in late 1945 they answered a knock at the door and found Dylan Thomas and his wife, Caitlin, carrying one of their children and a suitcase. The Thomases were in one of their nomadic gypsy periods, never staying anywhere long when it meant paying the rent. Margaret Taylor was a literary groupie who obsessively chased men she thought were geniuses. She was delighted to welcome Dylan Thomas (1914-53) to their college-owned home, though A.J.P. Taylor instantly recognized the poet as a shameless sponger, for Margaret was wealthy and of independent means.

The Thomases moved into a wooden summerhouse in the grounds of Holywell Ford and stayed for fifteen months. In that time Dylan made money broadcasting for the BBC but spent every penny of it on drink, usually before getting back to Oxford from the broadcast. The Thomases lived off Margaret. Each night the three of them would go out drinking in Oxford pubs, leaving the historian at home with all the assorted children and Margaret buying all the drinks. Taylor noted that, one by one, her paintings were disappearing, the Sickert, the Renoir, the Degas, as she found the means to feed her obsession. In the end, to get rid of them, Taylor found a run-down cottage at South Leigh, 25 minutes from Oxford on the train, and Dylan and family moved there – only for Margaret Taylor to visit every day. In fact, she virtually kept Dylan Thomas for the last eight years of his life.

Out on the banks of the Cherwell, like a modern Magdalen, stands St Catherine's College, the newest and most successful of modern undergraduate colleges. Built on six acres of Holywell Great Meadow bought from Merton College, it stands today in a wonderfully secluded, rural, setting, the harsh lines and contours of its severe design now softened a good deal by the growth of trees and shrubs.

Catz, as it is known in Oxford, was a much-needed college. Its history goes back to 1868 when, at the suggestion of a Royal Commission that the university should be opened to "a much larger and poorer class," a gathering of "unattached students" was formed for those who couldn't afford to live in college while studying for their degrees. The "unattached" label was always seen as slightly derogatory and so, in 1884, they became "non-collegiate students," by which time they had formed a students' social club known as St Catharine's Club after one of Oxford's medieval halls (the name was changed to Catherine in 1919; St Catharine's still survives in Cambridge). In the early part of the twentieth century, the number of non-collegiate students continued to grow and the St Catherine's Society took on all the trappings of a college, having its own river barge, sports ground and societies. The revolutionary 1944 Education Act, which ensured that all students accepted by the university would get financial support, meant that the original purpose of having unattached students no longer applied, and so Catz started thinking of becoming a college. The mastermind of the college's entry into the university was the historian Alan Bullock (b.1914), who became the founding Master when the first students arrived at the new buildings in 1962.

Unlike the medieval colleges, Catz was able to be designed as a complete entity, and the man chosen for the job was the Danish architect Arne Jacobsen. He was given the task of producing a modern building with traditional features like quadrangles and staircases, and his completed design was widely acclaimed; the *Guardian* described it as "Oxford's most classical building." But it did not appeal to everyone. The uncompromising lines seemed out of place in its rural setting, and Jan Morris, most perturbed, described its hall – the largest in Oxford – as "like an assembly shed in a munitions plant, or a trolls' gymnasium."

Thanks largely to Alan (now Lord) Bullock, Catz very quickly established itself among the much older colleges and their long traditions. By 1978 it was the university's biggest college, with more students than any other. Today it feels as though it has always been there. Famous early undergraduates include Eric Williams, the first Prime Minister of Trinidad and Tobago, Lord (Stuart) Blanch, former Archbishop of York, J. Paul Getty, the industrialist and philanthropist, and David Hemery, the Olympic gold-medal hurdler.

Rhodes House

Rhodes House in South Parks Road serves a dual purpose, as a permanent memorial to Cecil Rhodes and the headquarters of the Rhodes Trust. It has a distinctive appearance, built like a Cotswold manor house except for an imposing portico, and with a green, copper-covered dome topped by a bronze Zimbabwe bird. What Rhodes House is not is a social centre for Rhodes Scholars, for they are very much part of their colleges like all other Oxford students. The building was finished in 1929 on land bought from Wadham College next door. It is the Rhodes Scholarships which helped open up Oxford to the world in the twentieth century. Rhodes left the bulk of his mining fortune to establish 57 annual scholarships, 20 to come from the British Empire, 32 from the United States and 5 from Germany. He chose these three elements because, at the turn of the century, these were the major powers in the world and he believed "an understanding between the three strongest powers will render war impossible." The German scholarships inevitably disappeared during the Second World War and more have been created for Commonwealth applicants. Among eminent Rhodes Scholars have been (Lord) Howard Florey (1898-1968) from Australia, William Fulbright (1905-95), founder of the reciprocal scholarships, Robert Penn Warren (1905-89) and Dean Rusk (1909-94) from the U.S. and Dom Mintoff (b.1916) from Malta (later to be Prime Minister).

Both Presidents John F. Kennedy and Bill Clinton (b.1946) included a number of Rhodes Scholars in their White House administrations and, of course, Clinton was himself a Rhodes Scholar at Oxford in 1968-70. He was attached to University College on an (uncompleted) B.Phil course in politics. For the first term, he lived in an converted almshouse in Kybald Street behind Univ, but for the second year took lodgings at 46 Leckford Road, North Oxford. In an unguarded moment when President, Clinton joked to a BBC journalist: "If they ever find out what I got up to in Oxford, then I'm in deep trouble."

Luckily for the President, those who knew him well or even intimately during his Oxford days proved more honorable than his cronies in his later political career and, despite a small army of investigative jounalists descending on the city, no-one was found willing to reveal any of the details that would get Clinton in deep trouble. His

Republican opponents in the 1992 presidential campaign thought they were on to something when he admitted that he had smoked cannabis while at Oxford, although he claimed that he had never inhaled it. Even suggestions that he had come to Oxford in order to avoid being drafted for the Vietnam War failed to stop him being elected.

In June 1994, President Clinton, who had said: "My first views about England were forged at Oxford. They were based on respect: they have never changed," returned to Oxford to collect an honorary degree at the Sheldonian Theatre. All the pomp of the university was out in force and the Latin welcome appeared to bemuse him. He admitted to a sense of intimidation as he had walked into the Sheldonian, proving that the university had lost none of its self-certainty in the late twentieth century, for there are very few institutions in the world that can intimidate the President of the United States – even when he is ostensibly one of them.

Between Rhodes House and Mansfield College, the university is building the Rothermere American Institute, a £13 million project to create a centre of research into American history, government, politics, culture and diplomacy. It is named after Viscount Rothermere, owner of the *Daily Mail,* who died in 1998 before being able to see his dream become reality. He was one of the biggest benefactors of the new Institute, along with the Rhodes Trust and the Annenberg Foundation. The first director of the Institute will be Professor Alan Ryan, a former professor of politics at Princeton

Mansfield College is traditionally Oxford's institution for training non-conformist ministers. It came to the city in 1886 when the Congregational churches closed their Spring Hill theological college in Birmingham and took the name Mansfield after the family who had originally founded Spring Hill. There were at the time a considerable number of non-conformists in the recently, and reluctantly, non-denominational university and it was felt that there should be a Free Church faculty in theology to train their ministers.

Mansfield was non-residential until 1946, and students were matriculated through other colleges. The bulk of members, however, were graduates who went on to study theology in order to be ordained. In 1955 Mansfield became a Permanent Private Hall and was thus allowed to matriculate its own students. Since then it has expanded into

Bill Clinton in Oxford, 1994 (Oxford Times)

the pleasant and spacious buildings in Mansfield Road, where there is even a sign inviting members of the public to wander around – you will not see many of those outside university buildings. Undergraduates now take a wide range of degree subjects, and about one-fifth carry on to study theology. The most notable name associated with Mansfield was

Albert Schweitzer (1875-1965), the Nobel Peace Prize winner, who was here briefly as Dale Lecturer in the 1930s.

Tucked in between Wadham and Mansfield and with a domestic frontage on to Holywell, lies Harris Manchester College, traditionally Unitarian but founded to accommodate students "of every religious denomination, from whom no test or confession of faith was required." Known as Manchester College, it was based successively in Manchester, York, Manchester again and London before coming to Oxford in 1889, after the university was opened to non-conformists. It has always offered both theological and general courses. Among its early tutors (though not at Oxford) was Joseph Priestley, the discoverer of oxygen. In 1995 the college governors announced that it would change its name to honor the carpet magnate Capt Charles Harris, whose son had donated £3.6 million to college funds.

Wadham College

Wadham College, founded in 1609, is the youngest of the pre-Victorian colleges. On his deathbed in Somerset, the West Country landowner Nicholas Wadham gave instructions for the foundation of a college he had been planning for years. Those instructions, however, were very vague; happily Wadham's widow, Dorothy, was a formidable lady who, within months, had acquired from Oxford Council, the site of the former Augustinian Friary dissolved in Henry VIII's time and then leased as allotments. Dorothy Wadham was a practical woman who had the sense to insist that the library be built above the kitchen to keep the books dry. Like many other colleges, it had an early bias towards men from its founder's region, in this case the West Country, and became a fashionable stepping stone for sons of the gentry, including Sir Walter Raleigh's son Carew who came up in 1619, just a year after his father's execution.

Seventeenth-century members included Robert Blake (1599-1657), one of Britain's greatest admirals and the young Christopher Wren. Here, too, at the time of the Restoration in 1660 came the young John Wilmot, later Earl of Rochester (1647-80), who died young after a short and almost permanently drunken life. Even so, he managed to establish himself as one of the most gifted poets of his age although, if any of his work is remembered today, it must surely be his pornographic verses. Rochester was very much an Oxfordshire man, being born at Adderbury in the north of the county, schooled at Burford in the west, and dying in Woodstock Old Park, after an amazing deathbed transformation from licentious libertine to pious worthy. It was Rochester who gave Charles II the epithet the Merry Monarch, and who pinned on the king's bedroom door, the now famous lines:

Here lies our great and mighty king,
Whose promise none relies on.
He never said a foolish thing
Nor ever did a wise one.

The Victorian diarist Francis Kilvert (1840-79) got a poor fourth-class degree in the 1860s, but revisited Wadham a decade later and left an account that will strike a chord with anyone who has ever been disappointed by a return to the haunts of their youth:

The fabric of the college was unchanged, the grey chapel walls still rose fair and peaceful from the green turf. But all else was altered, a change had come overt the spirit of the dream. the familiar friendly faces had all vanished, some were dead, and some were out in the world and all had gone away. Strange faces and cold eyes came out of the doorways and passed and repassed the porter's lodge. One or two of the college servants remembered my face, almost all had forgotten my name. I felt like a spirit revisiting the scenes of its earthly existence and finding itself strange, unfamiliar, unwanted.

Other illustrious undergraduates include F.E. Smith (1872-1930) who, as Lord Birkenhead, was Lloyd George's reforming Lord Chancellor, and the great England cricketer, C.B. Fry who, on his first Sunday in college, accepted a dare to climb up the great centrepiece of Main Quad and kiss the statue of Dorothy Wadham. Also here was the conductor Sir Thomas Beecham (1879-1961), the left-wing leader of the Labour Party Michael Foot (b.1913), the Poet Laureate Cecil Day Lewis (1904-72) and Melvyn Bragg (b.1939), the novelist and TV arts guru.

Holywell Street

The Kings Arms pub on corner of Holywell Street opposite the Indian Institute is on the site of the Augustinian friary. It became an inn, named after James I, in 1607 and was in the eighteenth century another of Oxford's major coaching inns. In 1962, the upper floors of the pub were converted into student accommodation for Wadham. Until 1973, a small bar off Holywell Street was reserved for men only and was a haven for misogynist academics slipping out for a lunchtime drink from their research in the Bodleian. It was once said that it had more brains to the square inch than any other bar in the world.

Holywell Street is one of the glories of Oxford. It has been closed to through-traffic since 1975, and this helps give it its own historic flavor, rather like the medieval feel of cobbled Merton Street. Holywell is, however, of a later vintage, for most of the houses are wonderfully preserved seventeenth- and eighteenth-century structures. Only New College's massive Victorian Gothic intrusion spoils the delicate beauty of this street. Gilbert Scott's 1872 monstrosity was described by one authority as "the most terrible of all the outrages on modern Oxford." The conversion of the King's Arms stables at the Broad Street end, to create Blackwell's excellent music shop hiding behind strange concrete shutters is also out of character, but the street is full of individual and collective gems. One is the Holywell Music Room, the oldest surviving concert hall in the world, opened in 1748 and restored to its original interior in 1960. Regular recitals are held here, accommodating audiences of some 250. The acoustics are excellent.

Try walking down here at twilight when the lights are going on in ground-floor rooms and curtains are not yet drawn and you will get glimpses of panelled rooms that seem not to have changed for centuries.

Holywell Cemetery

St Cross Road leads from the gated end of Holywell to the University Science Area and passes the best small cemetery in England, tucked behind St Cross Church, which was the scene of the marriage of Lord Peter Wimsey and Harriet Vane in Dorothy L. Sayers' 1936 novel *Busman's Honeymoon*. The entrance to the little cemetery can be hard to find and the wooden gate difficult to open, but persevere, for Holywell Cemetery is worth finding. At first sight, it seems overgrown and dilapidated, but this is also a nature reserve and therefore the grass around the graves is not regularly shorn as in other municipal cemeteries. Brambles and bushes are allowed some room and in spring and summer a host of wild flowers bloom; small mammals, even foxes, can be sighted here and the trees are alive with birdsong. This overgrown look makes it hard to imagine that there can be 1,266 graves here, including 32 college heads and 156 assorted dons and professors. Holywell was one of three public cemeteries opened in Oxford in the mid-nineteenth century to ease the pressure on the city's churchyards.

Centrally placed is an information board, showing the sites of some of the most famous permanent residents. But it is sometimes more interesting just to wander and be surprised as familiar names come into view. Be careful, though, not to be caught out; the Christopher Wren whose tombstone is near the entrance, died in 1953 and was not an architect. Maurice Bowra's big low slab cannot be missed; he was Warden at Wadham for 32 years and dominated the Oxford intellectual scene in the post-war years. There are two of Tolkien/C.S.Lewis's Inkling friends here: the poet Charles Williams and Hugo Dyson, the Merton English don. Science-fiction fans and Trekkies will recognize the name of James Blish. Born in New Jersey, he was a star of the genre in the 1950s and moved to Oxfordshire in 1963. In his later years, he achieved his greatest popularity with a long line of novels based on the TV cult series *Star Trek*. The Victorian composer Sir John Stainer, whose *Crucifixion* is still regularly performed at Easter, also lies here, not far from Benjamin Blackwell, the founder of Oxford's famous bookshop, and Sir Henry Acland, who built up the reputation of the University Medical School and was the driving force behind the establishment of the University Museum.

The family grave of the Bradleys contains the philosopher F.H. Bradley, whose work inspired T.S. Eliot and, alongside him, his brother A.C. Bradley, Professor of Poetry and a major Shakespearean critic. One can only wonder what their elder brother J.H. Bradley, also buried here, might have achieved had he not been "drowned in the Isis, aged 18 years." Ken Tynan, the most influential British drama critic of the 1950s and 1960s is buried here, although he died in California. He was the most flamboyant student of his generation when he studied at Magdalen after the war, and achieved notoriety in the 1960s by being the first person to say fuck on television and then by producing the musical *Oh, Calcutta!*

An ivy-threatened path has been cut to the grave of Walter Pater. Ironically, the man who inspired a generation of young Oxford men to love "art for art's sake" and who was the stimulus behind the Aesthetic Movement, is marked by a very dull, mass-produced marble cross. Close by, however, is a glorious, low, art-nouveau, terracotta headstone in memory of John Rhys, Principal of Jesus College and Professor of Celtic. Less familiar is the name of Theophilus Carter, an Oxford tradesman who was the original on whom Lewis Carroll based the Mad Hatter. And, though the name of John William Burgon is relatively unknown, most people will recognize a single line from his best-known poem *Petra*: "A rose-red city – half as old as time."

But probably the most important and certainly the most sought-out grave here is that of Kenneth Grahame, the author of the children's classic, *The Wind In the Willows*. His headstone reads: "To the beautiful memory of Kenneth Grahame, husband of Elspeth and father of Alastair, who passed the river on the 6th of July 1932, leaving childhood and literature through him the more blessed for all time." At the bottom is added "And of his son Alastair Grahame, Commoner of Christ Church, 1920." I have seen people take rubbings of this stone as if it were a church brass and there are usually fresh flowers on the grave.

Kenneth Grahame (1859-1932) was born in Edinburgh, but when he was only four his mother died and his father sent the children south to live with their maternal grandmother by the Thames in Berkshire. Kenneth went to St Edward's School in Oxford and was not happy with "the barrack-like school, the arid, cheerless classrooms." St Edward's was then very much a second-string school and so disorganized that the boys were allowed to wander around Oxford rather than do games. Grahame fell in love with the place that he called his golden city of the imagination:

> The two influences which most soaked into me there, and have remained with me ever since, were the good grey gothic on the one hand and, on the other, the cool, secluded reaches of the Thames – the 'stripling Thames', remote and dragonfly-haunted before it attains to the noise, rhythms, and flannels of Folly Bridge.

He wanted to stay on and go to the university, but money could not be found to support him and instead he was found a job as a clerk at the

Bank of England, in London. Here he rose effortlessly to become the youngest-ever Secretary to the Bank. He was trapped into marriage at forty and was unhappy again, except for his one spark of hope, his only child Alastair, a sickly half-blind boy, to whom his besotted father started telling stories about a mole and a water rat and a toad living by the river. But Alastair was a strange, awkward boy. The only child of older parents, he had a dreadful habit of lying down in the middle of the road when he heard cars approaching.

The bedtime idyll of a pastoral England, already disappearing in Edwardian times, turned inevitably into *The Wind in the Willows* and Kenneth Grahame became an internationally celebrated writer, although not all reviewers loved it: "As a contribution to natural history, the work is negligible" said *The Times*.

Meanwhile the boy Alastair was sent to Rugby School, where he lasted only one term and then to Eton, where a nervous breakdown forced his removal. In the end Kenneth Grahame, determined that his son should have what he never had, pushed the boy into Christ Church in 1918. His ailing sight made all his work a struggle and in May 1920, only days before his twentieth birthday, Alastair was found dead on the railway track at Port Meadow. A kind verdict of accidental death was recorded but, in fact, the youth – like the boy before him – had simply lain down across the rails when he heard a train coming.

His father was devastated and lived another twelve years, an ever more unhappy man. He died in 1932 and was buried here with his golden boy in his golden city.

Beyond the cemetery, St Cross Road and Manor Road are always busy with building work as different faculties and departments find new homes on the edge of the Science Area. At the top, opposite what looks like a multi-storey car park but is actually the Zoology and Psychology building, stands Linacre College, occupying the late-Victorian building formerly known as Cherwell Edge. This was the home of J.A. Froude, the Exeter College don who scandalized Oxford's Anglican academic community with his novels of lost faith in the 1840s but was reinstated as professor of modern history in 1892. Ironically, it was then used as a convent by the Society of the Holy Child Jesus, with a chapel by Basil Champneys (architect of the Indian Institute) and, later, as a large residential block for women undergraduates attached to St Anne's College. Linacre College was established from Linacre House, a society of graduates from other universities reading for advanced degrees in Oxford. The college was established in 1962 and moved to Cherwell Edge in 1977. It became a fully independent college of the university in 1986, and about half its student members come from overseas.

At the bottom of Longwall Street, where the city walls bring to mind places like York or Chester, stands Longwall Garage, the building where, in 1912, William Morris built his first car, the prototype for the Bullnose Morris Oxford. The garage has been converted to student accommodation, but the frontage has been retained with a display window explaining the importance of the building in the development of Oxford.

St Edmund Hall

Tucked into the corner of Longwall and the High but best approached from Queen's Lane is St Edmund Hall. Behind the simple doorway on to the lane lies one of the most satisfying sights in Oxford. For one steps off the dull street into the Front Quad of the college (Teddy Hall as it is known in Oxford-speak) and here is the whole collegiate life in miniature, a small, inescapably pretty scene with fine, largely domestic-style buildings pushing in from all four sides without making the whole space seem overcrowded. It is flower-filled and creeper-lined. There is a delightful sundial in the wall of the northern range and Oxford's only surviving college well in the middle of the lawn. (It is no longer used, of course, but its thirteenth-century shaft is intact.)

This small scale and the fact that Teddy Hall is, quaintly, the last survivor of the hundreds of academic halls which crowded Oxford before the colleges took over, leads many to think it must be Oxford's smallest college. But this is not so; since it was granted full college status in 1957, St Edmund Hall has grown and grown, although the student residences and new buildings are tucked away beyond Front Quad and hidden from visitors by the college-owned houses on High Street.

St Edmund Hall is named after a thirteenth-century Archbishop of Canterbury, St Edmund of Abingdon. In the 1190s, before his elevation to head the Church in England, the saint is said to have taught in a building on or near the site of the present hall. If only the link could be confirmed (the academic halls had no written statutes and so dated records were not kept), little Teddy Hall could give a fright to the giants claiming to be Oxford's oldest established educational establishments. The hall survived when all about were closed down or subsumed into the larger colleges (St Edmund itself took over White Hall and St Hilda's Hall), mainly thanks to a co-operative relationship with its larger neighbor, Queen's.

Because it held a minor status for so long, St Edmund Hall does not have the long roll-call of influential and successful graduates that the other colleges can claim. Perhaps the most famous is the eighteenth-century antiquary Thomas Hearne (1678-1735) who, after astonishing work as assistant keeper of the Bodleian Library, turned down the post of librarian to the Royal Society, because he could not bear to leave Oxford. He was a bit of an old reactionary and refused to take the oath of allegiance to the German king George I. This cut short his career, so he retired to St Edmund Hall for the last twenty years of his life, to study and write. He is remembered today for his 145-volume diary (in the Bodleian) which offers an acerbic, not to say jaundiced, view of Oxford life in his time.

With perhaps the exception of Lincoln College, St Edmund Hall has the most interesting of any college library in Oxford. For it is housed in the medieval church of St Peter in the East, and students have to walk through a graveyard to use it. It is in the East to distinguish it from St Peter-le-Bailey in New Inn Hall Street in the west of the city. It is one of Oxford's oldest and most interesting churches and in medieval times was the richest living in the city. Sadly, the only part of the church open to visitors today is the crypt, although this is the oldest part, dating from the early twelfth century (key from college lodge). Among those buried in the churchyard are Thomas Hearne and James Sadler, "the first English aeronaut."

Since the war, graduates of the college have included the comedian/writer Terry Jones (b.1942), one of the *Monty Python* gang, and the doyen of political interviewers, Sir Robin Day (b.1923), who came up to Teddy Hall in 1947 at the advanced age of 24. It was, he says, Oxford's Golden Age. The Second World War had kept three or four generations of undergraduates in uniform and now, with hostilities over, they flooded into Oxford together. "A brilliant array of characters went up during those years 1945-50, but only in later years, as reputations were won, did one begin to realize what an abundance had been gathered together at Oxford." Up with Day were the likes of Ken Tynan, Tony Benn, Jeremy Thorpe, Dick Taverne, William Rees-Mogg, Shirley Williams and Jan Morris (James Morris as she was then).

St Peter in the East, St Edmund Hall (private collection)

CHAPTER SEVEN

Archbishop Cranmer's Oxford

*"Forasmuch as my hand offended...may I come to the fire,
it shall be first burned"*

Thomas Cranmer (1489-1556) was by education a Cambridge man and by employment closely allied to the Royal court in London, but it is in Oxford that his memory is kept alive, for he came here to die an appalling death in what was probably the city's and the university's most shameful moment.

There is, in the centre of Broad Street, where the road narrows towards the western end, a simple cross in the road, marked out in unsophisticated stones. When repairs are carried out in Broad Street, this spot is left alone and it has never been tarmaced over like the rest of the road surface for, whatever one's religious inclination, this is as close to a holy spot as you are going to find in Oxford. It is a place where visitors and locals alike maintain a pensive dignity. A plaque in the wall of Balliol College opposite explains that, on this site, the English State, with the connivance of Oxford University, brutally executed its leading churchmen by burning them alive.

The picture we are usually given of Cranmer is that of an old man (67 was then old) dragged bare-headed and in a thin rough gown through the streets of Oxford from the University Church, weeping, to be put to death in front of courtiers, clerics, academics and townspeople. Yet we should not lose sight of what Cranmer was, nor of why he arrived at this piteous end.

Thomas Cranmer was born the son of a village squire in Nottinghamshire on July 2, 1489. He studied and then taught divinity at Cambridge, and caught the attention of King Henry VIII in 1529, when he told the troubled monarch that he need not wait for the unlikely announcement from the Pope that he would be allowed to divorce his queen of twenty years, Catherine of Aragon, who seemed unable to bear him the son and heir he so desperately wanted. Cranmer told the king that the matter of the marriage's legality (Catherine was his sister-in-law, having been married to his elder brother Arthur, who died before coming to the throne) could be decided by university scholars. Henry delighted in Cranmer's loyalty, made him a royal chaplain and gave him a post in the household of Anne Boleyn, who was destined to become Catherine's replacement as queen. Henry sent Cranmer to Rome to plead his case before the Pope and then made him ambassador to the Holy Roman Emperor, Charles V, only to call him back in 1533 to take over the vacant post of Archbishop of Canterbury, the most powerful priest in the land. Within two months of his enthronement as archbishop, Cranmer, who had himself married while abroad and was now keeping his wife a secret, declared that Henry and Catherine had never been legally married. This meant that their only child, Mary Tudor, was now declared illegitimate, something she was unlikely to forget when her turn came to occupy the throne.

Whatever Henry wanted, Cranmer supplied, and in return he became the most powerful archbishop England had ever known. He was the undoubted leader of the Reformation in England, forswearing allegiance to the Pope, wiping his name from every prayer book and pronouncing the King to be the true head of the English church. He swept away Catholic practices and doctrines, promoting the distribution of Miles Coverdale's English Bible and revising the liturgy of the Church of England. His *Book of Common Prayer*, published during the reign of

Henry's successor Edward VI, was a masterpiece of both language and content. Cranmer's Prayer Book, together with the King James Authorised Version of the Bible in 1611, were the texts on which 300 years of British Empire were built. In addition to all this, Cranmer devised the articles of religion which became the doctrine of the Protestant Church of England and which, known as the Thirty-Nine Articles, were used for centuries to determine who was fit to study at the University of Oxford.

When the boy king Edward VI was dying in 1553, Cranmer knew that Henry's will made the Catholic "bastard" Mary next in line for the throne. He must have known what was coming for, upon Edward's death, he threw himself behind the hopeless campaign for Edward's cousin, the young, but Protestant, Lady Jane Grey. Jane was queen for only nine days before Mary stormed in and took the crown that was rightly hers. Within a few months, ex-Queen Jane was separated from her head at the Tower of London and Mary turned her anger on Cranmer. He was taken to the Tower and tried on two counts of treason, for which it was decided he should be hanged, drawn and quartered. But Mary, swiftly re-establishing the Roman Catholic faith, wanted a worse fate for him. In March 1554 the queen rounded up the leaders of the English Reformation, Archbishop Cranmer, Nicholas Ridley (c1500-1555), Bishop of London and Hugh Latimer (c1485-1555), Bishop of Worcester and packed them off to Oxford to be proved heretics.

One by one, the bishops argued their beliefs, in Latin, in the Divinity School and all three were told in St Mary's that they had been proved wrong. They were given the chance to recant; they all refused, and Parliament swiftly passed an act reviving the traditional punishment of burning at the stake for heretics. With the evidence of the disputations, the three could now be tried and sentenced as heretics. As an archbishop who had originally been approved by the Pope, Cranmer had to be tried before papal commissioners. He was, of course, found guilty but his sentence had to be endorsed in Rome. Without telephone, fax or e-mail, this was going to take some time, so Cranmer was locked in the Bocardo prison which stood alongside the church of St Michael at the North Gate. From there he was forced to watch as Latimer and Ridley, after a swifter trial, were taken to the stake in Canditch, as Broad

Street was then known, standing outside the city wall and overlooked by the early buildings of Balliol College. Ridley's brother had brought some gunpowder for the men to hang around their necks so that, when the flames reached it, their deaths would be reasonably quick. Before Latimer's exploded he managed to call out his famous cry which has echoed across the centuries as a slogan for the revived Church of England: "Be of good comfort, Master Ridley, and play the man! We shall this day light such a candle, by God's grace, in England, as I trust never shall be put out." Ridley found it difficult to play the man, for the wood piled about him was freshly cut, full of sap and refused to blaze. As his lower limbs smouldered away, the Bishop was heard to cry in his agony: "Lord have mercy upon me: I cannot burn...I cannot burn."

After witnessing this appalling spectacle, Cranmer was locked again in the Bocardo to await confirmation of his own death sentence. Eventually word came from Rome and on March 21, 1556, having been told that, even though he had six times recanted his Protestant faith, he was still to be burned, Cranmer was led in a pitiful procession into St Mary's where, raised on a platform for all to see, he was berated for his old heresies and given the chance to declare that he now believed in the Catholic doctrines approved by the Queen. Despite everything, the old man had one trick left and pulled out a speech he had hidden in his tunic. Amid uproar in the church, he repudiated all his recantations and declared that the Protestant beliefs had been right all along: "Forasmuch as my hand offended in writing contrary to my heart," he said, "therefore my hand shall first be punished for, may I come to the fire, it shall be first burned."

And so, on a cold, wet and windy March Saturday morning, the Archbishop of Canterbury, once one of the most powerful men in the land and the author of one of the most influential works of English literature, was taken out of St Mary's, past the Divinity School, beyond the city wall, to the stake in Broad Street where, true to his word, he held his hand into the flames first before he was consumed. Such were the wind and the flames upon that day that the gate of Balliol College was scorched. When the college was rebuilt in the nineteenth century, the gate was preserved and its blackened timber can be seen to this day, hanging on the wall of the archway that leads from one Balliol quad to the other.

Martyrs' Memorial and the Randolph Hotel (Oxford Times)

In the 1830s, the traditional Anglican church was feeling rather edgy, particularly in Oxford, where Pusey, Newman and Keble were advancing their Anglo-Catholic high church ideas and enjoying some success. So when, in 1838, a rally was arranged to discuss a way of commemorating the Protestant Martyrs, Cranmer, Latimer and Ridley, most people recognized it as a political act by the old church faction.

The original aim was to build a completely new church, dedicated to the Martyrs, but this fell through and it was agreed to launch a nationwide appeal for money to be spent on two projects: a new north aisle for the church of St Mary Magdalen, the closest church to the site of the Broad Street martyrdom, and a cross to stand outside the church. The situation of this cross would also be a poke at the Anglo-Catholics, for it would stand within sight of St John's College, the spiritual home of the Catholic martyrs St Edmund Campion and Archbishop William Laud. The cross, which was designed by the young Sir George Gilbert Scott, was based on the Eleanor Crosses, the series of stone monuments erected by the distraught King Edward I after his wife, Eleanor of Castile, died in 1290.

The foundation stone was laid in 1841 and a year later the much-needed north aisle at St Mary Magdalen was completed. The door from the Bocardo prison where the martyrs had been confined before their executions, was placed in the aisle. Ironically St Mary Mag's is now the most Catholic of Oxford's Anglican churches; if it is incense and vestments you want – symbolizing all that the martyrs stood against – this is the church for you. The door has since been removed to St Michael at the North Gate.

In 1842 the statues of the three martyrs were put in place halfway up the memorial. It was originally surrounded by iron railings, which were removed during the Second World War. In its 150-year history, the memorial has become one of Oxford's major landmarks. It is now most often used as a meeting place for parties of tourists waiting to be shown around the historic city centre.

St Giles'

Broad Street may be broad, but it is nothing compared to St Giles', the widest street in Oxford, a dual carriageway before such things were ever invented and occupied today – behind the twin lines of lime trees – by some of the most splendid buildings in the city. It takes its name from St Giles' Church at the northern end, where the route divides into the twin northern roads to Banbury and Woodstock.

St Giles' Fair has for centuries been one of the highlights of the Oxford calendar. It is held, confusingly, on the first Monday and Tuesday after the first Sunday after St Giles' Day, September 1. This means that it is largely a Town rather than Gown affair, for the students do not come up to Oxford University until the end of September. Even so, almost everyone else in Oxford turns up to join in the fun and revel in the sense of a great occasion. The fair fills the whole of St Giles' and the road is closed to traffic causing awkward diversions but, for once in Oxford, no-one complains.

St Giles' Fair (Oxford Times)

In the south-west corner of St Giles' stands Blackfriars, the Priory of the Holy Spirit. This was the creation of Father Bede Jarrett, leader of the English Dominicans who, in 1916, set about realizing his dream of bringing the Dominican brothers back to Oxford for the first time since they had been suppressed in 1538.

Oxford's Dominicans can trace their history back to St Dominic himself. In 1221, the Order's General Chapter, presided over by the saint, decided to send friars to England, with the principal aim of establishing a base at Oxford. They set up a small chapel in the area of the present Town Hall and included among their earliest members Roger Bacon. They went on to produce some of England's greatest theological writers, and, by 1305, there were 96 Dominican brothers in the city. Under the Dissolution, Thomas Cromwell sent in his men to rid the city of the Dominicans and the monks stayed out until Father Bede raised the money to build the Priory and its beautiful chapel, which is entered through the attractive but easily overlooked wrought-iron gateway underneath the statue of the Madonna (which, upon its erection in 1924, was criticized for having too small a head and too few clothes). There are today some thirty Dominican friars in residence in Oxford, many teaching in the university.

Pusey House, next door to Blackfriars, was founded in 1884 in memory of the recently deceased leader of the Oxford Movement, Edward Pusey. The present Gothic building was built in 1912-14 and was first known as the Dr Pusey Memorial Library, with the aim of housing Pusey's large collection of theological books and manuscripts associated with the Anglo-Catholic revival. In 1981, much of the St Giles' frontage of Pusey House was given over to St Cross College, founded as a graduate college in 1965. A good deal of the money for the new buildings behind St Giles has come from a connection with the Blackwell family of Oxford booksellers and publishers

Regent's Park College, on the corner of Pusey Street, did in fact move to Oxford in 1927 from Regent's Park in London as the country's main source for training Baptist ministers. At first, the Baptists shared the buildings of Mansfield College with other non-conformists, but the first part of these buildings on St Giles' was completed just before the Second World War in 1939. Regent's Park became one of the university's permanent private halls in 1957 and has continued to train Baptist ministers and theology teachers, although now it is fully ecumenical and international in its intake. Many of the world's leading Baptists received their training here.

Tucked in among St Giles' religious houses is a place of genuine pilgrimage, for the Eagle and Child, known locally as the Bird and Babe, is Oxford's most famous literary pub. Still remarkably unspoiled, it was the favorite destination for the diarist Anthony Wood in the seventeenth century, but is more famous as the place where the so-called Inklings met to discuss their own and other people's literature. The best-known of this group, which used to meet every week between the 1930s and 1960s were, of course, J.R.R. Tolkien and C.S. Lewis. Probably the third most important member of the group was Charles Wiliams (1886-1945), the poet and religious writer who was a star of the literary scene in the 1930s and 1940s. Other members included Hugo Dyson (1896-1975) and Neville Coghill (1899-1980). They used to meet in a small room to the rear of the pub. Lewis, describing their conversations, wrote:

Those are the golden sessions; when four or five of us after a hard day's walking, have come to our inn; when our slippers are on, our feet spread out towards the blaze and our drinks at our elbows; when the whole world and something beyond the world, opens itself to our minds as we talk; and no one has any claim on or any responsibility for another.

Roman Catholics were technically allowed into the university in 1871, when the need for all students to subscribe to Cranmer's Thirty-Nine Articles was removed. Still, the Church forbade them to attend until 1895, after which the Benedictine monks of Ampleforth monastery in North Yorkshire set up a teaching house, St Benet's Hall, at the top end of St Giles', thus ending the Benedictines' 300-year exile from Oxford. At the time of the Dissolution, the order had run Gloucester, Durham and Canterbury colleges. Some thirty or forty students reside here, half monks and half laymen. Notable among St Benet's graduates is Cardinal Basil Hume (1923-99), who went on to run Ampleforth before being elevated to Archbishop of Westminster and leader of the Roman Catholics in Britain.

On the other side of St Giles' is the Lamb and Flag pub, owned by St John's College, which became an ale house in 1695. Alongside is a cobbled path through to the Science Area. Part of the building is student accommodation.

St John's College

St John's College is not noisy like Christ Church or Balliol, but for 400 years it has sat snugly and smugly beside St Giles', safe in the knowledge that it is one of the richest of all Oxford colleges. Most of the middle-class suburbs of North Oxford are built on land owned by St John's – there was once a time when you could go from St John's in Oxford to St John's in Cambridge without leaving St John's land. In recent years, its academic successes have outshone even those of its neighbor on the corner of Broad Street.

St John's was created in the zeal of Catholic England under the reign of Mary Tudor, coming into being only two months after Trinity and only weeks before Ridley and Latimer were burned nearby for their refusal to accept Catholicism. It stands on the site of the monastic college of St Bernard, founded in 1437 for Cistercian monks at Oxford and closed and destroyed during the Dissolution. St John's was founded in 1555 by Sir Thomas White, who had led the support in the City of London for the Catholic Mary Tudor's accession over the claims of Lady Jane Grey on the death of Edward VI. White apparently had a dream in which he was advised to build a college at "a place where three trunks of an elm grew out of one root." This he found at St Bernard's (the tree survived for 100 years more before being cut down by the bursar).

The first of St John's own martyrs was St Edmund Campion (1540-81), a brilliant scholar whose theological studies gradually brought him around to support the Catholic cause, which was to become a treasonable act in Elizabeth's England. In 1581 he wrote *Decem Rationes*, a short book giving ten reasons for the Catholic faith which, he said, he would "set before the famous men of our universities." Copies were placed in the University Church and caused great controversy. A fortnight later Campion was betrayed and arrested and taken to the Tower of London where, after torture, he was dragged through the mud and rain on a hurdle to be hanged, drawn and quartered at Tyburn on December 1, 1581.

Twelve years later, William Laud (1573-1645) was created a Fellow of St John's. Laud spoke out against the Calvinist leanings of the university, and his own leaning towards Catholicism was soon obvious. He became President of the college in 1611 and, under Charles I, moved through the bishoprics to become Archbishop of Canterbury. By this time he was already Chancellor of the university and determined to restore discipline in the colleges. So he drew up what is known as the Laudian Code of rules by which the university was supposed to govern itself. It covered academic dress, the length of hair, the content of sermons and it banned scholars from playing dice, cards and football. Undergraduates were forbidden to go hunting with hounds or ferrets and "they shall not idle and wander about the city or its suburbs, nor in the streets or public market or Carfax." The code, though much diluted, remained the basis of the university's laws until 1854.

Laud's dominance over Oxford was mirrored on a national level. He was a great influence on King Charles I and favored by Charles's Catholic wife, Henrietta Maria. King and queen face each other today across Laud's Canterbury Quad at St John's. When discord arose between king and parliament, Laud was widely blamed for his influence on Charles. Before war broke out, he was impeached by the Puritan-dominated Commons on a charge of high treason. He was kept in the Tower of London, largely forgotten, for nearly five years until, in the midst of Civil War, he was beheaded at Tower Hill, the last Archbishop of Canterbury to meet a violent death and the last to dominate the government of England. The historian Hugh Trevor-Roper observed: "Few men in our history have been so loudly and apparently so universally vituperated." But the vituperation did not extend to his old college and, after the Restoration, Laud's body and head were brought back from their immediate resting place to lie in the college chapel next to its founder. Relics are still preserved including the cap he wore to his execution, with a ragged hem where souvenir hunters have snipped away at it over the centuries.

Among other famous St John's men were Jethro Tull (1674-1741), the great agricultural reformer, the poets A.E. Housman (1859-1936) and Robert Graves (1895-1985), Lester Pearson (1897-1972), Prime Minister of Canada and Dean Rusk (1909-94), Jack Kennedy's Secretary of State.

In the 1940s three young men together at St John's were the writers Philip Larkin (1922-85), Kingsley Amis (1922-95) and John Wain (1925-94), who in the 1950s led the literary group known as the Movement. Larkin was the finest poet of his generation, although his reputation has slumped since his death in 1985, with the publication of his diaries and letters, which showed him to be most politically incorrect, a misogynist and a holder of right-wing opinions. The poems are still as wonderful as ever, but the man's views do not fit our times. Amis, one of the most successful English novelists of the late twentieth century, was similarly irascible, but John Wain, though holding forthright views, was a decidedly more pleasant character. He stayed in Oxford after graduating, was Professor of Poetry in the 1970s and, in the last years of his life, wrote a trilogy of novels, *Where the Rivers Meet, Comedies* and *Hungry Generations,* set in his beloved Oxford and chronicling the twentieth-century development of city and university in the shadow of the Cowley car factories:

> *In the late 1920s one man, W.R. Morris, later Lord Nuffield,...by the introduction of large-scale industry, laid waste the rural setting and disrupted the intellectual forum. Once hailed as/ ushering in a glorious future, Nuffield's empire has now collapsed, leaving a grimy detritus which forms the setting of our lives.*

Kingsley Amis first arrived at St John's in 1941, with the threat of conscription into the Armed Forces hanging over him. The right-wing views for which he was later to become notorious had clearly not yet developed, because he joined the student branch of the Communist Party (Iris Murdoch was a branch officer at the time), though he claimed this was just to rebel against his father. He soon found that he could not keep up with the earnestness required of the comrades and disliked the meetings and the necessary reading and quickly dropped out.

Music, particularly jazz, became important to him, and he made up for a shortage of cash by borrowing a jacket which had a "poacher's pocket" on the inside just big enough to take a ten-inch gramophone record. "I feel rather bad," he admitted later, "about saying that some of the Oxford shops lost several deleted jazz discs by this route." In 1942, the call-up papers came and Amis joined the Army. When hostilities were over in 1945, he returned to complete his studies. His novelist son, Martin Amis (b.1949), got a First at Exeter.

"All the time I was at Oxford I felt like an outsider," said Tony Blair (b.1953) who came up to read law at St John's in 1972 from Fettes, the Edinburgh public school known as "Eton in a kilt." Young Blair fitted well into the pattern of future Labour Prime Ministers that had already been established at Oxford. Like Clement Attlee of Univ, he never spoke in a debate at the Oxford Union, the traditional politicians' training ground and, like Harold Wilson of Jesus, he was contemptuous of the university Labour club: "I couldn't be bothered with that...student politics at Oxford never seemed very practical."

What he did do at Oxford, apart from earning a respectable Second, involved sex, rock 'n' roll and religion. Young Blair was a handsome sort, had a string of girlfriends throughout his Oxford days and was once summoned by the Dean of St John's to explain why he had had a woman in his rooms outside the permitted hours (things are more relaxed now). A lipstick found in his room was produced as evidence but with a straight face, Blair instantly replied "Oh, that's mine." Rock 'n' roll was a much more serious business, and Tony became lead singer with a band of students calling themselves the Ugly Rumours. Basing himself on his hero Mick Jagger, the long-haired Blair would stomp around the stage in wide-open shirt, purple loon pants and Cuban-heeled boots, performing old Eagles and Doobie Brothers numbers. The band used to rehearse at Corpus Christi, and on one occasion the thudding beat infuriated some members of the college so much that the power supply was cut off.

It was in Oxford that Blair became a practising Christian. He had been brought up in an ostensibly Anglican atmosphere at Fettes, although the religion was so institutionalized that few boys ever passed through the place inspired by faith. But at St John's he met an older Australian student, Peter Thompson, who was an ordained priest and who introduced him to a philosophy of practical Christianity which immediately struck a chord. Blair was confirmed into the Church of England at St John's, and it is a faith he has never lost and which folds easily into his own brand of socialism.

The future Prime Minister had an unexpected brush with the law during one of his few political activities. Taking part in a demonstration against the fascist National Front outside Oxford Town Hall, he was singled out as a revolutionary type, grabbed by the police and flung through the air. According to friends, he had never experienced anything like it in his life and his respect for the law was not exactly enhanced by the event.

Jane Austen's (1775-1817) father had been a Fellow of St John's, her grandfather a Fellow of All Souls and her great uncle, Theophilus Leigh, Master of Balliol but her own experience of the university city was less happy. In 1783, at the age of seven, Jane and her older sister Cassandra were sent to Mrs Cawley's school in Oxford. Mrs C was widow of a principal of Brasenose. It was not a happy experience for Jane; she later complained of having been

> *dragged through numerous dismal chapels, dusty libraries and greasy halls.*
> *It gave me the vapours for two days afterwards. I never was but once in*
> *Oxford in my life and I am sure I never wish to go there again.*

Balliol

If ever proof were needed that one should never judge a book by its cover, Balliol College can supply that proof. For the most respected, most successful and most prestigious of all the Oxford (or Cambridge) colleges is housed in the most uninspiring and drab set of buildings imaginable. During Balliol's great renaissance at the end of the nineteenth century, it was decided to pull down all the medieval buildings and replace them with first-rate modern architecture by first-rate modern architects. Waterhouse and Butterfield, both of whom had proved themselves elsewhere in Oxford, were among those called in, but the finished result is dull and plodding.

Balliol's nominal founder, John de Balliol, a County Durham landowner, rented a house just outside the city wall in 1263 and paid for the continual education of a handful of poor scholars. He did so, so the story goes, as penance for insulting the Prince Bishop of Durham during a territorial dispute. Balliol himself died in 1269 and it was his widow, Dervorguilla, who officially founded the college in 1282.

Although the reformer John Wyclif was Master of the college for a year, its early history was unremarkable. It had no ties with any particular school or region, so there were no restrictions on a trio of formidable and far-seeing Masters who sought to give it a reputation for excellence in the nineteenth century. The first of these was John Parsons (Master 1798-1819), who took the radical step of opening up Fellowships to outsiders rather than just scholars of the college, insisting that academic excellence should be the first reason for a man to get on at Balliol. Competition among tutors led to an increase in quality, which led to competition for places as undergraduates, with an increase in quality there too.

Parsons was followed by Richard Jenkyns (1819-54) who started awarding scholarships in open examination and made other reforms which resulted in Balliol already being pre-eminent in academic excellence by the time the great Benjamin Jowett took over in 1870. Jowett (1817-93), who was already Regius Professor of Greek, had been at the college for 35 years and made time to see every undergraduate there once a week. He also did all he could to make sure that clever young men from poor homes were able to attend the university.

Jowett's avowed intention was to produce from his Balliol men the new ruling class in England, a class that had nothing to do with wealth and privilege, but was based on education, intelligence and ability. He admitted he wanted to "inoculate England with Balliol men." He wanted to produce a cultivated and responsible elite, remarking: "One must remember how important it is to influence towards good those who are going to have an influence over hundreds of thousands of other lives."

But Jowett's dedication did not fully cover up his own social ineptitude and being in his company was inevitably hard work. One pupil, Augustus Hare, said he was "at once the terror and the admiration of those he wished to be kind to." Silence seemed to be his harshest weapon; another student, J.A. Spender, wrote of tutorials where undergraduates read him their essays:

> Sometimes he rewarded you with a brief 'good essay' or 'fair essay', but there were other occasions when he looked at you for an interminable minute and then slowly shifted his gaze to your neighbor and said 'Next essay please.'

Jowett never married, but for many years, carried on an intimate and passionate correspondence with Florence Nightingale, also unmarried. When asked what she was like, his reply was: "Violent, very violent." He was, according to Jan Morris, a powerful influence on the frigid sexual standards of the Victorians: "In his translation of Plato, he even managed to imply that, when Plato wrote of uninhibited homosexual bliss, he really meant a respectable Christian union between man and wife." Yet Jowett was an inspired teacher, whose pupils showered him with unending love and admiration after they had left the college.

Balliol's policy of making room for the best certainly paid off for the poet Gerard Manley Hopkins (1844-89), who came up from Highgate School in 1863 with a reputation as a fine classical scholar. He went on to get a double First and was described by one examiner as "by far the best man in the first class." Hopkins absolutely adored Oxford and has left us some of the most-often quoted poems about the city and its environs, though these mainly came from his second stay. In an early poem *To Oxford*, he said his love for the place "grew more sweet-familiar" every term and affirmed "this is my park, my pleasance."

Though Balliol was the centre of religious liberalism in Oxford and Jowett himself went on to typify the Broad Church, it was to the High Church that Hopkins was drawn. John Henry Newman had only recently defected to the Roman Catholics and the Tractarian banner was kept flying in the city by Edward Pusey, but young Gerard perceived the Tractarian cause to be flagging and, at the end of his second year at Balliol, he wrote to Newman asking to be received into the Roman Catholic Church. During his final year he decided to take holy orders and settled on joining the Society of Jesus (Jesuits). Fearing that his poetry might distract him, he burned all his early poems after leaving Balliol and resolved to write no more unless at the bidding of the Jesuits. For seven years he wrote nothing as he underwent the long, arduous training to be a priest. But he returned to his beloved city in 1878 when he took up the post of assistant priest at the new church of St Aloysius in Woodstock Road.

The novelist Graham Greene (1904-91) was at Balliol in the 1920s. He was a deep and emotional young man, who claimed that for at least one term he was never sober, waking with a hangover and immediately starting to drink again. It was while he was at Oxford that Greene experimented with Russian Roulette. On at least five occasions, he walked out of the city towards Elsfield, carrying a revolver which once belonged to a cousin killed in the First World War. "It was a sodden, unfrequented country lane," he remembered. "The revolver would be whipped behind my back, the chamber twisted, the muzzle quickly and surreptitiously inserted in my ear, beneath the black winter trees, the trigger pulled." Greene's own explanation was his sense of youthful boredom "as deep as love and more enduring"; he either died or experienced "an extraordinary sense of jubilation."

During his last term at Oxford, Greene wrote an article for the *Oxford Outlook*, a magazine founded by Beverley Nichols and which Greene for a time edited, including contributions from such as Edmund Blunden, Louis MacNeice, W.H. Auden, C. Day Lewis and Emlyn Williams. This particular piece contained a throwaway reference to the Virgin Mary. This brought him a letter of sharp rebuke from Vivien Dayrell-Browning, a recent convert to Catholicism, who was working in Blackwell's bookshop. Greene wrote back apologizing and invited her to tea in his Balliol rooms where, within minutes, he fell in love with her. Two years later, Greene had converted to Catholicism for her and they were married. It was, though, a doomed relationship and they lived apart for most of their lives (as Catholics, they could not divorce). Vivien returned to Oxford where she has lived ever since, becoming best-known in the city for her remarkable collection of doll's houses which she occasionally put on public view – although no children were ever allowed near them.

Cyril Connolly (1903-74), who was up at Balliol at the same time, was 22nd in descent from John de Balliol. He hated the place and, for the rest of his life, loathed the sound of bells which reminded him of dank, dismal, tedious, Oxford afternoons. Aldous Huxley (1894-1963) was of an earlier generation. Though his sight was severely impaired, he had read everything. He always stood at lectures and took no notes. One colleague remembered him "standing by a pillar, near the doorway, against the window, just listening." But he got a First. Other distinguished Balliol men include the writers Robert Southey, Matthew Arnold, Arthur Hugh Clough, Algernon Charles Swinburne, Hilaire Belloc and Anthony Powell and the politicians H.H. Asquith, Edward Heath, Roy Jenkins and Denis Healey.

Harold Macmillan (1894-1986), Prime Minister 1957-63, came up to Balliol from Eton, but had first been in Oxford as a young boarding pupil at Summer Fields prep school at the turn of the century. He got a First in Classical mods, but the First World War intervened before he could take his finals and he never came back to study at what he said had become "a city of ghosts." He did, however, return in triumph in 1960, when he was elected Chancellor of the University, a role he filled for more than a quarter of a century. His friends generally agreed that he was more proud of this post than of being Prime Minister, and he refused steadfastly to retire saying, at the age of 88, that he would only give way to an older and wiser man.

St Mary Magdalen, with its enclosed churchyard, stands on an island at the junction of some of Oxford's busiest streets and backing the Martyrs' Memorial. Unusually, it is wider than it is long. The present building reaches back to the twelfth century, and is today the most atmospheric of all Oxford's churches. A stronghold against the Evangelical movement gaining strength at St Aldate's and, even more forcefully, through Sunday meetings in a nearby cinema, its dark interior glimmers with the flames of candles and retains the smell of incense. There is a portrait of the "martyr-king" Charles I and, once a year, his memory is honored here. On the far wall, a recently erected tablet confirms the burial here of the antiquary and gossip-merchant John Aubrey (1626-97).

Aubrey was a Wiltshire man but spent as much time as he could in Oxford. He was at Trinity during the Civil War and delighted in the company of the celebrities of Charles I's court. All his life he wrote, collecting especially details of the lives of those about him, including the most eminent men and women of the time. He was one of the original members of Christopher Wren's Royal Society and was at Whitehall when Cromwell ran the country and after the restoration of Charles II. His writings, together with those of the diarists Samuel Pepys and John Evelyn, give us our best picture of life in the higher circles of English society in the second half of the seventeenth century.

In Oxford he was for many years a friend of Anthony Wood, although they later quarrelled. It was not until many years after his death that his famous *Brief Lives* was published. W.H. Auden said of this collection of short, gossipy biographies of the great men of his age: "Aubrey can tell us more about a person in a sentence than most writers in a page." In 1697 Aubrey set out from London to visit his friend Lady Long in Wiltshire and stopped off in Oxford to spend the night with his chemist friend Kit White in Holywell. During the night he died, probably of an apoplectic fit, and he was buried in St Mary Mag's, in the space reserved for the men of Trinity College. All his manuscripts are now in the Bodleian Library.

Between 1918-21, the poet W.B. Yeats (1865-1939) moved to Oxford, where he had rooms in Broad Street, where Boswell's store stands today. He had no connections with the university but was invited in 1921 to speak at the Oxford Union on the motion "This House would welcome complete self-government in Ireland." Yeats reportedly walked up and down the aisles, waving his arms and shaking his fists. Sinn Fein, he said, had brought real justice into his part of Ireland for the first time for centuries.

Trinity College

Trinity College offers a face to the passer-by quite unlike that of any of Oxford's other old colleges. Its ceremonial entrance on Broad Street is through the wrought-iron gates next to Balliol, but students and visitors alike step into one of the university's most attractive colleges through an undistinguished hole in the wall by a row of humble seventeenth-century cottages (rebuilt in 1969). Beyond this entrance, Trinity appears to open out, thanks to the wide expanse of lawn in Front Quad. In fact, the college holds itself in and well away from the noses pressed up against the Broad Street gates, for the bulk lies in the distance beyond the chapel (the first in Oxford not built in the Gothic style).

Trinity was founded in 1555 – six months before Latimer and Ridley were burned at the stake a hundred yards away, but it was not the first college on this site. Durham College had been established here in the late thirteenth century as a place of training for the Benedictine monks of Durham Cathedral, but the brothers were kicked out during the Dissolution. The treasurer, and second-in-command, of the department dealing with the disposal of the monastic lands was one Thomas Pope, an Oxfordshire man. Being on the inside, he was able to buy up a lot of the former monastic sites at low cost, including that of Durham College, and he determined to found a new college here, much to the pleasure of the new Catholic queen, Mary I.

Trinity was never a hotbed of anything – certainly not academic excellence – but it was a resting place for both the Catholic and Jacobite causes. Indeed, it is said that the magnificent wrought-iron gates on Parks Road, will never be opened until a Stuart monarch returns to the British throne. The joke here is that they are not gates but a railing and can never be opened. Trinity is, appropriately, on a three-armed site, stretching its lawns down to Broad Street and to Parks Road and sneaking a finger through to St Giles' between St John's College and Balliol.

In the late seventeenth century, Trinity became a fashionable college for aristocratic and landed families and that attachment has never worn off. American visitors to Oxford often find special interest in Trinity, because among former students were both William Pitt the Elder (1708-78), during whose term as Prime Minister the expansion of the American colonies took place, and Lord North (1732-92), Prime Minister at the time of the War of Independence and the man credited with losing the colonies for Britain. George Calvert (1580-1632), the first Lord Baltimore and founder of Maryland, completed his education here too.

Buried in the college chapel is Thomas Warton (1728-90), the most complete Oxford man among the Poets Laureate, half of whom have connections with the university or city. Warton, who was a great friend of Dr Johnson, spent all his adult life at Trinity. He was the first great historian of English literature, and was elected Professor of Poetry before he was thirty. Interestingly, among his publications was an early guidebook to Oxford which included information about coffee-houses and inns, billiard tables and skittle-alleys.

Two of the college's most famous sons were actually forced to leave without degrees because of their behaviour. The writer, Walter Savage Landor (1775-1864) was described by his contemporary at Oxford, the poet Robert Southey, as "a mad Jacobin" and caused a great stir in college by refusing to have his hair powdered before dinner like the other undergraduates. He was expelled in 1794 when a slanging match between two student drinking parties on opposite sides of the quad ended with Landor taking a shotgun and blasting it at the shuttered window of the other group. "It was thought a good trick," wrote Landor...but unfortunately not by the college authorities.

The explorer, writer and translator of erotica, Sir Richard Burton (1821-90) was his own master throughout his life and did not fit well into college life at all, feeling he had "fallen among grocers." He wrote:

I began a 'reading man', worked regularly 12 hours a day, failed in everything, threw up the classics and returned to the old habits of fencing, boxing and single-stick...and sketching facetiously, though not wisely, the reverend features and figures of certain half-reformed monks calling themselves Fellows.

On one occasion he was let down on a rope into the garden of the Master of next-door Balliol, uprooted all the prize specimens and replaced them with common marigolds. He was eventually sent down for a term for attending a race meeting which had been expressly banned, but decided, while he was away, not to bother returning. Other famous names associated with Trinity include John Aubrey, John Henry Newman, the playwright Terence Rattigan (1911-77) and the poets James Elroy Flecker (1884-1915) and Laurence Binyon (1869-1943).

In 1998, Trinity bought for its library the signed manuscript of the poem *For The Fallen* by Binyon. The poem, first published in *The Times* in 1916, in the middle of the First World War, has largely been forgotten, except for one verse, which is, in Britain at least, one of the most famous poetic pieces of all time:

They shall grow not old as we that are left grow old
Age shall not weary them, nor the years condemn.
At the going down of the sun and in the morning
We will remember them.

These are the lines which appear on countless war memorials across the land and are repeated at Remembrance Day services in towns, villages and cities each November.

Blackwell's

The White Horse between Trinity and Blackwell's in Broad Street, is one of Oxford's most famous pubs and one of the oldest, tracing its records back to 1591. It is said that Winston Churchill used to drink here on visits to Oxford. It is owned by Exeter College. Blackwell's is, of course, one of the most famous bookshops in the world. It has been at no. 53 Broad Street since 1883, when the founder of the family firm, Benjamin Blackwell moved the business from nearby Holywell Street. In those days, Blackwell's was chiefly a second-hand bookshop, but in the hands of Sir Basil Blackwell (1889-1984), Benjamin's son, it grew towards the stature it holds today. Sir Basil, who was born in this building, also developed the publishing side of the business and his magazine *Oxford Outlook* was staffed by people like Dorothy L. Sayers, who went on to make names for themselves as writers. Today, Blackwell's is a successful chain of more than fifty bookshops, catering largely to university communities.

The small Broad Street frontage hides a shop in which it is still a delight to browse, with a stock designed to appeal to the members of the university and the intelligent general readers in whom Oxford abounds. The recent advent of Dillon's and then Waterstone's into Broad Street has perhaps affected Blackwell's takings, but will never be able to replace it in the hearts of generations of students, for whom it represents an essential part of Oxford life. Any number of new graduates have left the city to start on their path to fame and greatness with a Blackwell's bill still to be paid off.

The staggering ugliness of the New Bodleian Library, on the corner of Broad Street and Parks Road, has been at odds with the beauty of the buildings that surround it since it was completed in 1940. It was described by Jan Morris as "resembling a well-equipped municipal swimming baths." More than half the cost of building this much-overdue annexe to the Bodleian came from the Rockefeller Foundation. It can accommodate five million volumes. A tunnel beneath Broad Street connects the extension with the old Bodleian and contains a conveyor belt to take books from one side to the other. Part of the D-Day landings operation was planned by the Admiralty intelligence service in the vaults here.

At the opening ceremony, King George VI was presented with an ornate key to the main door but, as he turned it in the lock, it snapped in half. That door has never been used since.

CHAPTER EIGHT

Dr Johnson's Oxford

"We were a nest of singing-birds.
Here we walked, there we played at cricket."

Samuel Johnson (1709-1784) is one of the towering figures of English
literature, although it is hard to find anyone outside English Literature
departments who can name anything he wrote – other than the
Dictionary – let alone anyone who has read anything by him – including
the *Dictionary.* Johnson's fame rests rather on his personality, as it was
intimately recorded by his first biographer James Boswell, and his well-
known aphorisms – after the Bible and Shakespeare, Dr Johnson is the
mainstay of most dictionaries of quotations.

Sam Johnson was never an academic; his doctorate was an honorary
one bestowed on the successful author by Dublin University. Although
he was certainly learned and enjoyed the company of Oxford and
Cambridge men, he never took his degree at Oxford. But it was poverty
rather than any intellectual disability that led to Johnson leaving the
university in his third year.

Johnson was born on Wednesday September 18, 1709 in Lichfield,
a market and cathedral town in Staffordshire. His parents were

respectable but never wealthy. His father Michael, who was 52 when his son was born, was a bookseller and went on to be elected sheriff of the town. His mother Sarah, was 40 and put the boy out to a wet nurse, in whose home he tragically picked up scrofula, a tuberculosis of the lymph glands, which damaged his eyesight and caused him trouble with both reading and writing all his life. In those times, scrofula was known as "the king's evil" and it was believed that the touch of the monarch could cure the disease. So, as a very young boy, Sam made the long coach trip to London where he was indeed touched by Queen Anne, but, of course, to no avail.

The boy proved receptive to the house full of books in which he found himself growing up and, at the age of 18, even though his parents could ill-afford it and relied upon the promises of funds from a friend, he was taken up to Oxford to be entered at Pembroke College. He later told Boswell that his secret had been reading "a great many books which were not commonly known at the universities, where they seldom read any books but what are put into their hands by their tutors." Indeed, he boasted: "When I came to Oxford, Dr Adams, now master of Pembroke College, told me I was the best qualified for the university that he had ever known come there."

Consequently, it was no surprise that he should have been disappointed in the teaching staff. Of his tutor, Dr Jorden, he said: "He was a very worthy man, but a heavy man and I did not profit much by his instructions." When John Taylor, one of his schoolfellows expressed the wish to join Johnson at Pembroke, Sam told him he could not, in conscience, "suffer him to enter where I knew he could not have an able tutor." Inquiring around the university, he found that the Rev Edmund Bateman of Christ Church was the highest regarded don in the place and persuaded Taylor to be entered there. In fact, Bateman's lectures were so good that Johnson used to meet Taylor after each one and make notes from Taylor's memory of what the great man had said.

While he was at Oxford, Johnson suffered the first serious attacks of "morbid melancholy," the depression that was to affect him throughout his life and account for some of the crabbier of his later outpourings. There was much to be depressed about, for his father became insolvent and the promised funds to keep him at Oxford never materialized. He had to stop going to see Taylor in Christ Church, when he found the other undergraduates there, largely the sons of gentlemen, casting scornful looks on his shabby clothing. His shoes became so worn that his toes were showing through. One friend, in kindness, left a pair of new shoes outside his door in Pembroke, but Sam, from his great well of stubborn pride, threw them away.

Eventually the bills became too high and the pressure too great and Johnson, one of the finest minds ever to pass through Oxford University, was forced to leave without a degree, and try to live off his wits in London.

Of course, he succeeded and made a name for himself as a writer but he retained fond memories of Oxford, going back again and again throughout his life. When he returned in 1754, the great *Dictionary* project was almost complete and he needed to do some late research in the college libraries. It was here that he met the young don Thomas Warton, soon to be installed as Professor of Poetry and in later life to become the first of Oxford's seven Poets Laureate. Warton arranged for the man who was never able to take his Bachelor's degree, to be made an honorary Master of Arts in recognition of his services to literature.

It was sweet justice and Johnson held back publication of the *Dictionary* so that he could add the letters MA to his name on the title page. His last visit to Oxford was in 1784, only a few months before his death. He was on his way back to London from Lichfield and stayed with the Rev William Adams, formerly Master of his old college. Johnson's rooms at Pembroke were on the second floor, over the gateway, according to Boswell. "The enthusiasts of learning will ever contemplate it with veneration," he said. The college still treasures Johnson's teapot and a portrait of him by Sir Joshua Reynolds.

Pembroke College

Pembroke College has always been Christ Church's poor neighbor across the road and an unequal rivalry has always existed between the two colleges. Back in 1964, when Pembroke's night porter went out for his first look around one morning, he found a ten-foot brick wall blocking the archway between Old and Chapel Quads, completely sealing them. At some time during the night, someone had moved 400 house bricks

150 yards from a building site and stacked them so professionally that it was impossible to knock them down. Propped against the wall was a placard saying "To dear old Pemmy, luv and kisses, Ch Ch." Christ Church undergrads have always referred to Pembroke as the Coal Scuttle.

Pembroke was founded in 1624, and credit for it is given both to James I and to William Herbert, Earl of Pembroke and Chancellor of the university at the time. More accurately, it was built on £5,000 left in trust by a rich brewer, Thomas Tesdale, in 1610. The new college was established on the site of Broadgates Hall in Beef Hall Lane, one of eight surviving academic halls at the beginning of the Stuart era and owned by Christ Church.

The Earl of Pembroke gave his name to the college on the promise of a generous benefaction – which never materialized, for the Chancellor died suddenly in 1630. There were no other endowments to keep the college running, so Charles I passed on a couple in the 1630s. Even so, Pembroke bumbled along in poverty for centuries. In the early 1830s the religious reformer John Keble called it the cellar and dust hole of the university,.

Apart from Sam Johnson, early members included Sir Thomas Browne (1605-82), author of *Religio Medici*, and John Pym (1584-1643), who played a crucial role on the Parliamentarian side in the Civil War. Eighteenth-century undergraduates included the Methodist George Whitefield (1714-70), the most eminent of the Wesleys' disciples who, according to his memoirs, sometimes prayed for two hours at a time flat on his face over in Christ Church Meadows. Here, too, was William Blackstone (1723-80) the British legal scholar whose work *Commentaries on the Laws of England* was for more than a century the basis of all legal education in both England and the United States.

In the 1780s James Lewis Smithson (1765-1829) had the reputation of "excelling all others in the university in chemical science." Smithson, who claimed to be the bastard son of the Duke of Northumberland and descended from the Percys, became a Fellow of the Royal Society at the age of 22 and had a craving for posthumous fame:

The best blood of England flows in my veins: on my father's side I am a Northumberland; on my mother's I am related to kings. But it avails me not. My name shall live in the memory of man when the titles of the Northumberlands and Percys are extinct and forgotten.

He was true to his word, for Smithson left his money and property to the U.S. government on his death, to found an institution "for the increase and diffusion of knowledge among men." That foundation became the Smithsonian Institute, the largest museum complex in the world and a centre for research for 150 years.

For much of its history Pembroke contented itself with two quads on a rectangular site between St Aldate's and St Ebbe's, but in 1960 a third quad was formed when, much to the alarm of some of their neighbors, the college got permission to close Beef Lane, the ancient narrow thoroughfare leading from the back of St Aldate's church to St Ebbe's and, using houses they owned in Pembroke Street, enclosed the area to form North Quad. Those Oxford citizens in the know – and some who never forgave Pembroke – still use the quad as a cut-through to St Aldate's. The Pembroke Street houses were, in effect, turned around to face into the new quad and consequently nearly all the doors on the south side of the street are false and cannot be opened.

The twentieth century has produced two senior politicians out of Pembroke, Senator William Fulbright (1905-95), whose Fulbright Act of 1946 led to the exchange of students, scholars and teachers between the U.S. and other countries, and the former Conservative deputy Prime Minister, Michael Heseltine. Heseltine (b.1933), who had had a bad time at Shrewsbury School, found Oxford more to his liking: "Oxford was the most wonderful, liberating experience. It's where I found myself really. Suddenly I was among my peers, operating in an environment I loved." He was reading PPE (Politics, Philosophy and Economics), although he had not come to Oxford for a good degree, but to shine in student politics and become president of the Oxford Union. Perhaps too much time was spent on union debates, because at the end of his second term, young Heseltine failed all three papers in his prelims. He passed the retakes on two of them but had to take the last a third time. Nowadays, Oxford colleges would have sent him down for failing a paper twice.

He was elected president of the Union as he had predicted and then set about raising funds to convert the Union's cellars into a nightclub.

The guests of honor at the new club's first night were Sir Bernard Docker and his wife, who were notorious in the 1950s for flaunting their wealth and driving a gold-plated limousine. Lady Docker took to the dance floor with the tall handsome president and, utterly charmed, came off and told her husband to write out a cheque to pay for the entire cost of the refurbishment. Julian Critchley (b.1930), the maverick Tory MP who was up at Pembroke with him, tells of the night he saw Michael Heseltine map out his future on the back of an envelope. From President of the Oxford Union, the ambitions became: millionaire, MP, minister, cabinet, Downing Street. His single-minded approach to self-fulfilment meant that he achieved every one of those aims, except the last. And in that he came within a whisker of success, being runner-up to John Major in the 1990 election for a Prime Minister to replace the dumped Margaret Thatcher. As a result, Heseltine was appointed deputy prime minister and, on one or two short occasions, in Major's absence, found himself to all practical purposes running the country.

At the St Ebbe's end of Pembroke Street is another of Oxford's hidden gems, the Museum of Modern Art, a vibrant enterprise with an international reputation. Housed in a former brewery storehouse, MoMA has for thirty years presented exhibitions by the former avant-garde like Richard Hamilton, Roy Lichtenstein and Yoko Ono, interspersed with a judicious selection of the best contemporary artists in all mediums from around the world.

St Aldate's

Pembroke tucks itself around St Aldate's Church, which stands on an ancient Christian site, for the church is one of only two in the country named after Eldad, a fifth-century martyr. It was the property of Pembroke until 1859, when it was sold to an evangelical trust and it has been Oxford's leading Evangelical church throughout the twentieth century. Even today, it offers a shock for anyone who believes church-going is a dying art, for each Sunday a huge congregation, of students and townspeople alike, packs the church until there is standing room only.

The Bulldog at 108 St Aldate's was an inn by 1397, making it one of Oxford's oldest surviving pubs, though its present brick and tile frontage gives no indication of this. One unusual feature is the toilets

Pembroke College and St Aldate's (private collection)

which are at least 30ft below street level. It takes its name from the nickname of the university police, identifiable by their bowler hats. In the days of strict curfews at colleges, they were busy every night apprehending students at large in the city after the tolling of Great Tom.

South of Pembroke is Brewer Street, where a plaque marks no.1 as the birthplace of the crime writer, Dorothy L. Sayers (1893-1957), Her father was headmaster of Christ Church Choir School, which is now further along the street. He was also chaplain to Christ Church and thus Dorothy was baptized in the cathedral. When she was four, the family moved to Huntingdonshire, but in 1912 she returned to attend Somerville College, where she got a First-class degree, or rather passed the examinations that would have given her a First if Oxford had given degrees to women. She later set her best and most famous novel, *Gaudy Night*, in Shrewsbury College, recognizably Somerville. In 1917 she was offered a job at Blackwell's, on the publishing side rather than the bookshop. She had to learn the whole business in the event of Basil Blackwell being called up for the war. She left Oxford in 1920, when Blackwell decided he no longer needed her.

After the 1850 Royal Commission, which suggested the University should provide cheaper accommodation for less-well-off students than the established colleges could supply, any MA over 28 could open a Private Hall for students. These would take the name of the Licensed Master and last only until he died or gave up his licence. Thirteen of these private halls were set up, but when it became clear that two of the halls, one run by the Jesuits and the other by the Benedictines, remained in existence with simply a change of name with every change of Master, it was agreed, in 1918, to allow Permanent Private Halls. At that time it was just these two denominational halls that survived.

The Jesuits named their new hall after St Edmund Campion, the Fellow of St John's who was martyred as a Catholic agitator during Elizabeth I's reign, and it was, in fact, first established as an annexe of St John's. Campion Hall, in Brewer Street, with its stunning, spare Romanesque design, was built by possibly the greatest English architect of the first half of the twentieth century, Sir Edwin Lutyens and represents his only work in Oxford. Lutyens actually volunteered for the job after seeing and criticizing the plans drawn up by another architect. For this he was sued for unprofessional conduct, but won the case.

Campion Hall achieved its greatest acclaim during the Mastership (1933-45) of Father Martin D'Arcy. D'Arcy was probably the most respected and charismatic of all twentieth-century English Jesuits, and he built up within Campion Hall a rich collection of sacred art, including works by Eric Gill and Frank Brangwyn and much early Spanish art. These became known colloquially as Campion's *objets D'Arcy*. The hall usually accommodates some thirty priests and student priests.

Ronald Knox (1888-1957), whose translation of the Bible is still widely used by Roman Catholics, lived in Oxford between1926 and 1939 in the Old Palace which stands on the corner of Rose Place and St Aldate's. Although it has been splendidly renovated, there was nothing palatial about the building in Knox's time. He slept in a second-floor room which had been condemned as unsuitable accommodation for undergraduates. It was named for Bishop King, who built it and was the first and last Catholic bishop of Oxford. Knox kept to his room for most of the day except between 3-4pm when he walked around Christ Church meadow with his prayer-book. He stayed in to make himself totally accessible for any undergraduate who might call:

Whole days may pass without so much as a man wanting you to sign a passport form for him, but I have not discovered any other way of making sure of the rare undergraduate, perhaps one in a month, who screws up his courage to come and talk about something important and might if I were out, not have the courage to come again.

In 1936 he was appointed Domestic Prelate to the Pope, a purely honorific position which entitled him to be known as Monsignor Knox.

While he was at Eton, preparing to go up to Balliol, the future Prime Minister, Harold Macmillan was taught by Knox. "He was the only man I have ever known, who was a saint," he said of his teacher.

Lewis Carroll included several real Oxford places in his Alice books. In *Through the Looking-Glass*, he depicted Alice Liddell's favorite sweet shop as the Old Sheep Shop, attended by the sheep "knitting with a multitude of needles." It survives in St Aldate's as Alice's Shop, still recognizable from Tenniel's drawing, and now sells Alice memorabilia.

Boars Hill

Follow St Aldate's across the Thames into Abingdon Road and follow that thoroughfare out of the city and you will come to Boars Hill. If East Oxford feels superior to Jericho and Headington feels superior to East Oxford, and North Oxford feels superior to all other suburbs, then Boars Hill lords it over everyone. It was from this wooded escarpment south of the city that Matthew Arnold gazed upon the "sweet city with her dreaming spires" and the supposed site of his vision is preserved now in the meadow known as Matthew Arnold's Field. About it and dotted across the slope stand some 350 roomy houses built by the nouveaux-riches, gentleman dons, poets and professors, all – in a postman's nightmare – known only by their house names and never, heaven forbid, by a street number.

The archaeologist, Sir Arthur Evans (1851-1941), the discoverer of the palace of King Minos at Knossos in Crete, was one of the earliest colonists in the 1890s. His fantastic construction "Youlbury," with its 28 bedrooms and Minoan marble hall, has since been demolished, but it acted as a magnet for other dream homes. These included those of two Poets Laureate, Robert Bridges (1844-1930) and John Masefield (1878-1967). Masefield let a cottage on his land to another poet, Robert

Graves(1895-1985). The great, Australian-born, classical scholar, Gilbert Murray (1866-1957) was a neighbor. Among the present "hill-folk" is Brian Aldiss (b.1925), probably the most acclaimed of all British science-fiction writers.

St Ebbe's

Much of the old parish of St Ebbe's now lies under the Westgate shopping centre, the multi-storey car park and a development of modern town houses. Records go back to 1005 when St Ebbe's church was dedicated to the daughter of a seventh-century king of Northumbria. It has always been a poor area of the city. Plague hit in 1643 and, in October 1644, a major fire destroyed much of it. In 1818 the council built its gasworks in the area, and for 125 years it was polluted with the acrid smell of gas, making the whole parish unpleasant to live in. The area was largely bulldozed in the 1950s, and very little remains of the old community. The city council pulled down what it thought were slums and built instead cheap, almost windowless, boxes with very little hope in them.

Anthony Wood claimed that Charles II's most famous mistress, Nell Gwynn (1650-87) was born near here in St Thomas's parish, where her grandfather was a canon of Christ Church, and the poet Rochester in his *Panegyrick on Nelly* said that her father had died in Oxford. In 1665, when the great plague hit London, the theatres closed and Nell, an actress as yet undiscovered by the King, came with her mother to the city. Shortly after this, the king followed with his court. By 1681 Nell was the King's first favorite and it was she who kept his bed warm when he summoned Lords and Commons to meet him in the Bodleian, only to dissolve Parliament and never call another in his reign. At one stage, Nell was mistaken in her coach by the Oxford mob for the French, Catholic Duchess of Portsmouth and called out "Pray, good people, be civil, I am the Protestant whore!"

The Westgate Centre is Oxford's premier shopping mall. It stands sandwiched between a frequently changing department store and the Oxfordshire central library, and runs back to a multi-storey car park. The centre was built about 1970 on the site of the old West Gate to the city, close by Oxford Castle. The site was excavated by Oxford

Archaeological Unit before building began, and traces were found of both St Budoc's Church, lost since the thirteenth century, and the Greyfriars Church, set up by the first Franciscan missionaries to the city shortly afterwards.

Roger Bacon lived in the Franciscan house on the site after his return from a period in Paris (1250-57) when his research alarmed the religious community and he was sent away. He travelled widely, writing his great works in Paris, but returned to Oxford, where he died and was buried in the Franciscan burial ground. There is a commemorative plaque to him, but few will ever see it, cemented into the wall between the service bay to the shopping centre and the multi-storey car park. It might be geographically the closest spot to Bacon's headquarters, but suggests a strange set of priorities when it comes to celebrating the city's connection with one of the greatest of all medieval thinkers and scientists.

Opposite the front of the Westgate Centre is Bonn Square, named after one of Oxford's twin cities, which has unfortunately become notorious as a no-go area for visitors because of the drunken and aggressive down-and-outs who monopolize the public benches there. The memorial garden to the north was formed in 1897 in what was the churchyard of St Peter le Bailey. The Tirah Memorial at its centre commemorates a little-known campaign on the north-west frontier of India in which several local officers and men were killed.

Oxford Castle

The shopping centre stands on land that was once enclosed by the great bailey of Oxford Castle, fragments of which remain and which would, in almost any other town or city, be turned into a feature. Oxford, however, hides its castle away behind the county council offices and what was, until recently, Oxford Prison. There has been a long debate in the city, since the decommissioning of the prison, over what to do with the site, with some wanting to emphasize its historic importance and others seeing it purely as a commercially lucrative piece of real estate close to the city centre.

Oxford Castle was built within five years of the Norman Conquest by Robert d'Oilly (d.1091), who had fought with William the

Conqueror at the Battle of Hastings in 1066. Its position on the bank of the Thames next to a fortified town, made it an ideal place for the occupying Normans to control the upper Thames valley, and the town walls were altered to accommodate it. The bailey, with its wooden palisades, was surrounded by a moat, the earth from which was packed to form the 65ft motte or mound which still dominates the area opposite Nuffield College. Within the castle precincts, d'Oilly founded the church of St George's in the Castle, which became what was quite probably Oxford's first college. Among the priests who studied here was the early historian Geoffrey of Monmouth (d.1154). The west tower of the church, known as St George's Tower, survives today; its walls are nine feet thick at the base and it is the second oldest building in Oxford.

Henry I, the Conqueror's son, built Beaumont Palace just outside the city walls and certainly spent some time at the castle. On his death he nominated his daughter Matilda to become queen, but the Barons, unwilling to be ruled by a woman, offered the throne of England to her cousin Stephen. Matilda took up arms to fight for her right to the throne and for ten years England was embroiled in civil war. In 1142, Matilda was encamped at Oxford Castle and was besieged there for three months by King Stephen. All history textbooks used to tell of her dramatic escape just before Christmas when the Thames was frozen and Oxford was covered in snow. Matilda dressed herself all in white, was lowered from the castle and, using the camouflage, escaped across the Thames to Abingdon, from where she could ride at speed to the safer castle at Wallingford.

A second siege took place here in 1215, when the Barons trapped King John in Oxford Castle shortly before forcing him to sign Magna Carta at Runnymede further down the Thames. But by 1388, this royal stronghold was in ruins and it was eventually destroyed by Parliamentary troops after the Civil War. It continued to be used as a courthouse and jail until 1577 when, during what is known as the Black Assize, a terrible outbreak of "jail fever" killed 300 prisoners and presiding officials. The courts were moved to St Aldate's, where they remain today, although prisoners continued to be kept at the castle. Probably the most famous inmate was the bloodthirsty French revolutionary, Jean-Paul Marat (1743-93) who, in his youth, was jailed for stealing coins from the Ashmolean Museum. Public executions were carried out until 1863 and prisoners were kept here until a few years ago, since when the empty building, with its gloomy Victorian interior, has been in great demand as a setting for TV and film productions

Opposite the Castle Mound is Nuffield College, which was built on the site of a wharf at the end of the Oxford Canal. The site was bought in 1937 by Lord Nuffield, who offered to build an undergraduate college specializing in engineering and accountancy. The university persuaded him, however, to make it a postgraduate centre for social sciences. Nuffield handed over the site plus £900,000, but he and the University were very wary of each other. As a working-class boy, he was always slightly suspect to the university and he, in turn, had an inbuilt suspicion of the academic authorities. From the start, his college was only a department of the university and did not become an independent college until 1958. At his death, he must have been satisfied with how things had turned out, for he left the college all his remaining wealth.

St Peter's College
St Peter's College, on the original site of the medieval New Inn Hall, offers the least-imposing facade of any city-centre Oxford college. Its dull, gray walls hide what has long been considered the poorest of the colleges, and it stands in a dingy backwater of Oxford. Like St Anne's and St Catherine's, St Peter's first came into existence as a service to students admitted to the university who could not afford to live in college. Unlike those others, however, St Peter's had its foundation in a specifically religious setting and has never managed to shake off the idea that poverty might be good for the soul. Ironically, part of it was built on the site of what was the Royal Mint while Charles I was in residence in Oxford.

The college itself is a hotch-potch of existing buildings that were gradually taken over as the twentieth century progressed. They include the church of St Peter-le-Bailey, which has become the rather over-sized college chapel. Also included are the offices of the Oxford Canal Company, the Central School for Girls and Hannington Hall, which was owned by a branch of the Church Missionary Society. St Peter's owes its existence and early history to the Chavasse family (indeed, had it been founded 600 years earlier, it would no doubt be known as Chavasse College). Francis Chavasse had been Rector of St Peter-le-Bailey and later principal of Wycliffe Hall theological college in Banbury Road, before being made Bishop of Liverpool. He and his friends in the evangelical wing of the Church of England were, in the 1920s, becoming rather alarmed at the dominance of the Anglo-Catholics and, fired with a missionary zeal, Chavasse founded St Peter's Hall in 1928. His son, Christopher Chavasse was installed as the first Master and later went on to become Bishop of Rochester. Christopher's brother, Noel, was indisputably Oxford's greatest twentieth-century military hero, T.E. Lawrence notwithstanding.

Noel Chavasse (1884-1917) was the perfect British Empire hero: strong and dutiful but fair and compassionate. He and his twin brother, Christopher, entered Trinity College, Oxford together in 1904, represented the university at athletics, rugby and lacrosse and, in 1908, were both chosen to run the 400 yards in the Olympic Games. Noel trained as a doctor and was tending the wounded at the front within a couple of months of the start of the First World War. In 1915 he was awarded the Military Cross after the Battle of Hooge, and the following year came the announcement that he had been awarded the Victoria Cross, the highest award for bravery any British soldier can win. It was awarded "for most conspicuous bravery and devotion to duty, tending the wounded in the open under very heavy fire." During this, he was himself hit by a shell splinter while carrying a wounded man to safety. The following year he was offered a transfer to a base hospital, which he refused, writing: "I don't think I could leave the young lads here to fight it out while I luxuriated in a coast town."

In August 1917, he became the only man in the First World War to be awarded two VCs. He was severely wounded in the head while carrying a wounded man to safety. "He refused to leave his post and for two days not only continued to tend those brought in but repeatedly and under heavy fire went out to the firing line with stretcher parties to search for wounded," read the citation. "He was practically without food during this period, worn with fatigue and faint from his wounds." After three days a shell exploded in his dugout and fatally wounded him. In the last hours of his life, he managed to get a message to his fiancée explaining why he had carried on for two days after his skull was fractured: "Duty called and duty must be obeyed." Noel Chavasse's decorations and medals are on permanent loan to the Imperial War Museum in London. St Peter's College possesses a full-length posthumous portrait presented to his father and the original simple wooden cross from his grave is preserved in the college chapel.

The robust Protestant ethic of the early days had to be diluted when St Peter's was admitted to the university in 1961, at which time, like St Catherine's and St Anne's, the early need for helping poverty-stricken students had been superseded by the 1944 Education Act which granted funds for any student accepted into the university. Among the alumni of its short collegiate life are Edward Akufo Addo, president of Ghana and Carl Albert, speaker of the U.S. House of Representatives, 1971-7.

Frewin Hall, off New Inn Hall Street, is an extension of Brasenose College and was built on a site occupied by St Mary's Augustinian College in the fifteenth and sixteenth centuries. It was here that the great humanist theologian Erasmus (1466-1536) stayed during his visits as a teacher to Oxford. In its second existence, Frewin Hall played host to the Prince of Wales, later King Edward VII, when he was a student at Christ Church in the 1850s.

One of the least appealing sights of modern Oxford is the little knots of alcoholics sitting on the few benches of the city streets, drinking their cans of strong lager or swigging from bottles of cheap wine. These have recently been joined by the pathetic spectacle of New-Age beggars, sitting on the pavements, often with a dog on a piece of string or sometimes a filthy child to add to the pathos. There is an almost constant chorus calling for these people to be moved off the streets – they are clearly attracted to a tourist city with plenty of consciences to prick – but those who manage or police the streets insist that these people, far from being offensive to visitors, are in fact victims of our modern society with a rightful place on the city streets.

Should you want to help Oxford's down-and-outs – there are many who genuinely need help; the mentally ill suffering "care in the community" and those heavily dependent on drugs or alcohol – there is more chance of your money really achieving something if, rather than handing it directly to the individual, you drop it into one of the Oxpat collection boxes which are appearing in more and more of the city's stores. This money goes to the Oxford Poverty Action Trust, an umbrella organization which then distributes it among the various groups working to help those in need in the city. Launching the idea in 1999, Oxpat's treasurer said: "Our dream is to collect a pound a year from every tourist, which should give us enough to solve all Oxford's problems."

Carfax

There has always been such an underclass on the city streets, and it was at Carfax that they were to be found in past centuries for, on the paved area by Carfax Tower, where once stood St Martin's Church, was the city's Penniless Bench in the sixteenth century, a lean-to against the east wall of St Martin's, used as a shelter by beggars. In 1667, the lean-to was replaced by a stone arcade but, by the middle of the eighteenth century, it had become "a great nuisance, a harbour for idle and disorderly people" and the council ordered it to be removed.

St Martin's, where William Shakespeare stood as godfather to the future Poet Laureate, William Davenant, was demolished in 1820, except for the thirteenth-century tower, now known as Carfax Tower, which offers splendid views down the High. A replacement church stood only until 1896, when it was removed for the Carfax Improvement Scheme. The seventeenth-century clock was moved to the outside of the tower at this time and still offers amusement to the crowds of visitors who tend to congregate here. Each quarter hour the quarter-boys, two men holding clubs and dressed in quaint Roman costumes, strike the bell.

On the opposite corner of Queen Street from Carfax Tower a stone in the wall of the Abbey National offices identifies it as the site of the medieval Swyndelstock Tavern, the setting for the start of one of the most momentous occasions in Oxford's history. For here on Tuesday February 10 – St Scholastica's Day – 1355, a dispute over the quality of the ale led to the biggest and most far-reaching town and gown riot in the city's history. Some reverend scholars, unimpressed by their beer started to argue with the vintner John de Croydon, eventually throwing the bottle and cups at his head. He complained to his friends and family, who had the bell of St Martin's rung to summon the townsfolk, who in turn went on to attack any scholars they could find. The Chancellor of the university failed to quell the riot and had the bell of St Mary's, the University Church, rung to call out the scholars in retaliation.

They fought till dusk that day though no-one was killed or maimed, but the following morning the townspeople hunted out scholars around St Giles' and one was killed with others mortally wounded. Word spread from Oxford and some 2,000 country people poured through the West Gate to join in and beat the students back to their lodgings. The uneven battle continued for another 24 hours before all the scholars fled the city. In all, 63 students had been murdered by the townspeople in a riot which had been the result of an accumulation of more than a century's discord between the two very separate sections of the city. Vengeance was swift and, from the town's point of view, terrible. The Bishop of Lincoln put the town under an interdict, and the Mayor and Bailiffs were sent to the Tower of London. Bishop and King granted new powers to the university Vice-Chancellor and his officers, powers which gave them almost total independence within the city for more than 500 years.

Each St Scholastica's Day, the Mayor and 63 citizens, one for each scholar killed, processed in penitence to St Mary's, where they had to bow before the Vice-Chancellor and pay a fine of one penny each before listening to a mass for the souls of the dead. The penance was modified at the Reformation and abandoned during the Civil War, although the attendance at church was not stopped until 1825. The Swyndelstock Tavern changed its name to the Mermaid, but in 1706 it was demolished – on the orders of the Vice-Chancellor.

Carfax takes its name, somewhat tortuously, from the Latin *quadri furcus* – four forks, and is the meeting place of the city's principal medieval streets leading from the north, south, east and west gates. In medieval times, this crossroads would have been surrounded by market stalls. In 1610, an enormous elaborate conduit was erected to receive water piped into the city from springs on Hinksey Hill to the south, carried through lead pipes and so into the Carfax Conduit. The upper part of this construction supplied water to the colleges and the lower part was for the use of the city. On special occasions, like the Restoration of the Monarchy in 1660, the water would be replaced with wine. At the end of the eighteenth century, with road traffic increasing, the conduit was in the way and no longer needed, so it was removed in order for the road to be widened and now stands in Nuneham Park, south-east of the city.

Cornmarket

Cornmarket Street, running from Carfax to the old North Gate and St Michael's Church, was exactly what its name suggests, and in 1536 a roof, held up by pillars, was erected down the middle of the street to protect the corn from rain. This was pulled down during the Royalist occupation of the city in the Civil War, so that the lead covering could be turned into bullets.

When Queen Elizabeth I made the first of her two state visits to Oxford in 1566, she was greeted at the North Gate and then rode the length of Cornmarket, which was lined by cheering students, to Carfax, where she received an oration in Greek. Later, she attended a performance of the play *Palaemon and Arcyte* at Christ Church, during which the stage collapsed and killed three people. The show, however, went on and "the Queen laughed heartily thereat," according to Anthony Wood..

Three of Oxford's oldest and most important inns stood in Cornmarket. The Crown Inn at 59a is one of the oldest remaining inn sites in Oxford. It was a private house from 1032 and known as Drapery Hall until 1364, a minor academic hall and tavern. It was a favorite haunt of Anthony Wood. In the eighteenth century, it became a major coaching inn. It still has an Elizabethan feel, but much of the present inn was originally stables and outbuildings. The main Crown Inn was under what is now McDonalds.

Not to be confused with the Crown Inn, although it often is, the Crown Tavern stood on the other side of the road and it was here perhaps that we have some evidence of Shakespeare in Love. William Shakespeare (1564-1616) was a friend of John Davenant, owner of the tavern, and would stop here with the family during his annual journeys from the theatres of London to his home in Stratford-upon-Avon. Davenant's wife, according to John Aubrey, was "a very beautiful woman, and of a very good witt." It was here that William Davenant

(1608-68) was born and Shakespeare acted as his godfather at his baptism in St Martin's Church nearby. Davenant, who went on to fame as a poet and playwright, liked to suggest that his talent was inherited and that he was in fact the illegitimate son of Shakespeare.

When Cornmarket was widened in 1744, the tavern lost its frontage. Those rooms belonging to it which survive are now shops and offices. In 1927 a tailor, E.W. Attwood discovered sixteenth-century wall paintings behind oak panelling. This room became known as the Painted Room, and the panelling was put back on rollers so that it can be moved to reveal the murals, which are viewable on request at no.3 Cornmarket.

The third great inn is the Golden Cross, the stables and courtyard of which were converted in the 1980s into a series of upmarket shops leading from Cornmarket into the Covered Market. The buildings here were used as an inn from about 1193, though they have been much rebuilt and added to over the centuries. In the sixteenth century the Golden Cross became Oxford's premier inn and it was here in 1555 that the bishops Latimer and Ridley were cross-examined for five days before being sentenced to death. In the sixteenth and seventeenth centuries the Golden Cross at Oxford was one of the most fashionable inns in England.

The name Golden Cross dates from 1564, but probably refers to an incident in the thirteenth century. On Ascension Day 1268, the Chancellor, along with Fellows and Students, processed to visit the holy relics of St Frideswide, carrying a large wooden crucifix. Outside the synagogue in Fish Street, near Carfax, a young Jew snatched the cross, threw it to the ground and stamped on it. Prince Edward, who was staying in Oxford at the time, reported the matter to his father Henry III, who ordered a hunt for the young hothead and imprisoned every Jew in Oxford.

As penance, and to gain their release, King Henry ordered the Jews at their own expense to make a silver crucifix for the university to carry on future processions and to erect a magnificent cross on the spot near the synagogue, where the offence happened. This cross was to be of marble and covered in gold. Once it was built, the Jews appealed to the king for it to be erected in a less offensive place and he agreed. The place where it was put up is open to debate, but there really was such a golden cross and the inn must have been named after it.

Oxford Union

A gateway in St Michael's Street, off Cornmarket, leads to a courtyard surrounded by red-brick Victorian Gothic buildings, which are the premises of the Oxford Union Society, the social centre of the university for at least part of the student population and the headquarters of the famous debating society. This is Oxford's traditional training ground for politicians, the weekly debates, conducted in a parliamentary style, offering a chance for the politically pushy to make a name for themselves in the cut-and-thrust of public argument. Five British Prime Ministers – Gladstone, Salisbury, Asquith, Macmillan and Heath – were officers of the society, and other undergraduates who have been President for a term include Quintin Hogg (Lord Hailsham), Michael Foot, Tony Benn, Jeremy Thorpe, Michael Heseltine and William Hague.

The Union has a national and international reputation, and that is at least partly due to the world press coverage given to a debate which took place here on Thursday February 9, 1933, when students voted by 275 votes to 153 in favor of a motion "That this House will in no circumstances fight for its King and Country." This debate is often cited as one of the most important pieces of social comment of the 1930s. It has even been suggested as a cause of the Second World War, for it has been said that, when Hitler heard of it, he became convinced that there was no will in Britain to stop his rampage across Europe. The debate itself was not seen as terribly important by those who were present, however, although the only journalist there, John Owen of the *Oxford Mail*, reports that a record number of members had given notice of their intention to speak. As was usual in debates, four students argued the case for and against and were followed by two guest speakers. For the motion was the philosopher C.E.M. Joad (1891-1953), and against, a former President of the Union, Quintin Hogg (b.1907), who would later become a Conservative Cabinet Minister.

No-one would have taken any notice of the debate were it not for a letter a few days later in the *Daily Telegraph*, planted by one of the paper's own leader writers, J.B. Firth, a former Union President, who alleged that the vote had been the product of "Communist cells in the colleges." The rest of the national press then launched in to batter the undergraduates, culminating in a diatribe of abuse in the *Daily Express* which raged:

"There is no question that the woozy-minded Communists, the practical jokers and the sexual indeterminates of Oxford have scored a great success." There was even a demand that Cambridge should cancel the Boat Race – now things were getting serious.

A group of life members of the Union, led by Randolph Churchill (1911-68), son of Sir Winston, demanded a debate to call for all details of the vote to be removed from the Union's record. But they were pre-empted at the very next debate, when a gang of undergraduates from St John's College Boat Club – supporters of Oswald Mosley's Fascist Party – burst into the chamber, seized the minute-book, tore out the page recording the debate and took it off to be ceremoniously burned at Martyrs' Memorial.

Great drama, but the irony of the event is that although, during the war with Germany, many looked back and pointed a finger of blame at the Oxford Union, the debate itself had nothing whatsoever to do with Germany. It took place only ten days after Hitler had become Chancellor and the only references in the speeches to a foreign power were all about Soviet Russia. It was clear, too, that those who voted for the motion did so on an anti-war platform rather than an anti-patriotic one, for they had in their minds the horrors of the First World War, which had ended only fifteen years earlier and had been promised as the "war to end wars." The final word on the subject, however, must go to the silent witness of the War Memorials in the Oxford colleges, which show that, when the call came, the "cowards" of Oxford did indeed fight – and die – for King and Country.

CHAPTER NINE

Alice's Oxford

"Catapulted into fame by simply doing absolutely nothing"

Perhaps this chapter ought to be called Lewis Carroll's Oxford, for the writer and his muse shared the same territory at the same time, but Alice herself was a much more charming and interesting figure than the unctuous paedophile Charles Dodgson, whose obsession with the little girl forced her into a sudden and not always welcomed literary immortality. There can hardly be a soul in the English-speaking world who, as a child, did not come across the story of Alice's adventures, in Wonderland or through the looking-glass. She is, quite simply. the most famous fictional character to come out of Oxford.

And yet, of course, there is more fact than fiction connected with Alice. The famous books grew out of stories told to a real Alice, a child who grew up in Oxford. They were told by a strange academic who spent almost his entire adult life at Oxford University; and the stories are full of references to the enclosed university world of Oxford as it affected the real Alice in the mid-nineteenth century.

The real Alice was Alice Liddell (1852-1934), the second daughter of Henry Liddell, Dean of Christ Church from 1855 to 1891. As head of the richest and most prestigious college in Oxford, Liddell was a man of immense influence, for over thirty years the top man in Oxford. His connections, though, went even higher for, before moving to Christ Church, he had been Domestic Chaplain to Queen Victoria's husband,

Prince Albert. British and foreign royalty visiting Oxford always paid a visit to Dean Liddell, and the Queen's youngest son, the haemophilic Prince Leopold, fell in love with Alice during his undergraduate days. Furthermore, by that peculiar genealogical calculation that hardly anyone seems to understand, Alice is fifth cousin, three times removed, of Queen Elizabeth II, for they share a common ancestor, one Thomas Lyon who lived from 1704 to 1753.

So Alice, although not exactly aristocracy herself, was far from an ordinary girl. She grew up in the most influential family in British education and mixed her whole life with Princes and Prime Ministers.

Alice Liddell was born on Wednesday May 4, 1852 (both day and month are identified by the Mad Hatter as the date of Alice's visit to Wonderland) in the precincts of Westminster Abbey (Liddell was then headmaster of Westminster School) in the heart of London. She was not quite four when she moved to the newly rebuilt Deanery at Christ Church.

So much sentimental claptrap has been written about the relationship of the "shy" academic Lewis Carroll and his ideal "child-friend" Alice, that it is easy to lose sight of the fact that Charles Dodgson (1832-98) was an emotionally retarded pervert from whom any sensible parents today would keep their children well away. Paedophilia was not a socially recognized syndrome in the mid-nineteenth century but, with the benefit of hindsight, we know what we would make today of a bachelor clergyman who wrote obsequious letters to the mothers of little girls, asking for permission to photograph their children naked. He loved to have the children up in his Christ Church rooms unchaperoned, where he persuaded them "in their innocence" to romp around in the nude "in their favorite dress of nothing on." In what is now recognized by police and psychologists as typical paedophile behaviour, Dodgson used to prepare puzzles, games and toys, which he would carry around with him in the hope of chance encounters with young girls. Details exist of many occasions when he would approach children unknown to him, in railway carriages or on seaside beaches and promenades and engage them in conversation, before suggesting to their mothers that he should meet them again.

Before his death in 1898, he wisely destroyed his collection of hundreds of photographs – many, though by no means all, taken by himself – of naked girls (he did not like boys, and girls lost their appeal for him as soon as they reached puberty). Dodgson gave up photography completely in 1880, almost certainly as a result of the stories that were rife in Oxford about his activities with the daughters of prominent families. But, unable to sublimate his desires, he then took up art classes where the models were – of course – naked little girls. His closest woman friend was the illustrator, Gertrude Thomson, a woman who shared his interests and made a living from drawing naked children as fairies and angels in the manner so popular with certain Victorian collectors. Miss Thomson arranged life-drawing sessions for Dodgson, and letters survive in which he tells her quite clearly what sort of children he wanted her to procure for him.

There is no surviving evidence that Dodgson ever molested his little "child-friends," and quite possibly his gratification came when alone with his photographic collection. And yet a huge breach occurred in his relationship with the Liddell family in June 1863. After his death, some member of his family carefully removed the relevant page from his diary, so we shall never know exactly what happened. However, in the days before the missing page, it is clear that all was harmonious between Dodgson and the Liddells and he was almost continually in the company of eleven-year-old Alice and her sisters. After June 27, almost all contact had been cut; Dodgson does not refer to the girls again for nearly six months and Mrs Liddell is adamant that none of her daughters is to be left alone with him, an attitude already taken by a number of other Oxford parents.

Nevertheless, Dodgson, in his alter ego of Lewis Carroll, is still remembered affectionately by millions who have grown up with – and often never put down – his two great books for children, *Alice's Adventures In Wonderland* and *Through the Looking-Glass.* He wrote other stories for children, but there is nothing in them to catch the imagination like the Alice books.

Those captivated by the books are usually also always captivated by the fact that their genesis can be accurately plotted. The Wonderland tale grew out of stories told by Dodgson to Alice Liddell during a boat trip on the Thames in Oxford. The occasion was Friday July 4, 1862, when Dodgson suggested to Alice and her sisters, Lorina and Edith, that they should take a boat trip on the River Thames. They chose a boat from the boatyard at Folly Bridge and set off upstream towards Binsey and Godstow. Dodgson and the Liddell girls often had trips on the river and most often they went downstream to Nuneham Park, where the owner, William Harcourt, allowed picnickers to land on Tuesdays and Thursdays to eat their lunch in special huts he had provided.

Dodgson, not famously athletic, usually invited a male friend to accompany them, to help with the rowing. On this occasion he invited the Rev Robinson Duckworth, who went on to tutor royalty. Accounts of the day show the fickleness of memory. Duckworth remembers Dodgson making up the story as they rowed up to Godstow; Alice insists that the three sisters pleaded for a story as they sat in meadows by the river. But then, Alice remembered the day as being so hot that they abandoned the river to seek shade, while local weather records showed that fourth of July to be overcast and tending towards rain.

Extemporary stories were the norm during these outings. But on this occasion, as they returned, Alice asked Dodgson to write them down. Besotted with the dark-haired ten-year-old, Dodgson agreed, knowing that, as Trinity term had just finished, he would have some time to work on it. It was not until mid-November, however, that he began to write it out. By February 10, he had completed the hand-written copy that has always been considered the manuscript. He gave this to Alice as a Christmas present in 1864 and the following year was able to give her a copy of the published work, twice as long and with its title changed from "Alice's Adventures Underground" to *Alice's Adventures in Wonderland*. Thankfully, he was talked out of an earlier plan to call it "Alice's Hour in Elfland." The book was well received in the Press, though the rift with the Liddells was so severe that Dodgson never recorded in his diary Alice's reaction to his gifts. Although in later life Dodgson affected a horror of being recognized as a famous writer, even returning letters addressed to "Lewis Carroll," the success of Wonderland inspired him to write its lesser sequel *Through the Looking-Glass*, which appeared in 1871.

Back at the Deanery, Alice and her family played hosts to the newly married Prince and Princess of Wales, later King Edward VII and Queen Alexandra, and an even more significant royal event occurred in 1872, when Queen Victoria allowed her youngest son, Prince Leopold, to study at Christ Church. Leopold spent a good deal of time at the Deanery, which was the social centre of the Oxford University world, and there, it is deduced, he fell in love with one of the Liddell girls – Alice has always been considered the most likely of the three, but, much to her mother's annoyance, it was clear that Queen Victoria was only looking for European princesses as wives for her boys.

In 1880 Alice married Reginald Hargeaves, who had been an undergraduate at Christ Church while Leopold was in Oxford, and had also been a pupil of Dodgson. He had taken six years of plodding to get his degree and it is clear that Alice, who had grown up among the sharpest intellects, chose a husband some way her intellectual inferior. She was now to become mistress of Cuffnells, Hargreaves' estate in Hampshire. The couple married at Westminster Abbey. By now the rift between Dodgson and Alice was clear; his wedding present was not included in the official list, and he was not at the wedding and had probably not been invited. She stayed in touch with her royal admirer though; in 1883 Alice's second son – Leopold – was born and a few weeks later, Prince Leopold's daughter was born – she was christened Alice.

Her family commitments made Alice's visits to Oxford infrequent and she had little contact with Dodgson. In 1891, however, just before her father's retirement as Dean of Christ Church, she came back to Oxford and was invited to tea by Dodgson. She declined the offer but did visit him briefly with her sister Rhoda: it was the last time the two would ever meet. Dodgson died in 1898 – by a remarkable coincidence, in the same week as Dean Liddell.

In 1928 Alice, now widowed, found she could no longer afford the upkeep of Cuffnells and so sold the Wonderland manuscript. It fetched £15,400 at Sotheby's and Alice's future was secure. Four years later, when she was almost eighty, Alice allowed herself to step into the limelight for once in her life, when she was invited by Columbia University in the U.S. to receive an honorary doctorate to mark the centenary of Lewis Carroll's birth. At the end of her first day in America, she recorded a radio broadcast: "America and New York City are such exciting places, that they take me back to Wonderland," she said diplomatically. At Columbia she saw again the original manuscript and was presented to a gathering of 300 people. She stayed in America for ten days, explaining while she was there that she had been "catapulted into fame by simply doing absolutely nothing." She died in 1934.

Rowing

In Oxford, the River Thames is synonymous with boating. Few now take out small boats as did Dodgson and the Liddell girls; today one is more likely to see cabin cruisers and narrowboats. But rowing on the river is still a popular sport among students. The Oxford and Cambridge Boat Race, held in early spring on the Thames in London, is an event of international standing. Recently, its stature has been diminished as other branches of – now professional – sport demand more headlines, but the Varsity race is still the best-known rowing event in the world.

All Oxford colleges have their own boat club and the Varsity crew is chosen from the cream of these. Twice a year the college teams or "eights" row against each other in spring and early summer competitions known as Torpids and Eights Week, where, rather than competing abreast of each other, they form a line and try to touch the boat in front. If they succeed, they move up one place for the next race. All the crews are placed in divisions, according to how they finished the previous year. The college which finishes the four-day competition in front of the first division is named Head of the River. The races are as much a social event as a sporting one, especially during the early summer Eights Week, a great excuse for picnics and parties. The Bump Suppers thrown by the college that finishes Head of the River are not for the faint-hearted, with a lot of young people getting very drunk and very silly.

The races form the background for the climax of Max Beerbohm's celebrated 1911 novel of Oxford *Zuleika Dobson* when, on the final day, every undergraduate bar one commits suicide for love of Zuleika, by leaping into the Thames from boats, barges and banks. Osbert Lancaster (1908-86), whose illustrations to the novel can be seen in the Randolph Hotel, saw the battle between the aesthetes of the Oxford University Dramatic Society and the hearties in 1926 and decided to give rowing a chance. But it did not really work:

After a few days on the river, it became abundantly clear to me why rowing had, in more rational societies, been confined to the criminal classes and prisoners-of-war. After a grim two weeks, I cast in my lot with the aesthetes, laid down my oar and joined the OUDS.

Godstow

The ruins of Godstow Nunnery stand near where Alice's boating party was heading on Wonderland day. This is the site of the grave of one of Oxford's most romantic characters, Rosamund Clifford, mistress of King Henry II (1133-89).

Godstow Nunnery was founded in 1138 by Benedictine monks and dedicated in the presence of King Stephen. Rosamund Clifford was Henry's favorite mistress before he married the divorced Eleanor of Aquitaine – some reports say she had been secretly married to him. Whatever the case, after his marriage, the king kept Rosamund at the royal manor of Woodstock in what is now the grounds of Blenheim Palace, a few miles north of Oxford. Near the royal buildings, Henry created a bower for Rosamund, and legend has it that it was protected by a complicated maze. One story goes that Queen Eleanor, arriving unexpectedly at Woodstock saw a silk thread leading into the maze. She followed it through the labyrinth and found the fair Rosamund. In her jealous rage, she either poisoned her or stabbed her to death.

The truth is probably not quite so romantic, with Rosamund eventually falling out of the king's favor and retiring to the nunnery at Godstow, of which her father was a benefactor. Whatever the case, what is undisputed is that Rosamund was laid in a magnificent tomb before the high altar in about 1175. But this was not to be her final resting place. When St Hugh, Bishop of Lincoln, arrived at Godstow while visiting the outposts of his diocese in 1191, he was horrified to discover a woman of easy virtue lying before the altar and gave orders that her bones should be removed and buried outside the church. The site of this second burial is lost, but the story of Rosamund, the "rose of the world," a king's lover, haunts the ruins at Godstow, where the murmur of traffic from the bypass cannot destroy the feeling of tranquility that must have been known by the nuns here for 400 years.

Port Meadow and Binsey

Godstow Nunnery is on the edge of the wild and wide expanse of flat land alongside the Thames to the west of Oxford known as Port Meadow and Wolvercote Common. Port Meadow is mentioned in Domesday Book of 1086, and it is typical of Oxford, says the environmental writer Richard Mabey, "that the city's oldest monument isn't some august monastic foundation but this pleasantly scruffy stretch of pastureland." Because it has never been ploughed or treated with chemicals, it is of immense importance in terms of conservation and has been much studied by wildlife groups. Grazing rights for cattle and horses belong only to Freemen of Oxford and the Commoners of Wolvercote who, of course, usually have nothing to graze here. Once a year at an unspecified date, the Sheriff of Oxford rides out with his merry men to round up all animals found grazing illegally and fine their owners. During the First World War, Port Meadow was used as a training ground for the university and public schools battalions and became a Royal Flying Corps training aerodrome on quite a grand scale, with a capacity for 1,000 trainees.

Across the river from Port Meadow is the hamlet of Binsey and along the river nearby is a double line of poplars. These trees were planted some years ago by Oxford Civic Society to replace similar rows on either side of the river, whose sudden, unexpected destruction in 1879, while he was assistant priest at St Aloysius Church in Oxford, inspired Gerard Manley Hopkins to write one of his most popular poems, *Binsey Poplars*:

My aspens dear, whose airy cages quelled,
Quelled or quenched in leaves the leaping sun,
All felled, felled, are all felled...

Hopkins had known Binsey since he was an undergraduate at Balliol and loved to take long walks along the Thames or across Port Meadow. On March 13, 1879 he scribbled a postscript on the bottom of a letter to one of his friends; "I have been up to Godstow this afternoon. I am sorry to say that the aspens that lined the river are every one felled."

Little Binsey is an isolated hamlet today, with no clue that once it was bustling with pilgrims attracted to St Margaret's Church. It was here that St Frideswide was said to have prayed to St Margaret and miraculously a spring burst from the ground. Its water had healing properties and restored the sight of Algar, Frideswide's unwanted suitor. The spring became renowned as a holy well and was the target of the pilgrims. There were so many of these in the thirteenth century that the nearby (and now lost) village of Seacourt once had 24 hostelries to give bed and food to the pilgrims who had come in search of a cure. The well became known as a treacle well, from the old word meaning a healing liquid, and this gave Lewis Carroll the inspiration for the treacle well in the Dormouse's story at the Mad Hatter's tea party. Alice Liddell and her sisters would have been familiar with Binsey's well and would have recognized the allusion.

Among the many pilgrimages that were made to St Margaret's Well was one by Henry VIII and his first wife, Catherine of Aragon (1485-1536). Catherine had been unable to give Henry the son and heir that he so wanted and he brought her to Binsey to be annointed with the sacred water. He did not obtain the result he wanted and, in his desperate search for a son, he divorced Catherine, breaking from the Church in Rome in order to do so. It was this that led to the English Reformation and the zealous abandonment and destruction of all "idolatrous" things in the land – holy wells among them.

The nearby church itself is tiny, but full of character. It dates from the late twelfth century and contains, hidden within the pulpit, a carved wooden panel of St Margaret. She is a very sensual sort of saint and this is hardly surprising as the panel is attributed to Eric Gill (1882-1940), an artist obsessed with sex, who committed incest with his sisters and sodomized his daughters. The most famous incumbent of the parish of Binsey was Nicolas Breakspear (1100-59), who was vicar here before going off to study in Europe, where in 1154 he was elected the only English Pope as Adrian IV.

The Railway Station

The area at the junction of Park End Street, Hythe Bridge Street and Botley Road, is being developed for the £20 million Said Business School, due to open in 2000, built with money from the Arab businessman Wafic Said and planned to create "an impressive western gateway to Oxford." This was the scene of a green protest in 1998, when it was discovered that there were plans to pull down the former Great Western Railway station building which for years most people had considered one of the city's worst eyesores. It had been used as a tyre and exhaust centre and then left derelict. Even though the building was to be taken down beam by beam and reconstructed at the nearby Quainton Railway Centre, the protesters suddenly decided it was a beautiful and important part of Oxford's heritage and squatters moved in to prevent it being dismantled. The endlessly accommodating Oxford public sat back and watched a series of confrontations between council and police on the one hand and protesters on the other, before a dawn raid eventually managed to evict them all and the station was carefully taken down and shipped to Quainton.

Oxford nearly did not get the railway at all. During the 1830s expansion, when lines were spreading across the country, university interests persuaded the House of Lords to turn down successive bills for bringing the railway to Oxford. The university feared it would imperil the morals of its students and the Chancellor, the Duke of Wellington, was opposed to all railways because "they might encourage the lower orders to move about." Eventually the university relented but only as long as they were allowed the right to check up on any student daring to travel anywhere by rail.

Opposite the new business school stands the Old Jam Factory, where one of Oxford's most famous delicacies, Cooper's Oxford Marmalade, was manufactured and bottled between 1900 and 1947. The business started when Frank Cooper sold his wife's marmalade to dons and undergraduates from his grocery shop in the High. It proved so popular with generations of students, that they had it shipped out to them, a reminder of their days at Oxford, when they worked in various outposts of the Empire for the Colonial Service. The family firm has long been part of a major food conglomerate, and Oxford marmalade is no longer made anywhere near Oxford.

Worcester College

Worcester College is the furthest west of the Oxford colleges and was, for a long time, even more isolated, for it was not until 1822 that Beaumont Street was built, a straight line leading out from the main gates of Worcester and the first real connection with the other colleges. Worcester has an air of antiquity which is rather deceptive, because the college was not founded until 1714. But it does stand on the site of one of the earliest Oxford establishments, Gloucester College, founded shortly after Balliol in 1283. Gloucester College was built by the Benedictines to serve all their abbeys in the south of England. Some sixty religious houses were under orders to send monks to study at Oxford. Like other monastic houses, it was a victim of Henry VIII's Dissolution of the Monasteries. However, Sir Thomas White, who had already bought the site of St Bernard's Cistercian college and turned it into St John's, also did a deal for the site of Gloucester and turned it into Gloucester Hall, which was to be an academic hall under St John's.

It never really flourished, and because of its remoteness from the other colleges, it became a retreat both for elderly fellows and recusant Catholics. The poet Richard Lovelace (1618-58) was its most notable undergraduate in the seventeenth century. General decline set in, and by 1701 there were no undergraduates left at all. At about this time, Sir Thomas Cookes of Worcestershire was thinking of founding a new college in Oxford and put up £10,000 for that purpose. There was a bit of a squabble for the money but eventually the cash came to the principal of Gloucester Hall, who changed the new college's name to Worcester after Cookes' origins. The name of Gloucester survives now only in Gloucester Green, the redeveloped piazza behind the bus station a short distance away.

That famous opium eater, Thomas De Quincey (1785-1859) was the most notable undergraduate in the first 100 years of Worcester's life. There have not been many more of great distinction, although the media tycoon Rupert Murdoch (b.1931) was here in the 1950s.

De Quincey was studying Latin and Greek at Worcester College, but spent a lot of time visiting his friends the Wordsworths and Coleridge in the Lake District. He came back from one such visit with his final exams only two months away and far behind in his work. He told Dorothy Wordsworth that he would have to read 33 Greek tragedies in a week if he were to catch up. So, with presumably the help of his drugs, he read for 18 hours a day, determined to get a good result. In those days (1808), the exams were largely oral and the candidates could be grilled on their knowledge for up to three hours at a time. De Quincey was due to take his Latin exam on a Saturday, with the Greek on the following Monday. The first of these tests was clearly an ordeal, but that evening one of the examiners told a friend that de Quincey was "the cleverest man I ever met with," adding that, if he were to repeat Saturday's performance on Monday, "he would carry everything before him." Unfortunately, De Quincey's reading of the examination clearly did not match this praise as, on the Sunday, he packed his bags and left the university, never to return, and so missed winning his degree by one day.

The glory of Worcester is its gardens, described as the only real landscape architecture in the university. They used to run far back down to the river, but were truncated in 1788 when the Oxford Canal was brought into the city. At around this time, Worcester's famous lake, the only one in Oxford, was created. Though famed for its picturesque beauty, it was in fact a practical solution to the waterlogged and smelly grounds between the college buildings and the canal.

Ruskin College

Ruskin College in Walton Street is one of Oxford's most remarkable success stories. Although named after the Christ Church graduate who was Slade Professor of Art at the university, it was the idea of a couple of rich young Americans, Walter Vrooman and Charles Austin Beard, who in 1899 had the revolutionary notion of setting up a "college of the people" for working-class students, where dockers, miners and laborers of all kinds could enjoy an education that had previously been the preserve of a privileged elite. It was created with the express purpose of being a place to educate "the working-class leaders of the future."

It started life in St Giles', where it was known as Ruskin Hall, and moved to its present site in 1903 (there is a second site in Headington). At first, funds came from private philanthropic sources, and then increasingly from trade unions. A number of university dons were closely associated with Ruskin from the outset, and the university has always allowed its students to use the Bodleian and sit in on university lectures. The scholars themselves, usually mature students who had missed out on the chance of education the first time around, often felt that the college should be run by the Labour movement and split completely from the university, but an uneasy partnership has been maintained. The Labour deputy Prime Minister John Prescott (b.1938) said: "It wasn't Oxford, but it was in Oxford." Prescott, an 11-plus failure, was working on North Sea ferries at the time he took up his chance to come to Oxford. "Ruskin College is the greatest thing that ever happened to me," he said. "It opened my eyes and my mind to ideas which thrilled me. There's nowhere like it."

Jericho

Walton Street is the main thoroughfare of Jericho, Oxford's first purpose-built suburb. The area was practically uninhabited until the start of the nineteenth century, when it was developed on a grid pattern between Walton Street and the canal. It was a working-class area of laborers employed mainly at Oxford University Press and Lucy's ironworks and soon became a slum, suffering three major outbreaks of cholera between 1832 and 1854. Despite this, it became a stronghold of the Oxford Movement, thanks in no small part to the efforts of Thomas Combe, superintendent of OUP.

Combe and his wife, Martha, were described by their friend, the Pre-Raphaelite painter William Holman Hunt, as: "The salt of the earth...two of the most unpretending servants of goodness and nobility that their generation knew." It was Combe who paid for the building of Jericho's main church, St Barnabas, in Cardigan Street. Its Venetian Romanesque exterior, with a 132ft campanile, is suitably austere, but inside the church blazes with gold and brightly colored paintings.

Jericho became the district of "Beersheba" in Thomas Hardy's Oxford novel *Jude the Obscure*, which dealt with a rural stone-mason's inability to get accepted into the university. Hardy paid his first visit to Oxford in 1893, and *Jude* was first published, in an abridged magazine version, the following year. The backstreets of Jericho have changed little over the years, but Walton Street and the northern end have become a fashionable place to live. The area is full of lively pubs; the Jericho Tavern, in Walton Street, now renamed the Philanderer and Firkin, was the birthplace of the music scene known as Ox-Pop and saw the advent of bands like Radiohead and Supergrass. The Bookbinders Arms, in Victor Street, is the only pub in Britain of that name. It served the OUP and is an essential part of the Inspector Morse Oxford trail but internally bears no resemblance to the set built in the studio. Combe Road, which is a tiny cul-de-sac ending at the canal was used in the very first Inspector Morse film, *The Dead of Jericho*. The home of Morse's murdered girlfriend, Anne Staveley, is right at end of the terrace.

Oxford University Press

The Oxford University Press building which dominates the lower half of Walton Street was built in 1830 to house the university's printing arm, which had been expanding since winning contracts to supply Bibles and prayer books to the newly converted peoples of the world. Before this time, it had been housed in Hawksmoor's Clarendon Building in Broad Street. It was after the move that the OUP – even today a university department without shareholders – became one of the world's leading publishers. After securing the Bible market, the Press next turned to producing much-needed textbooks for the new schools springing up after a series of educational reforms. In 1900 the *Oxford Book of English Verse* was launched, the first of a never-ending series of "Oxford Books of..." which were quickly recognized world-wide as authorities on their subjects. Today, though the great press has been removed from the heart of the Walton Street building, the business is still expanding and now produces a catalogue of publications to rival any publisher in the UK.

The best-known work published here is undoubtedly the *Oxford English Dictionary*, which has been appreciated as the ultimate authority on English usage for more than a century. When the idea first got off the ground in 1879, the dictionary was planned as a four-volume work that would include all English language vocabulary from the twelfth century onwards and it was estimated the project would take ten years. Five years later, the dictionary's mastermind, James Murray (1837-1915), announced that his team of lexicographers had reached the word "ant" and so schedules were revised. Eventually, in 1928, the last volume of the OED was published but the problems of a living, evolving language were obvious and within five years a single-volume supplement was published to update it. The updating process is never-ending and offers a lifetime's work to any lexicographer today, although now the whole thing is available on CD-ROM. The massive work that took up four feet of shelf space and weighed 150lb has been reduced to a single disc that can be slipped into a coat pocket and weighs only a couple of ounces.

Theatres

The area between George Street and Beaumont Street is Oxford's theatre-land, though this is no West End or Broadway. Records show that in 1681 Charles II came to Oxford for the opening of the Playhouse and the Poet Laureate John Dryden wrote an epilogue for the occasion, but no-one is quite sure where that Playhouse was.

The New Theatre in George Street was built in 1886, after a move by both town and gown for a theatre where both professional and amateurs could perform, and it became the showcase for OUDS, the Oxford University Dramatic Society. It was demolished in 1933, however, to make way for the new New Theatre, which was by far the largest in England, seating 1,700 and able to attract the world's greatest actors and actresses. This theatre was run successively by Charles, Stanley and John Dorrill, and shows like *West Side Story* and *Hair* came here first before opening in London. In 1977 the Apollo Leisure group bought and renamed it, since when it has been used both as a cinema and for elaborate stage shows and pop concerts.

Oxford's first repertory company opened in the "Red Barn" opposite Somerville College in Woodstock Road in 1923, but moved in 1938 to the purpose-built Playhouse in Beaumont Street. Early members of that company included Sir John Gielgud and Dame Flora Robson, but over the last sixty years the Playhouse has closed and reopened with monotonous regularity, able to entice big names to appear in Oxford, but unable to pay for the privilege. It is presently flourishing.

The most memorable week in the Playhouse's history was in February 1966 when, in a gesture still hard to believe, the couple who were then the most famous in the theatre and film world, Elizabeth Taylor and Richard Burton, starred in an OUDS production of Marlowe's *Doctor Faustus*, turning down work that would have earned them £700,000. Instead, they performed without payment in order to make enough profits for a studio-theatre extension, now known as the Burton-Taylor Rooms.

Richard Burton (1925-84) had appeared on the Oxford stage before. He took advantage of a scheme during the Second World War, whereby cadets from the Armed Forces could go to university on a special six-month course. He spent his time studying English under Neville

Coghill at Exeter College in 1944. Burton, who had only recently changed his name from Richard Jenkins, fell in love with Oxford, explaining at the height of his fame that "it had and still has, a curious, almost mystic impact on me." Whatever he learned on his course, he remembered the city first as the place he learned to drink, calling himself "Beer Burton." He boasted to his family that he could put away two pints faster than any other undergraduate.

Richard Burton and Elizabeth Taylor (Oxford Times)

Burton had already done some serious acting before reaching Oxford and was keen to appear on the University stage. Unfortunately, at the time he was up, OUDS was in decline – bankrupt and temporarily suspended. Coghill, however, was directing a production of Shakespeare's *Measure for Measure* and Burton auditioned for him. The play was already fully cast, but Coghill got Burton to understudy the lead part, Angelo, "backing my king with an ace," as he would say. The part was to be played by Hallam Fordham, an RAF officer who was posted away from Oxford before the first performance. Ruthlessly, Burton seized his chance, and night after night he received a standing ovation. Coghill was so impressed that he invited Hugh "Binkie" Beaumont, the most influential theatre manager in London, to come and see him. Beaumont was equally impressed and told Burton to go and see him in London as soon as he left the RAF.

Oxford never lost its attraction for Burton and he came back often, usually to see Coghill or another friend, Francis Warner at St Peter's. The actor was famous for his hard drinking and his tempestuous love life, but in Oxford he is remembered for his generosity. On reading of the imminent closure of the student magazine *Isis*, Burton immediately sent a cheque for £1,000 to pay off its debts; he gave thousands to the Playhouse and £100,000 to St Peter's, where he had dreams of becoming an English don. But his greatest gift was to play Faustus, again directed by Coghill, with Elizabeth Taylor, the world's most beautiful woman, stunning the packed houses with her non-speaking role as Helen of Troy.

Beaumont Street
Beaumont Street stands today almost as it was when first laid out in 1822 in its late-Georgian grandeur. Its long terraces of three-storeyed town houses were thought by Pevsner to be "the finest street ensemble in Oxford," and most of the houses are now occupied by firms of doctors, dentists, solicitors and architects.

Beaumont Street cuts across the site of Beaumont Palace, which was built by King Henry I outside the city wall. The first record of the king's occupation was at Easter 1133, and Henry II and his queen Eleanor of Aquitaine were certainly living here in the late twelfth century, for their sons, Richard the Lionheart (1157-99) and John (both to be kings) were born here. By 1275, Edward I, who certainly spent a good deal of time here, gave the palace buildings to one of his diplomats and they then passed through a succession of owners before the ruins were rifled by St John's College in the sixteenth century to build its library.

The elegance of Beaumont Street continues around the corner into St John Street, named of course after the local landlord. The plain frontages of these terraces hide some of the most elegant interiors in Oxford and, despite the fact that a number of the houses are in multiple-occupation for students, St John's Street is still one of the most prestigious addresses in the city. Among the present (or recent) occupants have been a number of well-respected writers, including Britain's present Queen of Crime, (Baroness) P.D. James, who was born around the corner in Walton Street in 1920.

At the end of the street, one finds Wellington Square, on the site of the former city workhouse. The square takes its name from the Duke of Wellington (1769-1852), victor of Waterloo, Prime Minister and, until just before this development was built, Chancellor of the university.

In 1994 the university created something of a stir when it announced that its Continuing Education Department, based in Rewley House in Wellington Square, was to be renamed Kellogg College after the corn flakes manufacturer from Michigan. Continuing education used to be known as External Studies and is the academic outreach branch of the university, offering courses, summer schools and diplomas to thousands of part-time students across the country. Over the last decade, the Kellogg Foundation has given the new college about £9 million.

On the south side of Beaumont Street, opposite the Ashmolean, stands the Randolph Hotel, Oxford's most famous overnight accommodation, the lodging-house of kings and princes, of statesmen and film stars. Opened in 1866, it takes its name from Dr Francis Randolph, whose sculpture collection was an important element of the Ashmolean Museum opposite. The great and the good are still happy to enjoy the Randolph's slightly faded glory, in order to stay so close to the heart of the city. The Spires Restaurant contains a series of paintings designed (but not executed) by Sir Osbert Lancaster to illustrate Max Beerbohm's *Zuleika Dobson*.

The Taylor Institution, on the corner of Beaumont Street and St Giles' is commonly known to the folk of Oxford as the Taylorian. It occupies the eastern wing of the immense neo-classical building that houses the Ashmolean Museum. The St Giles' facade has four gigantic Ionic columns, surmounted by dramatic female statues representing France, Italy Germany and Spain, the countries whose languages were the main ones studied there. Sir Robert Taylor's original bequest to the university stipulated that the building be used for "establishing a foundation for the teaching and improving of the European languages."

The Ashmolean

Dominating Beaumont Street is the vast, powerful, Greek temple which is the Ashmolean Museum, the university's collection of art and antiquities. The four huge pillars at its main entrance can leave no-one in any doubt that they are entering something important. And the reputation of the Ashmolean is well established. Any book about Oxford will tell you that this is one of the great British collections.

So why is it such a disappointment? Apart from the dedicated few, the people of Oxford rarely go to the Ashmolean except as somewhere to take the children or grandchildren on a wet day. While researching this book, I got into the habit of asking people how much they enjoyed the Ashmolean and, without exception, their response was unflattering. It is no good just pointing to the visitor figures and saying that it is a popular attraction. After all, every visitor to Oxford feels that they ought to "do" the Ashmolean. The telling figure would be how many people ever went back for a second visit.

It is not that wonderful things are lacking in the university collection; there are plenty. But no help is given to the visitor to find them. The Ashmolean is at least thirty years behind the rest of Europe when it comes to interesting and educating museum visitors – and in another century when compared to the United States – it ought to be in a museum itself. Almost everything is wrong; the entrance lobby is just a vast open space without information panels or direction pointers; one is left to just wander and see what one can find. Naturally, ninety per cent of visitors march straight ahead and find themselves amid unfamiliar Chinese and Korean ceramics – beautiful certainly and well displayed, but not what one expects to be greeted with in an Oxford collection. From there, things go downhill; the amount of information given in most rooms is woefully inadequate and, believe it or not, in some galleries, the exhibits are identified only by numbers, and anyone interested has to find a copy of the inventory left somewhere in the room. Cases are often stuffed with a collection of dozens of similar objects without a sign anywhere saying: "Hey! Look at this. It's important, It's exciting." There are whole galleries on the first floor in which I have never seen another visitor. This is because they are full of cases of finds from university archaeologists' digs, which might be important in the history of Cyprus or Crete, but which simply do not catch the public imagination.

Is the problem that the Ashmolean staff see the museum and its collection solely as an academic resource centre for researchers from other universities? Are the public simply a nuisance that has to be put up with? That certainly was an attitude the university used to take in the bad old days when it was a closed institution which never had to justify itself outside the college walls. But in recent years, university managers have come to realize that it is a public-funded and very heavily subsidized institution and, bit by bit, we have seen it opening up. At the University Museum of Natural History, there has been a conscious effort to make its collection more accessible and more informative, particularly to families.

It is time that the same attitude was echoed at the Ashmolean. Then there will be no more blunders like the Alfred Jewel. This exquisite piece of rock crystal over an enamelled figure, all encased in finely worked gold with the inscription (in Anglo-Saxon) "[King] Alfred had me made" is the most famous and best-loved exhibit in the collection. It needs to be displayed in the round, as it once was near to the entrance. But now it is tucked away in a wall case, in the far corner of a dull, little-visited gallery, off the back stairs, next to a case of early Scandinavian brooches. Academically it is fitting, because it is back in the Dark Age Europe room, but its move is a slap in the face for museum visitors.

The Ashmolean collection has been built over 350 years around Tradescant's Ark, a collection of "rarities" gathered from travellers around the world, by the John Tradescants, father and son, who were first and foremost royal gardeners. In reality, this ought to be the Tradescantian Museum, for Elias Ashmole (1617-92), a London civil servant who had studied at Brasenose, got hold of the Tradescant collection by rather devious means, which included the harassment of the younger John's widow. Eventually the new owner passed the collection on to Oxford University just as Tradescant had wished. It was housed first in the building in Broad Street which now houses the Museum of the History of Science, and was moved to its present purpose-built home in 1845.

The little room on the first floor housing some of Tradescant's original "rarities" is still one of the most fascinating parts of the collection. Here is Guy Fawkes's lantern, Cromwell's death mask, a lock of hair from Edward IV, Cranmer's shackles, possibly part of the post to which Latimer and Ridley were tied at their execution and Powhatan's Mantle – perhaps the most important Native American relic in Europe. It consists of four deer skins sewn together and decorated with patterns made from tiny shells and is traditionally claimed to have belonged to Powhatan, the father of Pocahontas.

The Ashmolean is an art gallery as well as a museum and, although there are very few masterpieces among them, the paintings are generally representative of movements in European art since the Renaissance. Among the most famous exhibits are Uccello's fifteenth-century panel, *Hunt in the Forest*, drawings by Michelangelo and Raphael and some very well known Pre-Raphaelite images. One of the very finest paintings is the portrait of the Scottish Jacobite heroine, Flora Macdonald, by Allan Ramsay, which has recently been rescued from the obscurity it suffered when hung eight feet up on the wall of the clocks and watches room. Its transfer to the main gallery was a stroke of genius; one only hopes that Gainsborough's portrait of George Drummond, similarly tucked away, will one day receive the same treatment.

J.R.R. Tolkien (Oxford Times)

CHAPTER TEN

C.S. Lewis's Oxford

"I never saw anything so beautiful, especially on these frosty moonlight nights; though the hall at Oriel is fearfully cold at about four o'clock in the afternoon."

Clive Staples Lewis (1898-1963), with his pipe and tweed jacket and set in his ways, seemed the typical bachelor Oxford don. Nothing could have been further from the truth. Far from the donnish stereotype, he was an exceptional individual. He was one of the finest lay Christian writers of the twentieth century, he wrote a series of children's books that remain an exquisite timeless classic, and he had extraordinary relationships with two overpowering women.

C.S. Lewis, or Jack as he was known to his friends, was born in Belfast, Ireland, on November 29, 1898, the younger of two sons of an Protestant solicitor. When he was nine, his mother died and, within a fortnight, he was sent away to a boarding school in England, whose headmaster would flog the boys in his care for the least fault. What effect that combination of events had on the boy can only be conjectured; certainly it turned him against his father for life. Lewis came up to University College, Oxford in 1917, one of only twelve students in college, because the rest were away fighting in the trenches of France. After one term, Lewis was sent for training at Keble College, where he was billeted with a young man called Paddy Moore. Lewis and Moore, before they were sent to the war, made a pact that, if one of them survived and the other did not, the survivor would take care of the other's single parent, Lewis's father or Moore's mother.

Moore, of course, was killed and, true to his word, Lewis, when he came back to Oxford to finish his degree after the war, used his meagre allowance to pay the rent for Mrs Janie Moore and her daughter, Maureen, to live in the city. He was to be their companion for more than thirty years, ostensibly Mrs Moore's "adopted son," but in reality the older woman's lover and, in some ways, her servant, always willing to drop his studies to cater for her domestic needs.

A brilliant double First in Greats, followed by a First in the new discipline of English, led in 1925 to a post as English Fellow at Magdalen College, where he took rooms in the New Buildings. He lived in college while Mrs Moore and Maureen continued to live at Hillsboro, a house in Holyoake Road in the centre of Headington.

Since his youth, Lewis had always considered himself an atheist, but in the summer of 1929 he had a mystical experience on a bus travelling up Headington Hill from Oxford. Later, he said: "I gave in and admitted that God was God, and knelt and prayed: perhaps, that night, the most dejected and reluctant convert in all England."

It was around this time too, as a young don at the university, that C.S. Lewis became friends with J.R.R. Tolkien, the young Professor of Anglo-Saxon at Oxford. They would meet regularly for drinks at the Eastgate Hotel and discuss Christianity and their writing. It was the first step towards the group of Oxford writers that would be known as the Inklings.

In 1930 Lewis bought the house where he would spend the rest of his life, The Kilns, standing then in an enchanting setting of eight acres at the foot of Shotover Hill beyond Headington. The grounds contained a wood with a pool where, it was said, Shelley had sailed paper boats during his time in Oxford. Jack moved in with Mrs Moore and Maureen and, soon afterwards, his brother Warnie, fresh out of the Army, joined them.

Lewis was not always a popular man; he developed a bluff persona that many people found off-putting and he was passed over by his colleagues for a professorial chair in the English department, even though he was clearly the outstanding candidate. Yet those who got to know him well were devoted to him. Even Lord David Cecil, the literary biographer, who had little cause to love him – Lewis had led the campaign that stopped Cecil becoming Professor of Poetry in 1938 – said he was a great man: "One felt one was in the presence of someone who made his contemporaries seem like pygmies."

By now, Lewis had started to publish: academic books like *The Allegory of Love* (1936), science-fiction stories such as *Out of the Silent Planet* (1938) and spiritual books like *The Screwtape Letters* (1942). *The Lion, the Witch and the Wardrobe*, the first of his classic Narnia books for children, was finished by 1949 and *The Voyage of the Dawn Treader* and *The Horse and his Boy* by 1950. In fact, Lewis once claimed that he had written all the Narnia books within a single year, and it was not much of an exaggeration.

Mrs Moore died in 1951 and, with her daughter now a grown woman leading her own life, Lewis and Warnie settled down to a men-only existence at The Kilns: but it did not last long, for Jack was already communicating with an emotional American writer, Mrs Joy Gresham. In 1954 Cambridge University invited Lewis to become Professor of Medieval and Renaissance English. He kept on The Kilns, returning for weekends and vacations. Joy had by now moved with her two sons to London and had often visited Lewis in Oxford. Her divorce came through in 1954 and, by now clearly in love with Lewis, she moved to Old High Street, Headington. She did not impress Lewis's friends, who saw her as arrogant and foul-mouthed. In 1956, the Home Office refused her a permit to remain in England. The only answer was for her to marry a British citizen like Lewis and be allowed to stay. Lewis assured Warnie that it would just be a formality and that she would continue to live in Old High Street as Mrs Gresham.

On April 23, 1956, they were married in a civil ceremony at the register office nestling between the Quaker Meeting House and Army Recruitment Centre in St Giles'. He was 58, she was 41. But they kept the news from his Inkling friends. Shortly after this, Joy was diagnosed with bone cancer and given a 50-50 chance of survival. Lewis wanted to take her back to The Kilns to die as his wife, but felt this would be wrong without a Christian marriage. But, as Joy was divorced, the Bishop of Oxford, Harry Carpenter ruled that a church marriage would be against canon law. Eventually, Lewis persuaded a friend in order to marry them at her hospital bedside on March 21, 1957. Somehow Joy went into remission from her cancer and was able to live a reasonably active life for three more years. Lewis, without being "fanciful" as he puts it, reported that the bone cancer halted in Joy at about the same time as he developed a minor bone disease himself. He had been praying for months to be allowed to share her pain.

C.S. Lewis died on Friday November 22, 1963, though his death went largely unnoticed in the wider world, as that same day in Dallas, Texas, JFK was assassinated. He was buried at Headington Quarry. Warnie missed the funeral and stayed at home drinking whisky all day.

A cult grew up around Lewis after his death, and particularly after Lord Attenborough's *Shadowlands* film about the Lewis/Joy Gresham relationship. Now coachloads of visitors arrive in the residential roads around Lewis Close – much to the annoyance of neighbors – to see the ordinary suburban house where the Narnia books were written and the Shadowlands story played out. The Kilns is now a C.S. Lewis study centre, run by the California-based C.S. Lewis Foundation and restored with much of Lewis's own furniture. But the area around the house would be unrecognizable to its former owner. The kilns from which it took its name are gone and the Lewis Close/Kiln Lane area has been built up with housing. But one treasure remains unspoilt: behind the house and reached from Lewis Close, is an open-access nature reserve run by the Berkshire, Buckinghamshire and Oxfordshire Wildlife Trust, some seven-and-a-half acres of woodland and ponds, where one can wander at peace and share the landscape Lewis and Tolkien knew and which inspired both Narnia and Middle Earth.

To get from Magdalen to The Kilns, Lewis would travel the old London road through St Clement's and Headington. St Clement's was one of the poorest areas of Oxford during the nineteenth century, and a cholera epidemic in 1832 resulted in the death of many of its inhabitants. Earlier, during the Civil War, much of the St Clement's area was burnt or pulled down. The Black Horse pub at 102 St Clement's was one building that survived. During the seventeenth and eighteenth centuries, bull-baiting and bear-baiting were regular features here and, as late as 1826, there was still a University Bear-Baiting Club.

Headington

At the top of Headington Hill stands Headington Hill Hall in its extensive grounds. It is now part of the Oxford Brookes University campus, but was for many years the home of Robert Maxwell (1923-91), the publishing magnate and one of the most fiercely hated men ever to live in Oxford. Maxwell was born Jan Hoch of peasant Jewish stock in Czechoslovakia. During the Second World War, when his parents, grandfather, three sisters and a brother were murdered by the Nazis, Hoch proved himself a reckless and ruthless soldier in the Allied cause, winning the Military Cross. He came to Britain, changed his name and set about becoming rich and powerful, setting up a printing empire known first as Pergamon Press and later as the Maxwell Communication Corporation. He ran it from Headington Hill Hall, which he rented from Oxford City Council.

In his quest for power, Maxwell became a Labour MP from 1964 to 1970, but never progressed beyond the back-benches. As he built up his millions and his power, he tried to become a newspaper tycoon, but his ventures usually foundered quickly. It was only when he bought Mirror Group Newspapers that he found himself able to control an important part of the national press. From his position of power, he interfered endlessly in editorial decisions, and someone once counted that the *Daily Mirror* had 231 references to him in just three days.

Almost everyone who came into contact with Maxwell loathed him. He was a bullying employer and, as it was later revealed, a crooked businessman. But if anyone criticized him, he was swift to sue, and eventually, although every journalist in the land knew he was a crook, they were cowed into silence. When he died on November 5, 1991 (he fell, jumped or was pushed off his yacht near Tenerife), the announcement was greeted first with disbelief and then with unbridled joy. In thirty years in journalism, I have never known anyone else whose death was welcomed by cheers.

In the days and weeks following his death, the facts about Maxwell's business deals came out. To bolster his flagging personal finances, he took hundreds of millions of pounds from the Mirror Group Pension Fund, and thousands of Pergamon Press pensioners in Oxford found that their payments had been plundered too. Maxwell's widow had to auction the entire contents of Headington Hill Hall before moving out and slipping quietly away from Oxford. A year after his death, enough had been found out about the man for an *Oxford Mail* leader to say "Robert Maxwell was a devious crook, who would have sold his family for a quick buck."

Robert Maxwell and Oxford United fans (Oxford Times)

If there is anywhere in Oxford where the name of Maxwell is still held in any regard it is further along Headington Road at the Manor Ground of Oxford United Football Club. The club – formerly Headington United – was only elected to the Football League in 1962 and, after a series of boardroom wrangles, was on the point of bankruptcy twenty years later when Robert Maxwell bought it, paid off its debts and poured in some much-needed money. Almost immediately, the team won the old Third Division championship and then, incredibly, the Second Division championship the following season, putting them for the first time in the top flight of English football, competing with the likes of Manchester United, Liverpool and Arsenal. In 1986, United won the Milk Cup final at Wembley and Maxwell's joy was both genuine and complete as he joined in the celebrations when the trophy was paraded before the team's fans in the city centre. Yet he was always looking for new possibilities and, having succeeded at Oxford, unsuccessfully bid £10 million to take over Manchester United and then failed to get Tottenham Hotspur. He eventually bought Derby County and switched his allegiance from Oxford, where he temporarily installed one of his sons as the new chairman. Since Maxwell's departure, it has to be said, United fortunes have foundered.

Many visitors, marvelling at the buildings and history of Oxford University, are unaware that the city has a second, much younger, university based in Headington. Oxford Brookes University was among the first group of polytechnics allowed to upgrade to university status by John Major's Conservative government in 1992. As Oxford Poly, it already had a reputation and status unrivalled by any similar institution in the land and, following the recent increase in the number of universities in Britain, Brookes has, for the last three years, been judged top new university in the influential league table published by *The Times*.

The university is named after John Henry Brookes, the formative figure in the development of the Poly from a plethora of further educational establishments in the city. The School of Art, School of Science and City Technical School merged to form the Schools of Technology, Art and Commerce in 1934, and Brookes was its first principal.

The Headington campus site in Gypsy Lane was bought in 1949 ready for the establishment of a new Oxford Technical College, but the city council rejected the plan only to give way following a public outcry. The College of Technology expanded to become Oxford Polytechnic in 1967. The buildings, though important locally, are of little interest to visitors and the university has yet to turn out world-famous alumni, although Lord Nuffield studied at one of its predecessors. The university's first Chancellor is (Baroness) Helena Kennedy QC.

Headington is home to Oxford's renowned collection of teaching hospitals. As the inadequacies of the restricted site of the Radcliffe Infirmary in Woodstock Road became more and more obvious, new sites were sought in the developing suburb. The city's major hospital complex – and, in fact, the largest and most important hospital west of London – is the John Radcliffe Hospital (known in Oxford simply as the JR), on a 75-acre site behind Headley Way. Phase One, the maternity unit,was completed in 1971 and the main hospital in 1979. The Churchill Hospital, which stands on the site of a Roman pottery works in Old Road, was built in 1939 and named after the wartime

Prime Minister, Sir Winston Churchill. It was taken over by the U.S. Medical Services as a military hospital during the war. The Nuffield Orthopaedic Centre in Windmill Road made its reputation treating casualties of the First World War and then specialized in treating tuberculosis, polio and other diseases affecting mobility (it was here that the famous Oxford Knee, used in joint replacement, was developed).

The Irish-born writer Elizabeth Bowen (1899-1973) wrote her first four novels and two volumes of short stories while living in Old Headington. In 1925 her husband, Alan Cameron, was appointed secretary of education for the city of Oxford and they lived at Waldencote, a stone-built cottage facing on to The Croft. They took their place in Oxford society and became part of the writer John Buchan's circle at Elsfield Manor. Elizabeth soon became president of Headington Women's Institute, an organization which meant a lot to her. She told Virginia Woolf later: "I do very much miss WIs. Since I came to live in London, I feel I don't live in England at all.

While she was in Oxford she developed an intense friendship with Lord David Cecil, then a young don at Wadham and, through him, got to know most of the rising stars of the university scene. By 1932, she was writing "I spend most of my time in London as I don't like Oxford very much these days." But in 1960 she returned to the city and went back to a flat in Old Headington, trying to slip back into the social position she had held earlier. But, by now, a lot of the clever young men she had known in the 1930s were in senior posts at the university. She found to her chagrin that it was by no means easy to renew old friendships at the same level and that she was too old to take up the new generation of clever young men.

Tolkien

It is curious that, with the possible single exception of Iris Murdoch, Oxford dons have produced so little in the way of quality mainstream fiction. There have, of course, been plenty of fine poets but, from the detective fiction of J.I.M. Stewart (Michael Innes) and G.D.H. Cole, through the children's writing of Charles Dodgson and C.S. Lewis, to the fantasy worlds of Tolkien, most prose fiction has been genre work.

J.R.R. Tolkien (1892-1973) is perhaps the prime example, for his books of Middle Earth adventures were considered by his fellow dons to ill-become a senior academic. Nevertheless, they had a success of which all those less-publishable dons had reason to be jealous. In his own lifetime, fans besieged his Headington home so that he had to move into obscurity at Bournemouth to escape them. Since his death and the posthumous publishing of his works, his reputation has grown and grown. In 1997 Tolkien came top of three separate polls to choose the greatest book of the twentieth century, run by the booksellers Waterstone's, the Folio Society, and the science-fiction magazine *SFX*.

His popularity is quite astonishing and was, of course, achieved without any publicity machine, for Ronald Tolkien enjoyed a quiet life in Oxford and never gave magazine interviews or appeared on TV chat shows to promote his work. Yet today a considerable number of the visitors to Oxford come in pilgrimage to Sandfield Road where he lived, to Merton College where he died, and to Wolvercote Cemetery where he is buried.

John Ronald Ruel Tolkien was born in Bloemfontein, South Africa in 1892, where his father had recently moved from England in the hope of improving his banking career. However, Mr Tolkien Snr (the name is of Germanic origin) died when Ronald was just four, and he returned with his mother and younger brother to England, where he grew up and was educated in Birmingham. When he was twelve, his mother died and the orphan boys came under the care of their parish priest and an unsympathetic aunt. Before coming up to Exeter College in 1911, Tolkien had mastered Latin and Greek and was studying other, relatively obscure, languages like Gothic and Finnish.

He started at Oxford studying Greats, the classics, but after a Second in mods, he transferred to English Language and Literature where he immersed himself in Old English and philology, the study of language itself. From an early age, he had been making up his own languages, a preparation which paid off in his great elvish books. During the First World War, he developed trench fever while fighting on the Somme and was removed from active service. He came back to Oxford as an assistant lexicographer on the *Oxford English Dictionary*, but soon moved to a post of Reader in English Language at the university of Leeds.

Tolkien was not away from Oxford for long, however, because at the early age of 33 he returned as Professor of Anglo-Saxon. He was by now married with a family and settled into Oxford life, which included work on what he thought were his unpublishable elvish tales. It was during this time that he met the young C.S. Lewis, helped him with his conversion to Christianity (Tolkien was a devout Catholic) and started reading his work in progress with Lewis and other friends who had formed the drinking and writing group known as the Inklings.

In 1937, with Lewis's encouragement, he published *The Hobbit* – a tale of the perilous journey of Bilbo Baggins to recover treasure from the dragon Smaug – and was surprised to find himself with an instant success on his hands. Even so, he was a perfectionist as a writer and every sentence had to be squeezed out of him, and it was not until 1954/5 that the three volumes of the sequel, *The Lord of the Rings*, in which Bilbo's nephew Frodo sets out to destroy a powerful, dangerous ring in Mordor the land of darkness, appeared. Tolkien was by now the Merton Professor of English, a post he retained until his retirement in 1959.

Although *The Lord of the Rings* had been another immediate success, it took the advent of the flower-power generation of the 1960s for it to become a cult book, its stories of the battle between good and evil in a world of magic and make-believe appealing directly to a student generation which often found greatest empathy with the book while reading it under the influence of mind-expanding drugs. It was at this time that the fans started to invade Tolkien's private life, with phone calls in the middle of the night from American devotees who had taken no regard of time differences, and knocks on the door from total strangers who felt they had some sort of relationship with him simply by their devotion to his books. The flight to Bournemouth ended with the death of Tolkien's wife Edith in 1971, after which he returned to rooms supplied by Merton College until his own death in 1973.

As the twentieth century progressed, Headington expanded to absorb many outlying villages, including Headington Quarry, where stone suitable for building was first discovered in 1396 and which supplied much of the stone used for university buildings between the fifteenth and eighteenth centuries. In 1819, a local Marston parson, the Rev Jack Russell (1795-1883) of Exeter College, while on a walk to Elsfield, bought a fox-terrier pup called Trump from a milkman. It was from this dog that he developed the new breed of terrier which took his name.

The Headington Shark

Almost all the architectural treasures which pull visitors into Oxford were created two or three hundred years ago and nearly all of them are contained within the city centre. But since 1986, there has been one site which no visitor to Oxford ought to miss; a construction so bizarre and so original that it took the planning authorities completely by surprise. Oxford woke up one morning in August 1986 to find a 25ft fibreglass shark had plummeted – so it seemed – through the slate roof of a terraced house in one of its suburbs.

The Headington Shark was the work of the sculptor John Buckley and it projected from the roof of the New High Street house owned by the colorful, not to say eccentric, Bill Heine, the Illinois-born entrepreneur who had already re-opened two of Oxford's oldest cinemas and drawn attention to them with other fibreglass adornments: huge Al Jolson hands on the Penultimate Picture Palace and high-kicking can-can legs on Not the Moulin Rouge. Heine came to Oxford to read law at Balliol, but his studies were interrupted by the call-up to fight in Vietnam in 1967. He joined the Peace Corps and served in Nicaragua and Peru before coming back to Oxford to finish his degree.

Heine had to fight the city planning committee to get permission to keep the cinema sculptures, but that was nothing compared to the long battle he had over the shark. The council clearly did not know what to do, for Heine claimed it was a work of art and a "statement about CND, nuclear power, Chernobyl and Nagasaki." Councillors tried to prove it should never have been put where it was but, unable to find a precedent for a shark sticking out of a suburban roof, unable to prove it was a structural hazard and, above all, faced with the fact that it had become one of the most popular and best-loved of the sights of Oxford, they eventually backed down. By this time the Southern Arts Council had awarded the sculptor £1,000 in recognition of the work.

Heine went on to host popular and controversial local radio chat shows and write entertaining columns in the local press but he continued to upset the authorities and, even today, has at least as many detractors in the city as supporters. The shark, however, was swiftly accommodated by an Oxford public who are hard to surprise and impossible to shock.

The Headington Shark (Oxford Times)

CHAPTER ELEVEN

Lord Nuffield's Oxford

"It is much easier to amass wealth than to dispose of it wisely"

When Lord Nuffield (1877-1963) died, the *Oxford Mail* said he was "the maker of modern Oxford...Lord Nuffield made a greater impact on the city and university than any other single individual in the whole of their history."

Nuffield, who was born William Morris in a terraced house in Worcester, came to Oxford aged three and started work in a local cycle shop at fifteen. When he asked for a shilling-a-week pay rise, it was refused, so he left and started his own bicycle repair business from the back yard of the family house at 16 James Street, off Iffley Road. Soon he was building cycles as well as repairing them and, as motorized transport took hold, he turned to making motorcycles and servicing cars from a garage in Longwall. By 1912, he had decided he could build his own car. The first Morris Oxford, assembled from parts brought largely from manufacturers in Birmingham, cost £165 to buy. Although it was not the cheapest car on the road, it was attractive and dependable and Morris Motors was under way. Needing larger premises, he bought the former Oxford Military College in Hollow Way and, by 1914, some 13,000

Bullnose Morrises had rolled off the assembly line. After the First World War, Morris bought up large areas of cheap land in Cowley and simply kept on expanding. He was the first British industrialist to appreciate the benefits of the assembly line for the mass production of motor cars and, without his foresight, there would have been no British car industry.

Expansion continued until Morris Motors covered a huge area of Cowley. Oxford workers moved out to join him for high wages and regular employment, and migrant families from Wales and Scotland moved in. The city council built large estates to house them. The Morris works changed the face of Oxford by adding a third dimension to the Town and Gown split. It became "Motopolis" for John Betjeman, who grumbled: "East Oxford, where the works are, beyond Magdalen Bridge, is indistinguishable from Swindon, Neasden or Tooting Bec. The architectural development of Oxford since the war has completely changed the character of the city." Morris was also responsible for changing the city from a university town, where most of the working class existed merely to service the needs of the young gents at the colleges, to an industrial town where thousands found regular work, decent pay and a new self-confidence.

William Morris was not loved by all his workers; the factory was a sweat-shop, and the man who was amassing millions could be mean when it came to looking after his employees. He single-handedly kept trade unions out of the works until forced to give in by other pressures. The other side of Morris, though, was his generosity. He was a man of simple tastes, who cared nothing for the arts, for books or the theatre or for the countryside. He lived for his work and, as his millions grew, he eschewed the playboy lifestyle and retired to a reasonably modest country house with his wife and started working out how to use to best effect the millions he had made.

In his youth he had dreams of becoming a surgeon, and this perhaps explains his beneficence to medical research. "What I have been able to do for medicine and teaching in all walks of life," he said, "has given me more satisfaction than anything else." He gave millions to Oxford University to promote medical research. If he had not personally financed Howard Florey's work during the Second World War, penicillin might have remained just an idea put forward by Fleming. He also backed a revolutionary new design for iron lungs and issued them free to all major hospitals. He set up the Nuffield Foundation with £10 million, to spend money on social welfare and caring for old people. He founded the Nuffield Institute for Medical Research in 1936 and he rescued the Wingfield Orthopaedic Hospital, which is now the Nuffield Orthopaedic Centre.

Morris was created Viscount Nuffield in 1938 because of his donations to medical science. By the time he was eighty, he had given away almost £30 million, and every penny of it came from his own capital, his charitable contributions were never tax-deductible. But Lord Nuffield's greatest desire was to found his own undergraduate college within the university, devoted to engineering. Oxford did get its Nuffield College but, after an ill-natured fight with university grandees, Nuffield had to settle for it being a postgraduate foundation specializing in the social sciences, not what he had planned at all. Other colleges benefited though; he handed out largesse to St Peter's, Worcester and Pembroke, having chosen them because they were at the bottom of a list he was given, showing the colleges in order of their wealth.

Nuffield never courted publicity and steadfastly refused to allow a biography to be written during his lifetime. One famous author actually wrote one in the 1940s and sent the manuscript to Nuffield. He read it, paid the author a handsome sum and destroyed it. Perhaps he was embarrassed by aspects of his life like his dangerous flirtation with British fascism in the 1930s, or perhaps he was shy about revealing the full extent of his generosity. One little-known Nuffield account paid the rail fare for parents who could not afford to visit their sons locked up in one of the country's largest Borstals.

It is impossible for a visitor to Cowley today to appreciate the scale of Nuffield's car-building enterprise. At its height it employed many thousands of workers but, gradually over the last 25 years, this vast industrial complex has been diminished and disguised. Morris Motors gave way to the British Motor Corporation; that in turn became part of the disastrous British Leyland enterprise; BL turned into Austin Rover, then the Rover Group, and today Rover is a wholly owned subsidiary of the German car makers BMW. Most of the old Morris works has now been pulled down, and the site is now a large business park and retail estate.

William Morris's legacy lives on through Nuffield College and in the nationally important hospitals and medical centres that benefit the city. The suburb of Cowley is perhaps his permanent memorial – or perhaps it is the cars clogging the streets of the ancient city centre. Otherwise, there is little in Oxford to show the scale and the power of Lord Nuffield. His garage in Longwall has been converted into student accommodation, but with the facade preserved as it was when he left it. His office at Cowley has been reconstructed 35 miles away at the Heritage Motor Centre at Gaydon in Warwickshire. Plans for a statue or even a bust came to nothing – Oxford City Council would not find £500 to put towards one. Instead, today, the sole official memorial is a 30ft obelisk, dubbed the Nuffield Needle, which has been installed on the central roundabout in the Oxford Business Park, built on the site of the former works.

The Plain
The Plain is the great meeting place of roads coming into Oxford from the east. St Clement's, Cowley Road and Iffley Road meet here at the roundabout before being funnelled across Magdalen Bridge into the High. The church of St Clement once stood on the site of the Plain, and here too was St Edmund's Well, whose waters were allegedly responsible for so many miracles that the Bishop of Lincoln twice had to forbid its veneration.

The centrepiece of the Plain is the big roundabout, but between there and Magdalen Bridge stands the Victoria Fountain, built in 1899 to belatedly commemorate the old queen's diamond jubilee two years earlier. Water was provided here for both human and equine refreshment. It is sheltered under a circular roof held up by eight Tuscan columns but today only one tap remains and no water flows.

All Oxford University's constituent colleges are north and west of the crescent made by the confluence of the Thames and Cherwell, except St Hilda's. After the explosion of places found for women students in Oxford in the 1880s, Dorothea Beale, the principal of Cheltenham Ladies' College, opened a residential hall in Cowley Place in 1893, named after St Hilda of Whitby, the seventh-century abbess who was England's first great educator of women. St Hilda's Hall was intended as a stepping-stone for old girls of Cheltenham, and when Miss Beale opened her teacher training college – also St Hilda's – in Cheltenham in 1901, she created a neat little family of education units for women. This link became looser after women were finally admitted into the university in 1920 and when St Hilda's College was formed in 1926. It was only in 1960 that it became a full college within the university, and today it is the only single-sex college left. Its inhabitants, by the way, are still known as Hildabeasts. Miss Beale said of her embryonic college: "I want none to go for the sake of a pleasant life," and she installed a strict system of chaperones and iron grilles on the windows to make sure her wishes were respected. The young ladies were not all too pleased about this, and a famous rhyme about the founder and one of her associates runs:

Miss Buss and Miss Beale
Cupid's darts do not feel.
How different from us
Miss Beale and Miss Buss.

In the grounds of St Hilda's stands the Jacqueline du Pre concert hall, in memory of the great English cellist who died tragically young from multiple sclerosis. Jacqueline du Pre (1945-87) was born in Beech Croft Road, Oxford, and her passionate playing made her an instant star of the concert rooms at a very young age. She married the conductor and pianist Daniel Barenboim and converted to Judaism for him. After being diagnosed with multiple sclerosis at the age of 28 and soon confined to a wheelchair, she started a second career as a teacher of the cello. She died in London in 1987 and ten years later her brother and sister published a memoir of life with this "difficult genius," full of unflattering anecdotes. These included Jacqueline's demand that her sister allow her husband to sleep with her when she was seriously depressed (this became the central theme for the film *Hilary and Jackie*).

Because of its early association with a single feeder school, St Hilda's has never been a richly endowed college financially and has not produced many great alumnae, although the novelist Barbara Pym studied there and the literary historian Dame Helen Gardner was a Fellow. Barbara Pym (1913-80), who chronicled a donnish North Oxford milieu of intelligent women and unworldly clergymen, went up to St Hilda's in

1931 to read English. In 1930s Oxford, with one woman undergraduate to every ten men, she had a splendid social life and seems to have spent most of her time chasing men. Ironically, she never married; her most famous friendship in later life being with the bachelor poet Philip Larkin, who went on to choose her for a *Times Literary Supplement* feature in 1977 as his "most under-rated writer of the century." It was this feature (she was also the choice of Lord David Cecil) which gave her career as a novelist a late boost. In the same year, her novel *Quartet In Autumn* made the shortlist for the Booker Prize, Britain's most prestigious fiction award. Not surprisingly perhaps, Larkin was chairman of the judging panel and might have leaned on his fellow judges to include his friend. The top prize, as it turned out, went posthumously to Paul Scott for *Staying On*, his coda to the "Jewel in the Crown" *Raj Quartet*. Pym, who had set up home in Finstock, some fifteen miles from Oxford, with her sister Hilary, died from cancer in 1980 in Michael Sobell House, the hospice attached to the Churchill Hospital.

Cowley Road

East Oxford, between Cowley and Iffley Roads, was never a really poor area like St Ebbe's or Jericho, but started as an area of working-class people with pretensions to middle-class status – tradesmen and college servants. Now parts have become Oxford's bedsit land and many of the larger houses on Iffley Road have become small hotels.

Cowley Road itself is the busy urban artery of the city that is the complete antithesis to North Oxford and its university ways. The reserve of the Summertown middle classes changes here to an up-front social exchange, where life is lived on or close to the street rather than behind lace curtains. Although East Oxford is full of student bedsits and shared houses, these are more often the temporary homes of those studying at Brookes University and the Oxpens College of Further Education. This is not a purely student community though, but one of mixed origins into which students are easily absorbed. The linking factor between the groups seems to be lack of money. The houses are mainly small Victorian and Edwardian terraces, and the Cowley Road shops include discount and junk shops, and even the three brass balls of a pawnbrokers is evident across the road from the Tesco supermarket. Branching off from the main road towards Headington, however, are larger red-brick Victorian or Edwardian homes, mostly owned by people with young families or older residents.

The multi-ethnic, multi-racial mix is witnessed in food stores and eating places, with the usual kebab and balti houses joined by halal meat suppliers, a Jamaican eating house and Oxford's only Cambodian and Thai take-away. Here is the headquarters of the Afro-Caribbean Association, there the Bangladesh Islamic Education Centre and, somewhere between them, a traditional Chinese medicine practice. Cowley Road is the sort of urban village street that one finds on the run into West London or the centre of Birmingham or Manchester, a double row of small independent shops where leases change hands often and premises are left empty. "The Cowley Road isn't Oxford," comments the cynical narrator in Michael Dibdin's *Dirty Tricks*, "it's South London without the glamour." This is the sort of area where there is wall-to-wall bill posting but also window bars and steel shutters. Tesco – a hideous, great long brick wall of a frontage – and Boots are here, but otherwise national chain stores stay well away.

The road is full of interesting juxtapositions; Uhuru wholefoods, which was once run by a radical feminist collective and a place one avoided if one was male, is three doors along from the heavily shuttered sex shop, where one would not choose to go if one was female. Although the spire of the University Church and the dome of the Radcliffe Camera are in view as one walks down Cowley Road, this is a vibrant area of constant change that contrasts completely with the timeless permanence of the ancient college buildings of the city centre.

Students, and former students who have never been able to leave the scene of their youthful triumphs, are catered to by the futon shop, the several bicycle retailers, New Age beads and incense suppliers and the live music bars. The sound of rock music comes from open windows above the shops and battles vainly with the endless noise of the traffic, for this is the main route out of the city towards the suburbs of Cowley, Rose Hill and Blackbird Leys. Incredibly and disturbingly, even here in this run-down area where almost everyone is stretching what money there is, the young beggars sit on the pavement, pathetically importuning passers-by.

Past Magdalen Road, the shops thin out and Cowley Road becomes more residential, with newer housing. It is only here that the strange Oxford phenomenon of cycleways on footpaths begins. When this scheme was introduced in the late 1980s, many people were aghast that the safety of cyclists should be put before the safety of pedestrians. But in practice, it has to be admitted, it works throughout the city, with fewer cycle accidents and almost no tales of collisions between cyclists and pedestrians.

The Ultimate Picture Palace, built on an old brewery site, is Oxford's oldest surviving cinema and was first in operation at the beginning of the twentieth century. It was used as a furniture store for more than fifty years until Bill Heine re-opened in it 1976 as the Penultimate Picture Palace, with a large fibreglass sculpture of Al Jolson's hands in white gloves. In Marston Street, between the Cowley and Iffley roads, stands St Stephen's House theological college which, in its 125-year history, has produced a number of bishops for both home and abroad. The college is housed in the premises vacated in 1980 by the Cowley Fathers, the popular name given to the Society of St John the Evangelist, the first English monastic community since the Reformation, which was founded in 1866 by the Rev Richard M. Benson, vicar of Cowley and a disciple of Edward Pusey.

In the grounds of the Anglican All Saints Convent in Leopold Street stands what should be one of the saddest institutions in Oxford. But it is also one which is full of love and smiles and is proudly cherished through fund-raising and the prayers of the people of Oxford. Helen House was the first hospice in Britain (the second in the world) to cater solely for very sick and dying children. It owes its existence to the saintly Mother Frances Dominica. Mother Frances, daughter of a Surrey chartered accountant, trained as a children's nurse at Great Ormond Street Hospital before deciding to become a nun at the age of 23. Her decision shocked her family, who did not speak to her for eight years because they felt she had thrown her life away to live behind closed doors. But there are no closed doors at Helen House, except to provide privacy at moments of extreme anguish. Although the children who go there are almost all going to die soon, the place is full of fun. The staff wear no intimidating uniforms and there is light, music, toys everywhere. In her declaration of the aims of Helen House, Mother Frances said: "We want to make it possible for more families to have their sick children at home most of the time, in the knowledge that they can turn to Helen House for relief and support when necessary...it aims to be a home, not a hospital."

Just beyond Magdalen Road and on the other side of Cowley Road is a narrow unmarked lane leading to a stone cottage and a farmhouse. Through a gate marked "St Bartholomew's Chapel" is a row of almshouses and a small chapel. This was one of the first medieval isolation hospitals in England. St Bartholomew's of Oxford was founded by Henry I in 1126 as a refuge for lepers: in medieval times, leprosy sufferers had to carry a clapper to warn of their approach and were kept strictly segregated. St Bartholomew's, which became known as Bartlemas, was a mile east of Oxford, far enough from the city to be safe but close enough to cause the mayor to pay a weekly rent towards the upkeep of "twelve infirm leprose folk" and their chaplain. In the fourteenth century it became a major pilgrimage centre and a place of miracles, with a holy well in the grounds and a remarkable collection of "relics" including a rib of St Andrew, the bones of St Stephen and the flayed skin of St Bartholomew himself.

Later that century, Oriel College took over the site, moved the relics out and replaced the lepers with its own members, thus changing Bartlemas from an isolation hospital for the poor into an exclusive semi-rural retreat for scholars. Parliamentarian troops stopped up the holy well and pulled down the hospital buildings during the Civil War, although these latter were rebuilt within twenty years and were used once again as an isolation hospital in the early nineteenth century when cholera raged through Oxford and patients were brought there to convalesce.

Cowley

The name Cowley comes from the Anglo-Saxon meaning Cufa's wood, but the area was occupied by the Romans, just about the closest they got to Oxford, which was a forbidding wet marshland. The history goes back to the times when the ancient road from Dorchester to Alcester ran along its eastern boundary. Finds of pottery prove that people were living and working here more than 1,700 years ago. From the twelfth century to the Dissolution of the Monasteries, Cowley was owned by Oseney Abbey and the Knights Templar. Henry VIII, once he had suppressed the Abbey, added the land here to the foundation of Christ Church.

Until the late nineteenth century, this was a rural community, and a handful of ancient buildings can be found today in the area around Beauchamp Lane. In Victorian times, Church Cowley and Temple Cowley were joined by the parish of Cowley St John, whose first vicar was the Rev Richard M. Benson, the founder of the Cowley Fathers. Benson's successor, the Rev Coley, caused a scandal in the national press by refusing to bury one of his parishioners, claiming that he was "a notorious evil liver." The local community presented a petition calling for the funeral to go ahead, but Coley refused their request and locked himself in the church, whereupon a large crowd broke down the door. Coley was soon removed to another parish and was replaced by the Rev Georgie Moore, a former university boxer who was twice summonsed for assault. Moore was vicar here for 53 years and brought to the church the organ from St Martin's, Carfax, when it was demolished.

Beyond Cowley, beyond the ring road and – as far as much of Oxford is concerned – beyond the pale, lies Blackbird Leys. It is a sprawling, working-class estate of houses, largely rented, built in the early 1960s by the city council while it was busy demolishing the tight-knit community of St Ebbe's in the city centre and moving its population of laborers, factory workers and college servants out of sight, if not out of mind.

As council estates go, Blackbird Leys is certainly not a disaster area, with its wide, green spaciousness, its hard-working community associations and with the local Labour MP, Government Minister Andrew Smith, happy to make his family home there. However, the Leys also houses a disproportionate percentage of Oxford's unemployed and single-parent families and supplies a disproportionate number of the accused in the city's magistrates courts. Its otherwise delightful name became eternally synonymous with criminality in the early 1990s when, on a succession of hot summer nights, the national media became obsessed with the antics of a handful of misnamed "joyriders" who, often under the influence of drink or drugs, would steal big flashy cars from other parts of the city and drive out to Blackbird Leys. Here, to the delight of ever-growing numbers of the estate's youngsters, the drivers would show off their motoring "skills"; doing a series of hair-raising and heart-stopping manoeuvres – known as "hotting" – on a broad avenue in the centre of the estate, often culminating in the stolen vehicles being torched. When the police finally responded to public pressure to act, the heat and the drink and the drugs sparked a series of near-riots in the middle of the night, which both affronted and delighted the television news and the national press.

Iffley

The Iffley Road Sports Centre is the home of Oxford University Athletics Club and was, in 1954, the setting for one of the greatest moments in sporting history. The OUAC was founded in 1860 and, from the early days, produced world record breakers and Olympic champions. In 1876 the Hon. Marshall Brooks, a Brasenose undergraduate, achieved the first-ever high jump of over six feet, but even that paled into insignificance when compared with what happened on the track here on May 6, 1954, when Roger Bannister (b.1929), a graduate of Exeter College, broke the four-minute barrier for the mile race. No other athletics record had been awaited so anxiously and no other performance has been so lauded since.

Bannister, who came up to Exeter in 1946 to read medicine, was looking for a sport. He was no good at ball games and too light to make any impact in the college boat, but he liked to run. On his first evening in Oxford, he set off for the Iffley Road track, hoping to see "dozens of brilliant athletes on whom I could feast my eyes in hero worship." When he got there, it seems, the track was deserted except for a groundsman.

He made a name for himself while at Oxford and later as an international athlete, while he was a junior doctor at St Mary's Hospital, Paddington in London. By the spring of 1954, the sporting world was buzzing with the idea that the four-minute barrier for the mile was close to being breached. The Australian runner John Landy seemed favorite to get there first, but Bannister knew he was capable of doing it himself in the right conditions. The first opportunity of the year would be the Amateur Athletic Association's annual match against Oxford University at the Iffley Road track. So Bannister came back to race against his old club, but, more importantly, to race against time.

Weather conditions on the day were such that he almost decided to abandon the attempt but, as the runners approached the starting line, there was an unexpected lull in the wind and he decided to go ahead. He used his colleagues Chris Chattaway and Chris Brasher as pacemakers, and remembers that, as he faced the final bend out in front "the arms of the world were waiting to receive me, if only I reached the tape without slackening my speed. If I faltered, there would be no arms to hold me and the world would be a cold forbidding place, because I had been so close." He crossed the line in 3 mins 59.6 secs and the world went mad.

This was in the days when sport was an amateur business, and Bannister modestly celebrated his achievement at Vincent's Club in Oxford with a wine glass of tap water laced with salt, followed by a half-pint of shandy. Then he went back to work. As a doctor, he became a respected neurologist, but he remained close to his sport and was knighted for his work as the first independent chairman of the Sports Council, where he played a major role in starting the boom in multi-facility sports centres and was a key figure in drawing attention to the dangers of drug abuse in sport, long before the authorities began to stamp down on the practice. Between 1985 and 1993, as Sir Roger Bannister, he returned to Oxford to become Master of Pembroke College. "I have always felt that Oxford was, in a sense, my emotional home – academically and in other respects," he said on his installation.

At the end of Iffley Road is Iffley itself, a rural enclave within the city boundaries, the heart of which is protected as a conservation area. Within this village stands the beautiful Norman church of St Mary the Virgin, one of the most perfect twelfth-century churches in the south of England, and beyond this runs the River Thames through Iffley lock, still an island of tranquility and the site of one of the oldest existing locks in Britain, having first been built here in 1632.

Down the river a little further, stands Sandford Lock and just before the lock, at the weir, is a pool known as Sandford Lasher. This was the scene of a tragedy in 1921 which links Oxford with yet another children's classic. James Barrie's eternal children's play *Peter Pan* has no distinct link with Oxford like *Alice in Wonderland* or *The Hobbit*, but here, just outside the city boundaries, the boy who inspired Barrie's play, died in a tragic accident.

Michael Llewelyn Davies was the youngest of the five brothers to whom Barrie gave a home on the death of their parents, his friends Arthur and Sylvia Llewelyn Davies. *Peter Pan* developed from stories he made up for the boys, whom he loved like a father. After the death of his brother George, Michael, who had always been Barrie's favorite, drew even closer to him and they were to write letters daily to each other for the rest of the boy's life. Michael, up at Christ Church, was never a strong swimmer, but had come to the pool at Sandford with a college friend, Rupert Buxton, in May 1921 to swim. The pool was a known danger spot and Michael got into difficulties; Rupert tried to save him but both young men drowned. Michael's death was a blow from which Barrie never recovered, although ironically it ensured his status as a boy who could never grow up, just like Peter Pan.

Roger Bannister at Iffley Road, 1953 (Oxford Times)

CHAPTER TWELVE

Inspector Morse's Oxford

"We're all of us overqualified in Oxford"

The purists – and there are more than a few of them in Oxford – won't like it but, if anyone has kept the name of Oxford in the international spotlight in recent years, it is not an academic, a Nobel Prize winner, a politician or a writer, but rather a fictional policeman. Chief Inspector Endeavour Morse (as we must now call him – his father had a thing about Captain Cook) burst upon the world on January 6, 1987, when Central Television showed a two-hour adaptation of Colin Dexter's novel *The Dead of Jericho*.

The independent television companies were at the time desperately looking for a detective series to rival the successful adaptations of Agatha Christie's Miss Marple stories, which had been successful for some years on the BBC. Agatha Christie, of course, had lived only a few miles from Oxford and is buried in Cholsey churchyard. The list of Oxfordshire-based crime fiction writers is astonishing with J.I.M. Stewart, P.D. James, Michael Dibdin, James McClure, Iain Pears, Margaret Yorke and Dorothy L. Sayers all at one time based here.

In 1987 Colin Dexter (b.1930) was one among many, but Central producer Kenny McBain came up with a winning formula that involved

Dexter's clever plots, his appealing central character, Morse, and the limitless possibilities of Oxford as a backdrop. From the start, McBain intended something very special; the Morse films were shot on high-quality 16mm film rather than the usual videotape. And they were made to run for two hours, then a revolutionary idea and quite a gamble, as it asked viewers to stay interested for longer than the average feature film. The gamble paid off; more than 13 million British viewers tuned in for *The Dead of Jericho*, and came back with their friends for future episodes. The UK audience rose to 18 million, making Morse the ratings equivalent of a royal wedding or an F.A. Cup Final.

There have now been 32 television films, swiftly exhausting Colin Dexter's twelve full-length novels, moving on to develop some of his unfinished ideas and eventually coming up with entirely new Morse stories, whose connection with Dexter was minimal. It is hardly surprising, then, that the quality of the series has declined slightly over the years, with the written-for-TV episodes gradually filling with clichés and Morse's idiosyncrasies being exaggerated.

The novels themselves have changed little, although Sgt Lewis has become more like the TV character than he was in the early days and, for modern editions, Colin Dexter has gone back and swapped Morse's Lancia for the maroon Jaguar MkII 2.4 which became his television trademark. The success of the Morse series cannot be overestimated. There is little doubt that visitors to Oxford from all over the world recognize landmarks not because they have seen them in travel books, but because they know them from the Morse films. In Oxford one can now follow Inspector Morse trails and even take part in Inspector Morse pub crawls. There is, inevitably, an Inspector Morse society – run, ironically, from Cambridge.

The history of Endeavour Morse, ferreted out from the novels by Christopher Bird, runs parallel for much of its route with the history of Colin Dexter and there can be little doubt that the one is the alter-ego of the other. Although Dexter includes himself in one or two stories – anagrammatized as Rex de Lincto, "short, fat, balding and slightly deaf" in *The Inside Story* – he really appears as his own hero. Both were born in Lincolnshire in September 1930; both did National Service in the Royal Signals (Dexter, of course, became a Morse code expert); and both went on to university, though there their paths diverged, with Dexter going to Christ's College, Cambridge and Morse to St John's, Oxford. Both are lovers of crosswords – Colin Dexter was a compiler for *The Oxford Times* and a great fan of an earlier master, the banker Sir Jeremy Morse! He has been five times the national champion in the fiendishly difficult *Observer* Ximenes/Azed puzzle-solving competitions.

Inspector Morse on location (Oxford Times)

Morse never got his degree; an entanglement with one Wendy Spencer, an undergraduate at St Hilda's College, brought his academic hopes to an untimely conclusion. It was almost as a last resort that he tried his luck in the police force, working his way up to Chief Inspector rank but certain never to rise any higher. We know that his mother died when he was fifteen and that he detested (the feeling was mutual) his step-mother Gwen. There was a much younger step-sister, Joyce, but that is as far as family goes – he famously never married, though he was engaged to Susan Fallon who threw him over for a brilliant law professor. Susan turns up in the TV film *Dead on Time*, leaving her old lover anguished when she kills herself.

Morse is a typical North Oxford man; he lives in a ground-floor flat in a house in Leys Close, somewhere between the Woodstock and Banbury Roads. Don't go looking, it is not really there, but these streets are full of large villas, many split into flats, which swallow self-sufficient characters like Morse.

After Cambridge, Colin Dexter became a classics master, but increasing deafness caused him problems and he transferred to the University of Oxford Delegacy of Local Examinations, where he became senior assistant secretary. He was 44 when he published his first crime novel, *Last Bus to Woodstock*, and has gone on to win Silver, Gold and Diamond Daggers, the Oscars of the Crime Writers' Association. Like Morse, Dexter is very much a North Oxford man, living somewhere along the never-ending Banbury Road. He is not shy about his fame, lending his celebrity support at functions all over the city, but he can as often be seen pottering about the shops in Summertown, or walking home with his morning newspaper along Banbury Road.

North Oxford

North Oxford, Morse's instinctive habitat, was open countryside until the mid-nineteenth century. Suburban Summertown and Wolvercote were then remote hamlets. The familiar story of the whole area suddenly sprouting family-sized villas in the 1870s when the Royal Commission abolished the celibacy rule for college Fellows – and an army of dons rushing to get married and out of college – is only part of the truth. Building started around Summertown in the 1820s and around Norham Gardens, just north of the Parks, in the 1830s. During the course of the century, the two developments spread towards each other and westwards and northwards, the length of the Banbury and Woodstock roads, on the long thin stretch of land sandwiched between the Cherwell and the Thames.

This was, and remains, a decidedly middle-class area, quite unlike the rows of terraces growing up at the same time in Jericho or Grandpont to the south. There was a confidence about the new inhabitants that was matched by the confidence of the new architecture, partly Italianate palatial but mostly domestic Gothic, with villas of three and four storeys – detached along the two main roads and semi-detached in the side streets.

Those who did not live there mocked it, and "North Oxford" as an adjective came to be applied to a way of life which revolved around good works and earnest discussion. In his undergraduate days, the Irish poet Louis MacNeice wrote of:

> *the residential district of North Oxford, with its neo-gothic architecture and its population of cranks. Anyone driving into Oxford from the north could know where he was from the spectacle of fanatical and fantastic old maids upon bicycles...ecclesiastical porches, baronial turrets, bad stained glass in the lavatory window; the Englishman's home is his ragbag.*

To the young John Betjeman, however, this was a land of comfortable academic security. In his verse autobiography *Summoned by Bells*, the future Poet Laureate remembers his days at the Dragon School:

> *Show me thy road, Crick, in the early spring:*
> *Laurel and privet and laburnum ropes*
> *And gabled-gothic houses gathered round*
> *Thy mothering spire, St Philip and St James.*
> *Here by the low brick semi-private walls*
> *Bicycling past a trotting butcher's-cart*
> *I glimpsed, behind lace curtains, silver hair*
> *Of sundry old Professors. Here were friends*
> *Of Ruskin, Newman, Pattison and Froude*
> *Among their books and plants and photographs*
> *In comfortable twilight.*

Even today, when most of the larger houses have been taken over for non-domestic purposes or split into multi-occupation student flats, there is still a North Oxford type, and plenty of people, without any connection with the university, are happy to move in to share the intellectual and cultural atmosphere of the place.

Tucked into the parade of shops which marks out Summertown on Banbury Road is the headquarters of what is probably Oxford's most important gift to the world in the second half of the twentieth century. Oxfam, one of the world's great overseas aid charities, was born as the Oxford Committee for Famine Relief in 1942. It came about after a discussion at the Friends' Meeting House in St Giles' addressed the problem of starving children in Allied countries in Europe, suffering because of the blockade that was meant to keep provisions from the Nazis who were occupying most of the continent. The first Oxfam contribution of £3,200 was channelled through the Greek Red Cross in

1943. This was followed by a Famine Relief Week, with Greek dancing, films and concerts, organized by Oxfam's secretary, Cecil Jackson-Cole. It was Jackson-Cole, a self-made businessman, who realized that the charity would have to be run on business-like lines. He was a difficult and intolerant man, known to throw typewriters about the office when he got angry, but he went on also to found Help the Aged and Action in Distress. Fund-raising efforts continued to be focused on the plight of refugees in Europe after the war and Oxfam's sights were not broadened until 1951 when it launched an appeal to help ease the effects of a famine in Bihar in India. Since then, its operations, always implemented in partnership with local community groups, have brought positive change to almost every area of the developing world.

Norham Gardens in the nineteenth century (Oxford Times)

Lady Margaret Hall

At the bottom of Norham Gardens, the archetypal North Oxford road, lies the imposing gatehouse of Lady Margaret Hall. Behind the brick facade is a shrine of women's education, for LMH, as it is known throughout Oxford, was the first women's college in the city. It was possibly the University Reform Act in 1877 which thrust women's further education into the realm of public discussion in Oxford. For the learned, intelligent men who taught at Oxford, took wives who were often intelligent themselves, and they had daughters who grew up on the edge of the academic life, shone at local schools and wanted to share the education they saw around them.

In the 1870s women were allowed – on special occasions – to sit in on college lectures and even to sit for certain university examinations. In 1878 Elizabeth Wordsworth, the daughter and sister of Anglican bishops (and, more interestingly, great-niece of the poet William Wordsworth) was named as the first Principal of a hall of residence for women members of the Church of England. It was called Lady Margaret Hall, after Lady Margaret Beaufort, the mother of Henry VII and a great patron of education – she founded two colleges in Cambridge, endowed chairs of Divinity at both Oxford and Cambridge and was patron of the first English printer, William Caxton.

LMH opened the floodgates; the following year Somerville College was formed for women students not bound by the Anglican church and within fifteen years, St Hugh's Hilda's and Anne's were all established.

Early women students faced inevitable disapproval from traditionalists in the male preserve that was Oxford University. They would assemble in a group outside the gates of a college where lectures were to be held and then were escorted in by chaperones. They were, of course, forbidden to mix with the men. By 1892, LMH had begun to offer its own lectures, but it was not until 1920 that women were actually allowed to take degrees and be members of the university. In 1926 LMH officially became a college.

LMH graduates have been distinguished rather than household names. They include the educationist Baroness (Mary) Warnock, the biographer Elizabeth Longford and her daughter, the novelist and popular historian Antonia Fraser and the erstwhile Prime Minister of Pakistan, Benazir Bhutto. However, this bastion to women's education is now entirely emancipated. It allowed men in from 1979, is completely mixed-sex and even has a male Principal.

Somerville

Four of the five women's colleges were established in North Oxford. Somerville was the next to be founded and has always been the most prestigious. Built at the top of St Giles', it has, over the years, attracted women of fiercely independent minds possessing intelligence of matching ferocity. In the days before mixed colleges, Somerville and the other women's colleges dominated the Norrington Table, the annual and unofficial league table of Oxford colleges according to final degree results. This was because the cream of the country's Oxford-based women were pushed together in just five colleges, while the men were spread among more than twenty. Somerville is now mixed-sex, allowing men in from 1994, but not without a tremendous rearguard action from the existing women students who had chosen it largely because of its traditional all-woman atmosphere.

Somerville's independence of mind stems from its origins. When a committee was formed in the 1870s to set up a women's hall to accommodate women students from outside the city, it was split on whether the hall should cater simply for those who were members of the Anglican Church. In the end, it decided to go with the Anglicans and Lady Margaret Hall was founded. But the dissenters would not be beaten and set about opening a rival college, entry qualifications for which did not include any religious obligation. For its name, it did not go back to medieval saints or royalty but chose to be associated with the recently deceased Mary Somerville, who had been regarded as one of the great women scientists of the age, though self-taught and a wife and mother.

Somerville was the first women's college to set up its own teachers, the first to call itself a college and the first to offer research opportunities. Although it has been predominantly an arts-orientated college, two of its most famous members were chemists. The first, Dorothy Hodgkin (1910-94), was undergraduate and then Fellow and was awarded the Nobel Prize for chemistry in 1964 in recognition of her work on penicillin, vitamin B12 and insulin. The second, Margaret Roberts, was a pupil of Hodgkin, but gave up chemistry after graduating to go into politics and became the first woman British Prime Minister. Margaret Thatcher (b.1925) came up to Somerville in 1943 in the middle of the war and was, from the start, a member of the University Conservative Association, campaigning in the 1945 General Election for the city's Conservative MP Quintin Hogg – later to become her long-serving Lord Chancellor. In her fourth and final year at Oxford, Margaret was elected president of the Conservative Association, inviting prominent politicians to address the faithful; speakers who included two more future Prime Ministers, Alec Douglas-Home and Anthony Eden.

From Oxford, Margaret Roberts went to train as a barrister at

Lincoln's Inn, London, married the millionaire businessman Denis Thatcher and was elected as an MP in 1959 and leader of the Conservative Party in 1975. In 1979 she became Britain's first woman Prime Minister and served in the post longer than any other PM in the twentieth century.

Her old college remembered her and made her an honorary Fellow in 1970, but when it came to the university's turn to honor her, things went badly wrong. Traditionally all new Prime Ministers get an honorary doctorate within a year of taking office. It is a way of recognizing their achievement and also, no doubt, to encourage them to think favorably of Oxford. In Mrs Thatcher's case, the university dithered for five years before recommending her for the scarlet gown and velvet bonnet of a doctor of civil law. But by 1985 she had become the most socially divisive premier for decades – those who supported her doted on her, those who opposed her hated her. Her government was also perceived as having cut back sharply on funding for scientific and medical research and on student grants. So, instead of the university's nominations for 1985 Encaenia being nodded through by a dozen or so dons at Congregation, some 1,400 senior members of the colleges packed the Sheldonian Theatre for a long debate on her merits, and almost everyone was staggered by the strength of feeling against her as dons voted 738-319 to deny her the honor.

No decision taken in Oxford since the war caused so much controversy. Again the nation was divided. Thatcherites were apoplectic; the vote was seen as an indication of the inward-looking attitude of Oxford University and deplored as "reducing honourary degrees to mere politics." As for the the anti-Thatcher forces, they praised the University for its courage in making a political stand and for showing that honorary degrees "ought not to be regarded as an automatic right." Mrs Thatcher, though clearly stung by the snub, remained aloof and said: "If they do not wish to confer the honour, I am the last person who would wish to receive it."

Fences were never mended and after leaving office Mrs T. handed over all her personal and political papers to Cambridge University. She remained on good terms with her old college, however, returning to Somerville in 1991 to open the Margaret Thatcher Centre, a £4 million project into which she had put some of her own money.

Somerville had already produced another prime minister, for Indira Gandhi, of India, had been a student just before the war. Other graduates include a number of major literary talents, including Vera Brittain, Margaret Kennedy, Winifred Holtby, Rose Macauley, Iris Murdoch and Dorothy L. Sayers.

St Anne's & St Hugh's

St Anne's College was the last of the women's colleges and grew out of the Society of Oxford Home Students, which was formed in 1879 for the higher education of Oxford women themselves, those who could live at home as daughters or wives of dons or as students from the local girls' schools. They were taught for years in the houses of dons from the men's colleges who were sympathetic to the women's cause. By the Second World War the number of Home Students had swollen to more than 200. A benefactor enabled the Society to buy a site between Woodstock and Banbury Roads, where a library and lecture rooms were built, and in 1952 the landowners, St John's College, sold the freehold of the whole of Bevington Road at a knock-down price and St Anne's College was formed.

Former students include Ivy Williams, the first woman barrister in Britain, the poet Elizabeth Jennings and Baroness Young, Mrs Thatcher's Tory leader in the House of Lords. Among the Fellows for many years, as a philosophy don, was Iris Murdoch (1919-1999), one of the most accomplished of post-war British novelists. Dame Iris lived in North Oxford and said: "Oxford is the place I really prefer to be, because one is constantly surrounded by clever and imaginative people – they are all on the doorstep."

Since her death from Alzheimer's disease, Oxford's most important literary figure has been the novelist Ian McEwan, who lives in nearby Park Town, the city's smartest address. McEwan (b.1948) was named as one of Britain's twenty best young novelists in the early 1980s. Many on that list have sunk into obscurity but some, like McEwan, Salman Rushdie and Martin Amis, have matured to become the new literary establishment. McEwan gained full recognition in 1998, when his novel *Amsterdam* won the Booker Prize, the country's premier award for fiction...though most critics agreed the prize-winning book was far from his best.

In 1886, Elizabeth Wordsworth, the first Principal at LMH, rented a villa in Norham Road to accommodate young women unable to afford to be at her college. She called it St Hugh's Hall. Other houses in the area were bought to extend the hall and in 1916 the site between Banbury and Woodstock Roads was acquired when St Hugh's College was custom-built.

Among its graduates have been the veteran Labour politician, Barbara Castle, the writers Brigid Brophy and Mary Renault and the Nobel Peace Prize winner Aung San Suu Kyi, who for years has been under house arrest in Burma while her husband and sons continued to live in North Oxford.

The early days of St Hugh's saw it at the centre of an amazing story which we might today be tempted to think of as a huge publicity stunt. It involved the first Principal of the college, Charlotte (Annie) Moberly, a dour, stern-faced woman, and her successor and for many years, vice-principal, Eleanor Jourdain who, in 1901, took a holiday together in France and visited Versailles. In *An Adventure*, an account of the escapade published later, they claimed that they took a wrong turn and got lost and suddenly found themselves in the company of people in eighteenth-century costume. These included a woman who could only have been Marie Antoinette herself. The story was, of course, a sensation and has been argued over for decades. The boring explanation was that they had simply stumbled upon a tableau of locals in fancy dress, but the ladies themselves insisted on details which firmly placed the scene in the eighteenth century.

Those of a supernatural bent immediately decided that the two friends had slipped through a hole in time and, as they were distinguished academics, it was impossible that they could be trying to hoodwink the nation. Detractors, of course, pointed to two sexually repressed spinsters, full of romantic notions, whose story could not stand up to the closest scrutiny. The ladies themselves became furious if anyone disbelieved them, although Eleanor Jourdain's credibility slips a bit when one hears that, back in North Oxford, she also "saw" a medieval gallows, attended by executioners, priests and onlookers.

Postgraduate Colleges

North Oxford also contains three of the university's newest postgraduate colleges. Next door but one to Somerville lies Green College, largely in the grounds of the Radcliffe Infirmary. It was founded in 1979 to concentrate on training medical students, thanks to a huge gift from the American industrialist Dr Cecil Green (b.1900), who had made his fortune by founding Texas Instruments. Green was born in Manchester, but is a naturalized American citizen, and his generosity to all manner of schools and universities in the U.S., Canada, Australia and Britain have marked him as one of the great philanthropists of the twentieth century. He was given an honorary knighthood in 1991.

Although it is so new, Green College incorporates one of Oxford's great landmarks, the eighteenth-century Radcliffe Observatory. It was built by the young James Wyatt and is the first example of neo-classicism in Oxford, based upon the Tower of the Winds built in first-century BC Athens. Sir Nikolaus Pevsner believed it to be "architecturally, the finest observatory of Europe." When it stopped being used as an astronomical observatory in the 1930s, it was bought by Lord Nuffield, who donated it to the university.

Nuffield was also responsible for turning the Radcliffe Infirmary from a provincial teaching hospital into one of Britain's leading centres for medical research and treatment. It was built in the late eighteenth century with money from Dr John Radcliffe's will. Nuffield's £2m gift, in the days before the Second World War, set up professorships in Medicine, Surgery, Obstetrics and Gynaecology, Therapeutics and Anaesthetics, and others followed later in Orthopaedic Surgery, Social Medicine and Plastic Surgery. It was in this building in 1941 that Howard Florey first tested penicillin on a human patient.

For international prestige, little St Antony's College sets an example with which even the mighty Balliols and Magdalens cannot compete. For St Antony's, which became a college of the university only in 1965, is Oxford's centre for international studies and its Fellows, visiting professors and some of its students are among the most eminent experts in their fields in Britain. Whenever foreign affairs are discussed on television or Radio 4, listen to see how often the interviewed guru is described as "Fellow of St Antony's College,

Oxford."

The college was founded in 1948 by Antonin Besse, a French-born shipowner who made his great fortune in the Middle East. Deciding he had too much money, he was determined to found a college in France, but the French government said "no," so M. Besse came to Oxford, where he offered £1.5 million for a postgraduate college on the understanding that a third of its members should be French. This unworkable condition was soon dropped, although St Antony's has always had a very large proportion of non-British students.

Wolfson College was founded in the 1960s and grew up on the banks of the Cherwell at about the same time as St Catherine's to the south. It is a graduate college with an inclination towards the natural sciences and had, as its founding president, Isaiah Berlin (1909-97), the philosopher and one of the most influential Oxford minds of the twentieth century. Berlin's appointment attracted grants of £1.5 million each from the Wolfson and Ford foundations. What was going to be known as Iffley College promptly changed its name to Wolfson College after its benefactor Sir Isaac Wolfson, the Scottish philanthropist and businessman. In 1973 University College Cambridge was also renamed Wolfson College after he made a huge donation there too. Thus Isaac Wolfson became only the second man in history to have colleges named after him at both Oxford and Cambridge. The first was Jesus.

Keble College

Standing opposite the Natural History Museum, that temple to Darwinian thought, stands Keble College, conceived as a monument to the Oxford Movement. Edward Pusey said of it: "Keble lies as if it were to give a broadside for Christianity to the museum." And yet, ironically, Keble was to be a breaker of traditions in Oxford and the start of something new. In the years before his death in 1866, John Keble, the man whose 1833 sermon in the University church had launched the Oxford Movement, had been one of a group of influential churchmen who were worried about the Anglican church's loss of power and respect in Oxford and the country as a whole. Successive governments had opened Parliament and the Civil Service to non-conformists and had allowed civil marriages. In Oxford, non-conformists were now allowed to take degrees and the natural sciences were becoming established as suitable subjects for study.

After Keble's death, his friends decided to use some of the profits from the sale of his wildly popular book of verse, *The Christian Year* and to launch a public appeal for more funds to found a new college in his memory. Their other aim was to make an Oxford education available to young men of lesser means. Keble College was to be for those with brains but without enough money or influence to get into one of the old-fashioned colleges. It would be run by an external council with the power to decide the fate of the college and its members, even to the extent of removing the whole body from Oxford if they felt the university were going too far down the path to atheism.

This half-hearted attachment to the university had repercussions, and many Oxford traditionalists took a dislike to Keble College from the start. This antagonism increased as the college buildings took shape. The architect was William Butterfield and his design was radical. For a start, the college was to be built not of stone like all its predecessors, but of brick. There was to be a dramatic change, too, in the distribution of rooms; they were not to be, as in other colleges, clustered around staircases, but joined by internal corridors. But the most dramatic effect of all was to be in the design of the college's outer walls. As brick cannot be carved, Butterfield decorated its surfaces with bands of different colors.

For more than a century, smug undergraduates from other Oxford colleges have taken their visitors to laugh at garish Keble. Today's walls carry a patina of grime which subdues the original shocking impact. It was so dramatic that John Ruskin gave up his daily walks in the University Parks for fear of setting his eyes on this loathed construction. The children's author, Beatrix Potter, visiting Oxford, said of Keble:

It struck me as decidedly ugly. Why, with such beautiful old buildings to copy, cannot they get anything better than glaring red and white brick edifices, which remind one of a London suburb?

To get any idea of Butterfield's original intention, one has today to go into his chapel, with its mind-boggling polychrome busy-ness. The chapel was paid for by one William Gibbs of Bristol, whose fortune, to the delight of many of Keble's detractors, had been made from guano – bird droppings. So gaudy was Butterfield's chapel that he insisted no paintings should be hung there, so when Martha Combe, widow of Thomas Combe, director of the Clarendon Press, presented the college with William Holman Hunt's religious masterpiece, *The Light of the World,* Mrs Combe had to pay for the construction of a side chapel in which it could be displayed.

Holman Hunt's picture, painted strictly from nature in true Pre-Raphaelite style, had been exhibited at the Royal Academy twenty years earlier and was described then by Ruskin as "one of the very noblest works of sacred art ever produced in this or any other age." It was to become the best-known sacred image of Victorian Britain. When in later years Holman Hunt heard that the college authorities were charging visitors sixpence a time to view the painting, he was furious and had a copy made – a larger copy – which he presented to St Paul's Cathedral in London where it could be seen free of charge by a much larger public.

From the very beginning, the aims and ideas of Keble's founders were to be watered down. Their mistake lay in their choice of Edward Talbot as first Warden. He opened the doors of Keble to a wide range of ideas and insisted on admitting men reading the widest range of subjects. He even encouraged the teaching of science and welcomed the idea of evolution to theological thinking. Although in the first half of the twentieth century, Keble produced a formidable array of bishops, the ties with the Church of England were gradually loosened. By 1930, undergraduates no longer had to be Anglicans, the restriction was removed from Fellows in 1952, and the final change came in 1969 when it was decided that even the Warden no longer had to be a Church of England minister.

For most of the twentieth century, Keble was one of Oxford's largest undergraduate colleges and, besides the various bishops, famous alumni include the tenor Peter Pears, the poet Geoffrey Hill and Chad Varah, the founder of the Samaritans.

University Museum of Natural History

Opposite Keble, as the standard-bearer of the new Science Area that so affronted Pusey, stands the University Museum of Natural History. It came into being in the 1850s when the natural sciences were being accepted as an appropriate study for undergraduates. There were scattered facilities for scientists all around Oxford, but it was decided to bring them together under one roof and, in 1855, the foundation stone was laid in what was then part of the University Parks. Around the walls of the glass-covered quadrangle stand doorways bearing the titles of the university's most senior scientific academics. They are picked out in the stone rather as the earliest arts departments are highlighted in the Schools Quad. For how long the illustrious gentlemen were to be found behind those doors is hard to say: what is certain is that they have now all spread out to head their own empires in other buildings in the Science Area nearby.

The building is a vast neo-Gothic cathedral to the new god Science, the first major public building in the Gothic style since the Houses of Parliament twenty years earlier. The interior, which is stunning in its impact, owes much to the influence of John Ruskin. The glass roof is supported by slender columns of iron and a railway station-like vaulting, and this ironwork is decorated with delicately wrought foliage and fruits. The central court, overlooked by statues and busts of eminent scientists, is surrounded by a two-tiered arcade and here the columns of the arches are themselves exhibits, for each is carved from a different British rock. This is by far the most welcoming and most interesting of the university's four museums. It seeks to tell the story of life on earth, with cases full of stuffed animals and preserved exhibits, interspersed with magnificent skeletons, including a cast of the dinosaur Iguanodon. Oxfordshire's limestone is a particularly good hunting ground for fossil dinosaurs, and the largest expanse of dinosaur footprints in Europe was found at Ardley Quarry a few miles to the north of the city. Casts of the prints of Megalosaurus have been incorporated into the lawn in front of the museum.

The museum's other prize exhibit is the Dodo. An example of this flightless bird, which was hunted to extinction in the seventeenth century, was kept stuffed here for many years, alongside John Savery's remarkable painting. Eventually, the poor bird became so moth-eaten that its remains were burned, although the skull and one foot were saved and put back on display. It was this bird, well-known to Charles Dodgson, that he incorporated into the tale of *Alice's Adventures in*

Wonderland, taking its part himself for, with his stammer, he would introduce himself as Do-Do-Dodgson. Recent research by museum staff has suggested that early accounts of the Dodo exaggerated its grotesque features and a more likely representation is now displayed alongside the treasured relics.

The museum is a working university department, and behind the locked doors around the arcades lies the collection of millions of specimens of animals and plants which serve as a research facility for scientists from all over the world. At the back lies the route to the Pitt-Rivers Museum, a mind-boggling conglomeration of ethnological curiosities from the native peoples of the world, which has clearly proved impossible to catalogue or display in an organized manner. This is a collection where one must simply wander and find what treasures one can.

It was in a room at the Natural History Museum that one of the most famous events of nineteenth-century Oxford took place. Most people know how, in 1860, Science delivered a knockout blow to traditional church-dominated thinking in the argument over Charles Darwin's Theory of Evolution. It was here that "soapy" Samuel Wilberforce, the stuffy Bishop of Oxford, tried to ridicule Darwin's theories by asking the scientist T.H. Huxley whether it was on his grandfather's side or his grandmother's that he claimed descent from a monkey. Amid the laughter, Huxley hit straight back by proclaiming that he would rather be descended from a monkey than from a Bishop like Wilberforce. The meeting ended in uproar, with tight-laced old ladies fainting and the hero of the hour being chaired shoulder-high from the scene of Science's greatest victory.

It is a wonderful story, but unfortunately that is exactly what it is, a story. For this account of the proceedings was never heard until 38 years after the event. No-one who was there remembers things happening quite like that. Journalists from *The Athenaeum* and *Jackson's Oxford Journal* were present but neither of their reports make reference to this exchange, nor to its remarkable effect upon the company. Another disciple of Darwin, Joseph Hooker, recounting the events in a letter to Darwin himself, said

> *Huxley answered admirably, and turned the tables, but he could not*
> *throw his voice over so large an assembly, nor command the audience;*

and he did not allude to Sam's weak points, nor put the matter in a form or way that carried the audience.

The Oxford meeting was not meant to be a showdown between Darwin's followers and Wilberforce. It was a routine meeting of the British Association for the Advancement of Science, a group of people from all walks of life with an interest in science. But Darwin's book, *The Origin of Species*, had been published only a few months earlier and, though his ideas on natural selection and the survival of the fittest were already well-known, the book itself had sparked off a huge debate between those who believed that each species had gradually developed from some simpler one and those who felt sure that "rock pigeons were what rock pigeons always had been." So this June Saturday's "Botany and Zoology" meeting attracted a great crowd to hear Professor J.W. Draper of New York University talk on "Darwin and Social Progress," knowing that Bishop Wilberforce, a vice-president of the British Association, would no doubt wish to have his say. Between 700 and 1,000 people turned up at the museum, so many that the meeting was moved to the library.

Now Bishop Samuel Wilberforce was no reactionary cleric blustering fundamentalist certainties about the Creation. On the contrary, he was a prime example of those Victorian churchmen who were the backbone of the amateur scientific community. Wilberforce was, among other things, a respected ornithologist, and he had been asked to review *The Origin of Species* in the leading magazine *The Quarterly Review*. It was a serious review too; Darwin himself wrote of it to Hooker: "It is uncommonly clever; it picks out with skill all the most conjectural parts, and brings forward well all the difficulties." and to another friend: "The Bishop makes a very telling case against me by accumulating several instances where I speak doubtfully."

Back to the museum: Draper droned on, applying Darwin's hypothesis to human society, and Wilberforce did not speak until two boring hours had passed and Huxley himself had turned down an offer to speak. It is likely that the bishop tried to lighten the proceedings and he probably misjudged the mood of the meeting when he made his flippant remark about monkeys and grandparents. Huxley's own version of his reply was:

If then, said I, the question is put to me would I rather have a miserable
ape for a grandfather or a man highly endowed by nature and possessed
of great means of influence and yet who employs those faculties and that
influence for the mere purpose of introducing ridicule into a grave scien-
tific discussion – I unhesitatingly affirm my preference for the ape.

Hardly the great snub of legend. There was, he says, laughter rather than
uproar, and the debate continued for some time, though it is clear from
both contemporary reports that, at the end of the meeting, the majority
of the audience still agreed with the Bishop's objections.

However, the Darwinians were essentially evangelists, and, convinced
that they had struck a blow for the evolutionary theory in the very heart
of High Anglicanism, they proceeded to tell and retell the tale of that
summer afternoon in Oxford. As is so often the case, each retelling made
Huxley appear more heroic and Wilberforce more crushed. Darwin's
biographers said that the meeting "was destined to be blown out of all
proportion, to become the best-known victory of the nineteenth century,
save Waterloo." And J.R. Lucas, writing in *The Historical Journal,* called it
"in itself entirely unimportant, one of the many skirmishes which took
place in Oxford during the field days organised by the British Association."

The library in which the meeting took place is not open to the
public, although a plaque outside the door records the event. In fact,
once through the security-bolted doors, it is almost impossible now to
picture the scene, for the vast room has been sub-divided into smaller
rooms on two floors.

The University Parks, covering some 100 acres, were meadow walks
for centuries before the university bought the land from Merton
College. During the Civil War the area had been the main exercise area
for the Royalist troops and when King Charles II stayed in Oxford in
1685 to escape the plague in London, he exercised his new King Charles
Spaniels here. Shortly after the land was acquired, the University
Museum was built at its southern end and more land was given over to
accommodate the spreading Science Area.

Over the last 150 years, trees have been planted, flower beds
cultivated and lawns maintained. The Parks (it is always plural, for
apparently this is a combination of an old and a new park) is an area
for perambulation like none other in Oxford. At its heart stands the

University Cricket Ground with its pavilion by T.G. Jackson, architect of the Examination Schools. The university cricket team has given a fine training to many magnificent Test cricketers. Until quite recently, Oxford would play all the first-class county teams here each year and one could spend all summer in the Parks, watching first-class cricket free of charge, that would have cost a pricy season ticket anywhere else. The Oxford-Cambridge Varsity Match is still the high point of the cricket season, though, and is played at Lord's, home of the MCC. Among the great cricketing names who started out playing for Oxford University at the Parks, were Plum Warner (Oriel), C.B. Fry (Wadham), Douglas Jardine (New College) Colin Cowdrey (Brasenose), M.J.K. Smith (St Edmund Hall), the Nawab of Pataudi (Balliol) and Imran Khan (Keble).

North Oxford is littered with schools, most of them private, although The Cherwell School is the sort of state school that has middle-class parents wondering why they should bother paying for their children's education. Among the independent schools is Oxford High School for Girls, an establishment with a formidable record for producing girls of the highest intellectual capabilities. Since the Government introduced league tables of school exam results, Oxford High has consistently been rated one of the very best in Britain.

St Edward's, the boys' school in Woodstock Road, has never had the same reputation for exam results, although having a son here carries a high social cachet. The war-hero Douglas Bader (1910-82) won a scholarship to the school in 1923 when he was thirteen. On his very first day he was caned by his housemaster for kicking his new bowler hat – part of the uniform – around the hall. In 1926 his mother wrote to the school saying she would probably not be able to afford to keep him there and in 1927 he almost died from rheumatic fever caught at the school. Yet he recovered to become a prefect and captain of both rugby and cricket. The actor, Laurence Olivier was another old boy.

But Oxford's most famous school is for younger children. The Dragon School, between Bardwell Road and the river, is a remarkable institution which to some personifies the Oxford temperament – that is Oxford the community rather than Oxford the university. Among prep schools, Dragon was always revolutionary. Its origins go back to the 1870s when dons, newly freed from celibacy, produced sons who needed educating. A group of such fathers got together to found the Oxford Preparatory School.

This dull title and any indication of dullness was swept away when, in 1877, Charles Cotterill Lynam was appointed headmaster. Lynam, known throughout his 34 years as head as "the Skipper," had views about the education of young boys which were, to say the least, not in line with the principles generally accepted within the Victorian public schools system. Rather than herding his young charges into pre-ordained patterns, ready to move on to public school, university and colonial administration, Skipper wanted Dragon boys to be inquisitive, independent-minded and far-ranging in their studies and interests. When it came to uniform, he rejected the restrictive knickerbockers and Eton collars adopted by other prep schools and introduced the style that prevails to this day, faded blue corduroys, with no tie. Skipper – he encouraged, even insisted upon, the nickname – was followed successively as headmaster by Hum, Joc and Inky, but his ideals have survived, although after his time Dragons became a little more disciplined.

No-one is really sure how the school got its name, though it is widely thought that boys first called themselves Dragons when forming sports teams to play against those of the Rev H.B. George – Georges against Dragons. The school still takes half boarders, half day-pupils, as successive heads felt it helped make the school more part of the Oxford community. Academic prowess has been – seemingly almost accidentally – remarkable, and there are very few public schools which would not welcome Dragons into the fold, even though some masters still fear the Dragon independence of mind.

The roll call of school alumni is as impressive as that of almost any Oxford college; old boys include the Labour Party leader Hugh Gaitskill, Poet Laureate Sir John Betjeman, TV inquisitor David Dimbleby, comedians Derek Nimmo and Dave Allen, the biographer Humphrey Carpenter, the anti-nuclear campaigner E.P. Thompson, war hero Leonard Cheshire, dramatist/barrister John Mortimer and novelist Nevile Shute. Old girls – the Dragon has always accommodated a few – include Antonia Fraser, Baroness Young and Naomi Mitchison.

In the lower half of Banbury Road, the great villas, too big for today's smaller families without servants, have been occupied by a series of agencies, language schools and training colleges. Wycliffe Hall, at the junction with Norham Gardens, is an evangelical Anglican theological college, founded in 1877, which trains British and overseas students for a variety of qualifications. In its first 100 years, some 1,500 Anglican priests were trained here, including Donald Coggan who became Archbishop of Canterbury and Stuart Blanch, who was Archbishop of York.

Just beyond the entrance to Somerville stands St Aloysius' Church, Oxford's leading Roman Catholic church, and the second Oxford home of the Jesuit poet, Gerard Manley Hopkins. It was opened in 1875, having been built with bequests from leading Catholics including John Henry Newman, and was designed by Joseph Hansom, the creator of the Hansom Cab. At the ceremony of dedication, Cardinal Henry Manning preached a sermon berating the university for changes in its teaching. Manning (1808-92) got a First at Balliol and was President of the Oxford Union, where he had been a friend of William Gladstone. He was ordained an Anglican priest but was deeply influenced by Newman and followed him in converting to Roman Catholicism in 1851. In 1865, he became the first convert Archbishop of Westminster, and was made a cardinal in 1875, beating Newman by four years.

Only three years after St Aloysius' opened, Gerard Hopkins was sent as assistant priest. He was, of course, delighted to be back in Oxford, but found the city and university had changed. The University Reform Act of the previous year had abolished the celibacy rule for college Fellows, and in 1878 the first women's colleges, LMH and Somerville – next door to the church – started up. Hopkins was unsettled and he failed to hit it off with Fr Parkinson, the priest in charge and another Anglican convert. Despite all this, his ten months back in Oxford were fruitful for his writing, producing two major works, *Duns Scotus's Oxford* and *Binsey Poplars*.

Within a year, it was clear that he was quite unsuitable for the job. He took further parish postings near Manchester and in Liverpool before being sent to the Catholic university in Dublin in 1884 as Professor of Greek, where he died five years later from typhoid. The Jesuits stayed in charge at St Aloysius' until 1981, when they handed it over to the Birmingham diocese.

Little Clarendon Street is an unexpected outpost of student-orientated shops running from the junction of St Giles' and Woodstock

Road towards Walton Street. It comprises college buildings, the grossly ugly University Offices, bijou Chelsea-type shops and an ever-growing number of bars and restaurants. Perhaps the most remarkable thing in the street, however, is a small cast-iron plaque tucked among the dustbins in a service entry at the Jericho end. Its Latin inscription looks as though it might be a memorial tablet to some august academic. However, a translation reads "On this site, Irene Frude, the most kindly landlady of undergraduates of Keble College, provided each day for almost 35 years, enormous breakfasts. Some, with fond memories of this, undertook the placing of this tribute to her in 1976" – it is probably the only Latin memorial to a lodging-house landlady anywhere in the world.

Prince Leopold, Duke of Albany (1853-84), was the youngest of Queen Victoria's children and certainly the most intelligent. Unfortunately, he was also a haemophiliac and epileptic. One of his tutors as a young man was the Rev Robinson Duckworth, who had accompanied Charles Dodgson and the Liddell sisters on the boat trip that led to *Alice's Adventures in Wonderland*. With his Oxford connections, Duckworth helped persuade the Queen that Leopold should attend the university. The Queen was not amused by the idea; she had her doubts about Oxford because of the zealotry of the Anglo-Catholic followers of Newman and Pusey. Leopold did not live in at Christ Church when he came up in 1872, but had Wykeham House at 56 Banbury Road prepared for his use.

The Queen gave him a bad time:

I receive bullying letters and telegrams from 'home sweet home'...I may never drive out here...I can hardly ever invite more than four to dinner and I may never invite any of the softer sex, which is a great pity, as there are such awfully pretty girls here.

The centre of the Prince's social life was the Deanery at Christ Church, where Liddell and his wife and daughters were at home to anyone of note. Leopold fell in love with one of the Liddell girls, possibly Edith, but more likely Alice herself. There was talk of marriage but pressure was put upon the Prince from the highest quarters and he withdrew. During 1874 he was gravely ill on two occasions, coming very close to death, and he left Oxford in 1875, being awarded his degree by diploma.

At the top of Banbury Road, on the other side of the ring road, is Wolvercote Cemetery, now the city's largest, covering 134 acres and filling up since 1889. Its most famous permanent inhabitant is J.R.R. Tolkien, professor of Anglo-Saxon and author of *The Hobbit* and *The Lord of the Rings*. He is buried here with his wife Edith, and their headstone gives both their names and their pet-names for each other. Edith was Luthien and Ronald was Beren, names taken from one of Tolkien's own stories. The city council,which maintains the cemetery, has been forced to recognize how many visitors come to this vast necropolis wanting to pay homage at the Tolkien grave and have signposted it from the main gates.

Also buried here is the novelist Joyce Cary (1888-1957), whose books, including *Mister Johnson* (1939) and *The Horse's Mouth* (1944), made him hugely popular in the 1940s. Here, too, are the parents and brother of Lawrence of Arabia and a large burial plot with a stone inscribed "The Maxwell Family." It was here that the hated media tycoon Robert Maxwell buried his three-year-old daughter who died from leukaemia and his 21-year-old son who died from meningitis and where he planned to be buried himself. In the end, the children remained unaccompanied: after Maxwell's mysterious death at sea in 1991, he was allowed to be buried among the Jewish heroes on the Mount of Olives in Jerusalem.

Cutteslowe

Just before the ring road is the area known as Cutteslowe which, in the 1930s witnessed an almost unimaginable example of class prejudice. In 1933 the city council sold 22 acres of building land between Jackson Road and Banbury Road for the erection of a private estate of middle-class housing. This was right next to the corporation's new Cutteslowe council estate. The Urban Housing Company, which was to build the little private villas, claimed that there was a gentleman's agreement about the sort of tenants the city would allow to live on the Cutteslowe estate and expressed outrage when the council announced plans to house 28 slum-clearance families there.

The company immediately built two large brick walls to divide the up-market properties from their social inferiors. The walls, topped with metal spikes, simply lay incongruously across the roads like miniature Berlin Walls. As a result of this Oxford apartheid, the council tenants had to make a detour of nearly a mile to reach Banbury Road and the children's school.

Militants reacted to the anger of the council tenants and organized a march with bands and pickaxes to tear down the walls. But the crowd of 2,000 which had gathered to watch the event saw the demolition party turned back by a line of police, who warned them that they faced arrest.

The city council declared that the walls breached by-laws and tried, but failed, to get a compulsory purchase order on the two sites. Eventually, councillors took the campaign to Parliament, where in 1938 a committee ordered the company to destroy the walls. It refused, but the council sent in steamrollers to crash through them and workmen with sledgehammers and shovels to finish the job. The very next morning, housing company workmen arrived to rebuild the walls – with council employees close behind. Every time a few bricks were laid, they were immediately knocked down again.

The matter was taken to the High Court for a decision and, in the meantime, gates were put across the roads. The judge who heard the case decided that the company was quite at liberty to build the walls and up they went again. Astonishingly, they stayed up until the council paid £1,000 to buy the sites on which the nine-inch thick walls stood. That worked out at half-a-million pounds an acre and, on March 9, 1959, almost 25 years after they were erected to separate two classes of Oxford citizens, the walls finally came down, ending one of the most shameful episodes in the city's history.

Demolition of the Cutteslowe Wall (Oxford Times)

Further Reading

Batson, Judy G., *Oxford in Fiction*. New York: Garland Publishing, 1989.
Bell, Brian (ed), *Oxford: Insight City Guide*, Singapore: APA, 1990.
Betjeman, John, *An Oxford University Chest*. London: Miles, 1938.
Blair, John, *Anglo-Saxon Oxfordshire*. Stroud: Sutton Publishing, 1994.
Bloxham, Christine, *Portrait of Oxfordshire*. London: Robert Hale, 1982.
Brooke, Christopher and Roger Highfield, *Oxford and Cambridge*. Cambridge: Cambridge University Press, 1988.
Casson, Hugh, *Hugh Casson's Oxford*. London: Phaidon, 1988.
Catto, J. (ed), *The History of the University of Oxford*. Oxford: OUP, 1984-94.
De-la-Noy, Michael, *Exploring Oxford*. London, Headline, 1991.
Dougill, John, *Oxford in English Literature*. Ann Arbor: University of Michigan Press, 1998.
Eddershaw, David, *The Civil War in Oxfordshire*. Stroud: Sutton, 1995.
Hibbert, Christopher, *The Encyclopaedia of Oxford*. Basingstoke: Macmillan, 1988.
Honey, Derek, *An Encyclopaedia of Oxford Pubs, Inns and Taverns*. Oxford: Oakwood Press, 1998.
Jebb, Miles, *The Colleges of Oxford*. London: Constable, 1992.
Lobel, M.D. (ed), *The Victoria History of the County of Oxford*, vol 3, The University of Oxford. Oxford: OUP, 1954.
Morris, Jan, *Oxford*. London: Faber & Faber, 1965.
Morris Jan (ed), *The Oxford Book of Oxford*. Oxford: OUP, 1978.
Oxfordshire County Council, *The Story of Oxford*. Stroud: Sutton, 1992.
Pursglove, G. & A. Ricketts (eds), *Oxford in Verse*. Oxford: Perpetua, 1999.
Snow, Peter, *Oxford Observed*. London: John Murray, 1991.
Thomas, Edward, *Oxford*. London, Black, 1902.
Tyack, Geoffrey, *Oxford: An Architectural Guide*. Oxford: OUP, 1998.

Ten of the Best Oxford Novels

Tom Brown at Oxford: Thomas Hughes (Macmillan, 1861)
Sequel to the superior *Tom Brown's Schooldays*. The best fictional view of mid-19th century university life. Hughes emphasizes the hearty sporting side but, through his portrayal of the servitor Hardy, also highlights the gap between rich and poor at Oxford.

Jude the Obscure: Thomas Hardy (Osgood, McIlvaine & Co, 1895) Quality literature. Jude, a self-taught, working-class youth finds there is no place for such as himself at "Christminster" University, and plays out his tragedy in the city. Lots of recognizable Oxford landmarks, with only their names changed.

Zuleika Dobson: Max Beerbohm (Heinemann, 1911)
In its time, a wicked satire on the Edwardian university, but now it seems like

dreadfully dated tosh. Zuleika comes to stay with her grandfather, the Warden of Judas College and has a devastating effect on the undergraduates, all of whom (bar one) drown themselves in the Thames during Eights Week, for love of her.

Gaudy Night: Dorothy L. Sayers (Gollancz, 1935)
Oxford's first "Queen of Crime" (P.D. James was born here too), thinly disguises Somerville as Shrewsbury College, to which Harriet Vane returns
for a "gaudy" or reunion feast and stays on to solve the mystery of who is responsible for acts of spite upsetting the college's calm. The first Oxford novel to address the special problems facing women in the university.

Brideshead Revisited: Evelyn Waugh (Chapman & Hall, 1945)
Post-war Waugh looks back on his time at Hertford as Oxford's "golden age" and this retrospective novel re-creates the hopeless decadence of the 1920s. The TV adaptation in the 1980s heralded a boost for tourism in the city.

Jill: Philip Larkin (Faber, 1946)
Larkin is an incomparably better poet than novelist, but his first novel (of two) is a splendid evocation of an Oxford full of class divisions and social tensions – everything *Brideshead* avoids tackling.

The House in Norham Gardens: Penelope Lively (Heinemann, 1974)
Written as a children's book but as fulfilling as most adult fiction, this tightly written and intelligent book has a wonderful feeling for North Oxford as a real place. It is about the fantasy world of 14-year-old Clare, living in a Victorian-Gothic villa with her elderly great-aunts.

Last Bus to Woodstock: Colin Dexter (Macmillan, 1985)
The first Inspector Morse novel and a perfect introduction to Dexter's Oxford, which has always been more town than gown, unlike many of the specially written TV mysteries. Two girls are seen waiting for the last bus to Woodstock; one is later found there, raped and murdered.

Crampton Hodnet: Barbara Pym (Macmillan, 1985)
There is no middle way with Pym; you either love her or loathe her. This was her first novel but was not published until after her death. She writes about 1940s North Oxford and sends up the people who inhabit it. Some say she got it spot-on, others that North Oxfordians have tried ever since to live up to her caricatures.

Where the Rivers Meet: John Wain (Century Hutchinson, 1988)
The first and best of Wain's Oxford trilogy, his last fictional work. It is a rambling saga without the quality of his early novels, but is a superbly researched social document, focusing on the Leonard family of Osney Island, showing the town/gown tensions as one brother joins the old university and the other enters "Billy" Morris's new industrialized Oxford.

Index of Literary
& Historical Names

Index of Places & Events